WILL EISNER: CONVERSATIONS

D1526651

Conversations with Comic Artists   M. Thomas Inge, General Editor

Will Eisner: Conversations

Edited by M. Thomas Inge

University Press of Mississippi   Jackson

CANISIUS COLLEGE LIBRARY
BUFFALO, NEW YORK

www.upress.state.ms.us

The University Press of Mississippi is a member of the Association of American University Presses.

THE SPIRIT and WILL EISNER are trademarks owned by Will Eisner Studios, Inc. and are registered in the U.S. Patent and Trademark Office. Used with permission. All rights reserved.

All illustrations are copyrighted © 2011 by Will Eisner Studios, Inc. Reprinted by permission.

Copyright © 2011 by University Press of Mississippi
All rights reserved
Manufactured in the United States of America

First printing 2011
∞
Library of Congress Cataloging-in-Publication Data

Will Eisner : conversations / edited by M. Thomas Inge.
    p. cm. — (Conversations with comic artists)
  Includes index.
  ISBN 978-1-61703-126-7 (cloth : alk. paper) — ISBN 978-1-61703-127-4 (pbk. : alk. paper)
— ISBN 978-1-61703-128-1 (ebk.) 1. Eisner, Will—Interviews. 2. Cartoonists—United
States—Interviews. I. Eisner, Will. II. Inge, M. Thomas.
  PN6727.E4Z92 2011
  741.5'6973—dc22
  [B]   2011000935

British Library Cataloging-in-Publication Data available

For Ann Eisner
and
Donária Inge

"I was not attracted, even as a young man, to the dumb-but-pretty girl. My own thinking, my own tastes, were always very much in favor of the intelligent competent women."—Will Eisner, 1986

CONTENTS

INTRODUCTION

To study the life of Will Eisner, comic artist extraordinaire, is to study the origins, history, and development of the comic book and the graphic novel. They were profoundly interrelated and one could argue that the fate of the graphic narrative in general would not have been the same without the presence of Will Eisner. He demonstrated from the start that telling stories through words and pictures was not simply some ephemeral way of amusing readers in search of temporary pleasure. Rather he saw it as a new and exciting way to address the age-old questions about human nature and the human condition through a familiar but freshly energized and revitalized art form.

People have been telling stories with symbols and images from the earliest times of recorded history, through the development of narrative art, and into the twentieth century with motion pictures. It was not until the 1930s, however, that the small magazines we know as "funny books" or "comic books" began to engage millions of readers in the startling full-color adventures of larger-than-life heroes and caricatured comic figures. In an age of aesthetic elitism, their very popularity served only to have them labeled as trash, but slowly and surely the comic magazines turned into lengthier, more complex works which by the 1970s would come to be known as "graphic novels." As they have become a permanent part of our literary and cultural landscape here and throughout the world, no one calls them "funny books" anymore. Will Eisner made much of that happen.

It was two high school friends from Cleveland, Ohio, Jerry Siegel and Joe Shuster, who jump-started the comic book into national popularity with the creation of Superman in *Action Comics* Number 1 in the summer of 1938. Before that from 1933 on most comic books were composed of reprints of newspaper comic strips, but Eisner, a young nineteen-year-old artist from Brooklyn, was among the first to realize that the medium would soon require lots of new stories and features to fill its pages. Thus he and a friend, Jerry Iger, set up a shop to produce, package, and sell this new material. His imagination teeming with vivid ideas, Eisner soon was creating, with the help of a remarkable group of talented artists, numerous characters who would go on to an extended life of their own in the hands of others, such as Doll Man, Black Condor, Blackhawk, Uncle Sam, and Sheena, Queen of the Jungle. Eisner would not hit his stride, however, until he was presented with an unexpected opportunity to develop a brand new idea.

Intent on competing with the comic books for more readers, the Des Moines Register and Tribune Syndicate proposed that Eisner create a Sunday comic book supplement as an insert for their newspaper customers. Eisner was never one to imitate anyone else, so instead of creating the kind of flying, costumed, and muscle-bound superheroes who populated the comic books in the wake of Superman, he created a very human detective named Denny Colt who donned a simple mask and a blue business suit to fight crime and called himself the Spirit. The genius was not so much in the concept of the character but in his development and participation in a twelve-year series of adventures that remain among some of the best told stories in American literature—and among the best drawn for that matter. Inspired by classic and popular fiction of the time, Eisner brought a high level of sophistication to plot and characterization in his stories and illustrated them with an artistic skill that was extraordinary then and now. As an auteur of comic art, he stretched the limitations of comics and carried them into new literary and cultural territory.

Whenever Eisner was confronted with a problem or a challenge, he met it with a creative answer or innovative solution. A good example of this was the fact that *The Spirit* comic book supplement was to be only sixteen pages long and would have no separate cover. Most newsstand comic books then were sixty-four pages long and had a color cover printed on heavier stock. Rather than sacrifice a page of the first story to making a cover, Eisner incorporated the beginning of the story into a full first page design. But it was no ordinary beginning. Rather he created a vibrant symbolic illustration which included the title of the feature and kicked off the narrative. Sometimes the title of *The Spirit* would appear on the side of a building, as a poster in the background, against the door of a vault, on a boudoir curtain, in a gutter drain running down into a sewer, or on the drawing board of a cartoonist representing Eisner himself. This solution was so appealing that it not only served to attract readers week after week but it inspired other comic book artists to adapt it to their own use. Thus what came to be called a "splash page" became a standard part of the comic artist's visual vocabulary and narrative strategy.

Eisner's restless creative energy would lead him into other areas. While serving in the U.S. Army during World War II, he employed his skills in producing instructional materials for soldiers and thus began a lifelong mission to use comics as an educational tool. As the founder of American Visuals, he produced a long running magazine for the Defense Department devoted to preventive maintenance in the military and accepted contracts for other government and educational projects. In the 1980s, he developed a method for using comic book panels on television as a way of teaching children to read, but the funding he sought to develop the concept never materialized. One result of this proposal was the series of adaptations of world literature he began to publish in 1999.

Not only did Eisner want to educate through the comics, but he wanted to train young artists to carry on what he had started. Thus he taught at the School of Visual Arts in New York courses in producing comics for almost two decades and wrote two theoretical and practical textbooks based on his lectures, *Comics & Sequential Art* and *Graphic Storytelling*. In exploring the underpinnings and technical features of comic art in these books, he also accomplished another goal of his—to bring a higher degree of appreciation and respect for the comics as an influential force in American art and culture. From the very start of his career, Eisner believed in the power of the comics to compete with and equal any other accepted form of artistic expression be it fiction, painting, film, drama, music, or poetry. This he attempted to prove not by argument but by example.

Nothing demonstrates this more fully than his devotion for the last thirty years of his life to the production of extended graphic narratives, what have come to be called "graphic novels." His first effort was a series of linked short stories called *A Contract with God*, in the literary tradition of Sherwood Anderson's *Winesburg, Ohio*, Ernest Hemingway's *In Our Time*, or William Faulkner's *Go Down, Moses*. Not knowing what to call the book, and to escape the automatic disdain that would have come with "comic book," he put "graphic novel" on the cover. While the term had appeared in print earlier, it was his use of it that attracted attention. Soon it was adopted by others as an appropriate description for lengthy, complex, and thematically mature works of graphic fiction and nonfiction. As other artists and writers followed suit and produced their own graphic novels, Eisner went on to contribute over a dozen more fictional and autobiographical works to the new found tradition. He had come a long way from superhero comic books, by way of *The Spirit*, to complex works that address the struggles of ordinary people, the tragedies of history, and the human condition. Will Eisner was a genius for all seasons and in all forms of comic art culture. We will not see his like again.

* * *

When I first proposed this collection of interviews to Will, while he approved the idea, his immediate response was that he would want to revise and correct them. I told him that the intent of the series in which the book would appear was to preserve the historic record, not to amend it. But this was just like Will Eisner. He always wanted to improve on everything he had created, and he would frequently revise or redraw a piece of art he had done years earlier for a reprint. I hope I have not breached his trust by reprinting the interviews in their original form, except for the correction of typographical errors. He willingly shared his own file of interviews with me, but more importantly he shared his time, patience, and friendship for over thirty years with one of his lifetime fans and admirers.

This collection of interviews begins in 1965 with Eisner's rediscovery as a major force in the development of the comic book industry through Jules Feiffer's groundbreaking book, *The Great Comic Book Heroes*, in which he celebrated his former boss and mentor. It extends through the various reprint revivals of *The Spirit*, Eisner's contact with the underground comix movement which inspired him to return to producing comic art, and his devotion to educating young cartoonists, as well as producing his own series of graphic novels, in the last three decades of his life. Also included is an essay by Eisner written for the *New York Times Magazine* in 1990, "Getting the Last Laugh: My Life in Comics." While not strictly an interview, he appears to be answering in a more concise manner many of the same questions that were coming at him from the numerous interviews taking place at that point in his career.

Nearly all aspects of Eisner's life and art are covered in these interviews, and there is considerable overlap, but these repetitions are preserved as a part of the archival record. Eisner was generous in granting his time to the many people who wanted to interview him, so a complete reprinting of all those published was not possible. There were a few I would have liked to include, especially from fan magazines and foreign publications, but I was unable to locate their copyright owners to request permission. Among those who granted permission, helped me in the process, or did other favors, I would like to thank John Balge, John Benson, Stephen R. Bissette, Chris Couch, Michael Dean, Danny Fingeroth, Paul Gravett, R. C. Harvey, Tom Heintjes, Dale Luciano, Chris Murray, Will Murray, Bob Overstreet, Bill Pearson, Fernanda Rocha, Julia Round, Roger Sabin, Randy Scott, Dave Sim, Roy Thomas, J. C. Vaughn, Stanley Wiater, and cathryn yronwode.

A special word of gratitude goes to Eisner's friend and agent Denis Kitchen for negotiating permission to reproduce the illustrations and other material in this book. Kitchen is a gentleman, a scholar of the comics, and an accomplished artist himself.

The administration at Randolph-Macon College, especially President Robert Lindgren and Provost William Franz, continue to offer substantial support for my research in things comic and otherwise, as did previous presidents Ladell Payne and Roger Martin. My students have patiently listened to my lectures as Blackwell Professor of Humanities with polite forbearance. Rachelle Phillips has been one of the best student editorial assistants an editor could ask for. Her help has been crucial, as has that of student assistant Diana D'Amato, who skillfully prepared the index. At the University Press of Mississippi, former director Seetha Srinivasan, present director Leila Salisbury, and editor-friend Walter Biggins have made publishing books a pure pleasure. Together we have helped make comics history and criticism respectable, thus fulfilling one of Eisner's major dreams. My own dream, Donária, remains ever supportive and faithful.

MTI

CHRONOLOGY

1917   March 6—William Irwin Eisner is born in Brooklyn, New York, to Jewish immigrants, Samuel and Fannie Ingber Eisner. Samuel came from Vienna and Fannie was born to her parents on the boat bound for the United States from Romania.

1930s   Attends DeWitt Clinton High School but does not graduate. Publishes his first art work and comic strips in the school newspaper and literary magazine.

1934   Works in the art department of William Randolph Hearst's *New York American* newspaper.

1935   Attends classes at the Art Students League in New York in the summer and studies with artists Robert Brachman and George Bridgeman.

1936   Sells his first professional comic book work to *Wow, What a Magazine!* Forms with Samuel "Jerry" Iger the Eisner and Iger Studio to produce features for a variety of comic book publishers. Among the artists employed were Jack Kirby, Lou Fine, Bob Kane, Jack Cole, Joe Kubert, Alex Kotzky, and Mort Meskin, as well as others who would play an influential part in the development of comic books.

1937   December—Creates "Hawks of the Sea," written and drawn by Eisner for *Feature Funnies* No. 3.

1938   September—Creates Sheena, Queen of the Jungle, for *Jumbo Comics* No. 1, with story and art by Mort Meskin.

1939   Organizes a new shop with Everett "Busy" Arnold of the Quality Comics Group to produce a comic book supplement for newspapers to be distributed by the Des Moines Register and Tribune Syndicate. Creates the Doll Man for *Feature Comics* No. 27 written by Eisner with art by Lou Fine.

1940   May—Creates and writes the Black Condor for *Crack Comics* No. 1, with art by Lou Fine.

        June 2—The first issue of the *Weekly Comic Book* supplement appears and is distributed to newspapers nationally with the origin story of

"The Spirit" written and drawn by Eisner. Additional features created by Eisner are "Lady Luck," drawn by Chuck Mazoujian, and "Mr. Mystic," drawn by S. R. "Bob" Powell. At its peak, the publication would reach as many as six million readers.

1941   August—Blackhawk appears in *Military Comics* No. 1 created and written by Eisner with art by Charles "Chuck" Cuidera. Later in the fall, he creates and writes Uncle Sam in *Uncle Sam Quarterly* with art by Eisner, Dan Zolnerowich, and Lou Fine. On October 31, *The Spirit* daily comic strip begins for a three-year run ending March 11, 1944.

1942   May—Eisner is drafted into the U.S. Army and serves at Fort Dix in New Jersey and Aberdeen Proving Ground in Maryland primarily providing editorial cartoons and comic strips for military newspapers. Transferred to the Pentagon, he produces comics and articles designed to educate soldiers in arms and vehicle maintenance.

1945   Discharged from the Army in the fall, he returns to work on *The Spirit* and adds new people to his staff including Jules Feiffer and Wally Wood.

1948   Establishes a new company, American Visuals, to continue the work begun in 1942 in educational comics and features for the Defense Department. His favorite *Spirit* story, "Gerhard Shnobble," appears in the September 5 supplement.

1949   The first and only issues of *Baseball Comics* and *Kewpies* appear in the spring in an unsuccessful effort to start his own comic book publishing company. Two additional titles, *John Law* and *Pirate Comics*, were planned but cancelled before publication.

1950   June 15—Marries Ann Louise Weingarten with whom he will have two children, John David in 1951 and Alice Carol in 1953. Alice is lost to leukemia at age sixteen, a profound tragedy in their lives.

1951   American Visuals begins to produce for the Army a digest-sized magazine, *P.S. The Preventive Maintenance Monthly*, which would continue under Eisner's artistic and editorial guidance until 1972.

1952   October 5—The last issue of *The Spirit* supplement is published as Eisner devotes more time to military and educational projects.

1965   Serves as president of the Bell McClure Syndicate and of the North American Newspaper Alliance until 1968. *The Great Comic Book Heroes*, a book by former assistant Jules Feiffer, now a cartoonist and playwright, calls attention to Eisner's achievements.

1966   October—Harvey Comics begins publication of *The Spirit*, which reprints stories from the 1940s.

1971   Meets Denis Kitchen, an underground cartoonist and publisher, at a comic book convention in New York and forms a lifelong friendship and business association.

1973   Teaches comic art at Sheridan College, Ontario, Canada.

1974   Begins to teach comic art at the School of Visual Arts in New York and will continue to teach there until 1993. James Warren initiates a second effort to reprint *The Spirit* in a magazine which would continue until October 1976. Begins work on stories for *A Contract with God*.

1975   Receives a Lifetime Achievement Award at the Angoulême International Comics Festival in France.

1978   Baronet Books publishes *A Contract with God*, a linked collection of short stories which Eisner calls a "graphic novel." Although the term had appeared earlier, Eisner popularizes it as an appropriate term for a new form of comic art. Receives early academic attention by appearing on a panel with Art Spiegelman to discuss the future of comic art at a meeting of the Modern Language Association in New York in December.

1983   Eisner family moves from White Plains, New York, to a home and studio in Tamarac, Florida. Denis Kitchen begins a third reprint series of *The Spirit* under the Kitchen Sink Press imprint. *A Signal from Space* is published by the Kitchen Sink Press and reissued in 1995 under the title *Life on Another Planet*.

1985   *Comics & Sequential Art*, a theoretical and practical textbook, is published under Eisner's own imprint, Poorhouse Press. A continuation, *Graphic Storytelling*, follows in 1996.

1986   *The Dreamer*, an autobiographical graphic novel, and *New York, the Big City* are published by Kitchen Sink Press.

1987   *The Building*, is published by Kitchen Sink Press. A made-for-television film, *The Spirit*, is broadcast over the ABC network.

1988   Kitchen Sink Press publishes *A Life Force*.

1989   *City People Notebook* is published by Kitchen Sink Press.

1990   The first Eisner Awards are presented at the annual Comic-Con International comic book convention in San Diego, California, to honor comic book artists and promote the medium.

1991   *To the Heart of the Storm*, an autobiographical graphic novel, and *The Will Eisner Reader* are published by Kitchen Sink Press.

1992   Kitchen Sink Press publishes *Invisible People*.

1995   Eisner receives the Milton Caniff Lifetime Achievement Award from the National Cartoonists Society. Kitchen Sink Press publishes *Dropsie Avenue: The Neighborhood.*

1997   *The Spirit: The New Adventures* begins publication by Kitchen Sink Press with new stories authorized by Eisner and produced by contemporary artists and writers. Concluded after eight issues in November 1998.

1998   An International Graphic Novel Conference is held in his honor on the twentieth anniversary of the publication of *A Contract with God* at the University of Massachusetts Amherst. *Family Matter* is published by Kitchen Sink Press.

1999   *The Princess and the Frog by the Grimm Brothers* is published by Nantier, Beall, Minoustchine Publishing, the first of a series of classic literary adaptations followed by *The Last Knight: An Introduction to Don Quixote* (2000), *Moby Dick by Herman Melville* (2001), and *Sundiata: A Legend of Africa* (2003).

2000   DC Comics publishes *Minor Miracles* and begins issuing *The Spirit Archives*, a complete reprinting of *The Spirit* stories in twenty-seven hardcover volumes. *Last Day in Vietnam: A Memoir* is published by Dark Horse Comics.

2001   *The Name of the Game* is published by DC Comics. *Will Eisner's Shop Talk* is published by Dark Horse Comics.

2002   The first Will Eisner Symposium, a conference on comics and graphic novels, is held at the University of Florida in Gainesville in February. The National Foundation for Jewish Culture in New York gives Eisner its Lifetime Achievement Award. Interviews are conducted between Frank Miller and Eisner by Charles Brownstein to be published in 2005 as a book, *Eisner/Miller: A One-On-One Interview* by Dark Horse Comics.

2003   *Fagin the Jew* is published by Doubleday.

2004   December 22—Eisner has quadruple bypass surgery in a hospital in Lauderdale Lake, Florida.

2005   January 3—He dies from complications following the surgery. *The Plot: The Secret Story of the Protocols of the Elders of Zion* is published posthumously by W. W. Norton.

WILL EISNER: CONVERSATIONS

The Only Real Middle-Class Crimefighter

MARILYN MERCER / 1965

From *New York: The Sunday Herald Tribune Magazine*, January 9, 1966, pp. 8 and 55.

It started with Jules Feiffer saying in his book, *The Great Comic Book Heroes*, that in the golden age of comic books a seminal force in the industry, the comic artist most likely to be imitated by other comic artists, was Will Eisner, who, between 1940 and 1952 with a few years off for World War II, wrote and drew *The Spirit*, a comic-book-size seven-page supplement syndicated in Sunday newspapers. Not everybody remembers *The Spirit*, but those who do tend to remember it distinctly and with passion.

The Spirit was a burlesque of, among other things, the standard adventure comic. However, it started off (on June 2, 1940) in the classic comic book manner. In the first installment, Denny Colt, a young criminologist, is pursuing Dr. Cobra, a mad scientist. When Dr. Cobra's secret formula explodes all over the laboratory, Denny is immobilized, taken for dead, and buried in Wildwood Cemetery.

A few panels later, Denny arrives in Police Commissioner Dolan's headquarters, explains that he is alive but wishes to take advantage of his supposed death so that he can "go after criminals the law cannot touch." And so he puts on a blue mask and becomes The Spirit, operating out of Wildwood Cemetery with the assistance of Dolan, Dolan's beautiful daughter Ellen, and a small Negro boy named Ebony.

Eisner, however, could not play it straight for long. As the strip progressed, *The Spirit* as serious crimefighter gave way to *The Spirit* as not so serious focal point for whatever zany fantasy Eisner felt inspired to build around him that week. Crime became incidental; sometimes Eisner forgot to put it in. The stories ranged from adventures in the mysterious East to politics in Central City to living soap opera. They were always funny.

3

A lot of people in those days wanted to work for Eisner. Marginal types because of the fine, lunatic quality of his imagination; career comic artists because of his technical excellence—for one thing, he drew better than anyone else. I worked for him between 1946 and 1948, along with Jules Feiffer, in a five-man shop at 37 Wall Street where we turned out a weekly *Spirit*, assorted comic book features, and an occasional advertising brochure. As I remember it, I was a writer and Jules was the office boy. As Jules remembers it, he was an artist and I was the secretary. Will can't really remember it very clearly. It is his recollection that Jules developed into an excellent writer and I did a good job of keeping the books. Neither one of us could, by Eisner standards, draw.

When I discovered that Eisner, who had given up comic strips in 1952, was in New York, I called him. He had had other, similar calls since the onset of the Great Comic Book Revival. "It is," he said, "interesting to be a legend in one's time. What do you do when you're a grand old man before you even have a chance to be a grand young man?"

I found him, reasonably grand and still reasonably young, in his office at 421 Park Avenue South, with a wall of bookshelves displaying a row of old, bound volumes of *The Spirit*. Now a full-time businessman and commuter (he lives in White Plains with his wife and two children), he has been engaged for the past fifteen years primarily in publishing semi-technical instruction manuals. The principal client of his firm, American Visuals Corporation, is the Department of the Army, for which he turns out *P.S.*, a monthly magazine that explains and encourages the proper maintenance of equipment in words, diagrams, and comic strip sequences. He produces similar material for industry and other government agencies. He owns two other enterprises, Educational Supplements Corporation (social studies enrichment materials) and IPD Publishing Company (foreign language instruction manuals), and for two years ran his own newspaper syndicate, Bell-McClure-NANA.

But he didn't think that made an interesting story. "What you really want to say," he said, rising to the challenge—Eisner always wrote his own scripts better than anyone else—"is that after searching through the streets of the city you finally found Will Eisner, sitting on a box in an empty lot, turning out dirty books and selling them to little kids. And that, although you had to beg and plead with him, you finally persuaded the old tap dancer to do one more turn, before they rang down the final curtain."

That wasn't what I wanted to say at all, so we tried again. How did he feel about *The Spirit* now? Did he regret giving it up? "I gave up *The Spirit*," he said, "because I had to make a choice. There were too many other things going on and I hated to turn it over to other people. So I dropped it. I decided I'd rather be an entrepreneur than an artist."

Actually, Eisner started out as an entrepreneur. He was born in New York in 1917, the son of a Seventh Avenue manufacturer and, while in De Witt Clinton High School, had ideas of becoming a stage designer. However, when he got out of school he went to work ("encouraged," he says, "by starvation") as a writer- cartoonist for the advertising department of the *New York American*.

This lasted until he discovered comic books. He observed their great financial success. Comic book publishers were paying a flat $5 a page for material and Eisner and a partner, Jerry Iger, undertook to meet the rate by setting up a factory. "I would write and design the characters," he said, "somebody else would pencil them in, somebody else would do the backgrounds, somebody else would ink, somebody else would letter. We made $1.50 a page net profit. I got very rich before I was twenty-two."

When he was twenty-three, greater things beckoned. He conceived the idea of a comic book insert for newspapers and, with the Register and Tribune Syndicate, launched *The Spirit*. For this, he knew, no assembly line would do. He really had to sit down at the drawing board, and he did. "I tried to write well," he says. "I regarded it as serious writing. Others were cranking the money machine. With *The Spirit*, I didn't have to. I had complete freedom. He was my medium. It was like making movies. It gave me a chance to be actor, producer, author, and cameraman all at once."

The Spirit had barely got off the ground when, in 1941, Eisner went into the Army. Other artists took over while Chief Warrant Officer Eisner, attached to the office of the Chief of Ordinance in Washington, wrote, edited, and drew pictures for the ordinance journal *Firepower*.

Eisner came out of the Army feeling his strength, and his style shows off to the fullest in the postwar *Spirits*. He thought of comic strips as movies on paper and in *The Spirit* pushed this idea as far as it would go. He made his format work for him; he rarely stuck to the conventional nine panels to a page but geared panel size to speed of the action. Sometimes there were no panels at all, just words and characters wandering around loose. His repertoire of visual gimmicks was limitless and he had a way of writing sound effects so that you could almost hear them.

He also displayed great virtuosity in his writing. Most adventure comics were at best semi-literate, and this may be an overstatement. *The Spirit* was not only literate, it was literary in the exact meaning of the word. Eisner, as a child, read constantly, more often nineteenth-century short stories—Ambrose Bierce, O. Henry, de Maupassant were his favorites—and it showed in *The*

Spirit. He was a parodist by instinct. Some weeks he was Somerset Maugham. Other weeks Edgar Allan Poe. Or A. E. Coppard, or Norman Corwin, or Ben Hecht. He also took off from movie plots, confession magazines, news stories, hillbilly ballads, old-world folklore (the folklore he generally made up, but it always sounded right). But, almost always, the plots and the humor depended on reference to an established literary, or sub-literary, convention.

The pattern carried over into his characters. The major ones, superficially at least, came straight out of pre–World War II pop culture. Dolan was a classic Irish cop. Ellen was a classic Irish cop's pretty daughter. Ebony was a small Stepin Fetchit.

He had a gallery of minor characters who seemed to come from some overzealous Central Casting. There were the dangerous women: P'Gell, Silk Satin, Plaster of Paris. (After a while, some of them stopped being dangerous; The Spirit at one point had P'Gell get installed as headmistress of a girls' school. But he could never really trust her.) There were the villains: The Octopus, arch criminal (you only saw his hands), and Mr. Carrion who had an unnatural relationship with his buzzard Julia. There was Sam Klink, the honest rookie cop; Ward Healy, the political boss of Central City. There were the tragic heroines, Sand Saref (a strange choice of name for an anti-typeset, pro-visual man), The Spirit's childhood sweetheart gone wrong, and Sparrow Fallon, girl waif and all-time loser. There was Inspector Guillotine of the Sûreté, Pancho the talking bull, Zoltan P. Yafodder, who went around drawing mustaches on subway posters—well, the list could go on indefinitely.

The principal characters, in spite of their stock outlines, were quite real to *Spirit* fans, and to Eisner, too. Ebony, for one. He was the first Negro to play a major role in an adventure comic. "Ebony was really an attempt to introduce a Negro boy in a meaningful role," says Eisner. "He had a dignity all his own, even though he had a Southern accent." Ebony never drew criticism from Negro groups (in fact, Eisner was commended by some for using him), perhaps because, although his speech pattern was early Minstrel Show, he himself derived from another literary tradition: he was a combination of Tom Sawyer and Penrod, with a touch of Horatio Alger hero, and color didn't really come into it.

The Spirit himself was, in the long run, the realest of all. Despite the mask, which Eisner eventually found an impediment, he was human. He was harassed by criminals, but also by Ellen Dolan, his more or less fiancée, by Ebony's school teachers, and by the Department of Internal Revenue. There were times, many times, when he just couldn't cope. He wandered through

his baroque adventures sometimes with an air of disbelief, as if at any moment he might turn around and say to his creator, "Eisner, you've got to be
kidding."

"The Spirit is, you could say, a pure existentialist, if I understand existen-
tialism and I'm not sure I do. He was living in and dealing with the world as
it was and solving crimes for no apparent reason. He was always, like everybody else, a victim of circumstances. The Spirit was the only real middle-class
crimefighter."

Couldn't, I asked, the middle-class crimefighter come back? The old tap
dancer looked doubtful, although he allowed that a West Coast television outfit had been after him with that very request. "It would be fun," he said. "The
Spirit to me is like an old mistress—you hate her, but you still have a yen for
her."

Then Eisner the entrepreneur took over. "But I can't do anything about
that now. Do you realize," he said, "that by 1970 one-third of the population
of the United States will be in school? Did you know that?"—and he went
on to describe, enthusiastically, several new approaches he'd dreamed up for
teaching elementary school subjects through visual devices. "It's a wide-open
field," he said, "and it's getting bigger. That's the area I'm going to explore
next, if I can ever find the time to get started."

He always did have more ideas per week than he could ever possibly use.

Having Something to Say

JOHN BENSON / 1968

From *Witzend*, No. 6 (Spring 1969). Reprinted by permission of William Pearson and John Benson.

My first attempt to interview Will Eisner was in August 1961. I visited his offices in New York unannounced, and, although he was very cordial, he indicated that he was not interested in being interviewed. He said that he was very flattered that I still remembered *The Spirit*, but he had no plans to revive the feature and apparently had little interest in it.

It was not until seven years later that Eisner agreed to do the following interview, his first interview for a comics-related publication. The most significant development in the intervening period that led to his change of heart was the rise of interest in comics that had culminated in Phil Seuling's massive four-day SCARP [Society for Comic Art Research and Preservation] Convention two months before this interview, at which Eisner had shared the role of Guest of Honor with Burne Hogarth. During that luncheon event, Hogarth seemed to draw a line between "real art," that which was hung in the Louvre (which Hogarth's had been, at that time), and "commercial art." I thought Eisner should have a chance to respond, and, from the floor, I asked him if he thought that externally conferred acceptance had any relevance to what was real art. Eisner responded, starting with a heartfelt, "I'm *glad* you asked that question!" It may have been right after that event that I asked Eisner to do the following interview, which was recorded on September 10, 1968, and originally appeared in *Witzend* #6 (Spring 1969). His disagreement with Hogarth at the convention is touched on in the interview.

As I was ushered into Will Eisner's office, a contract was spread out before him and he was speaking on the telephone of "grand total projected annual market figures" and the like. This prompted the first question.

John Benson: Do you feel that your business acumen was a necessary aspect for you to create your art in *The Spirit*, or even before, when you were in comics?

Will Eisner: No, I think the business acumen is largely a result of an effort to market ideas. It's an outgrowth, really, of the fact that I was always generating more ideas than I could sell, or find a market for. After a while anyone in that position gets frustrated, so, out of sheer desperation, you go out into business. In the early days, in an effort to find somebody who would do selling for me, I latched on to Jerry Iger, and we formed a partnership—Eisner and Iger. Basic business acumen really comes from hunger. That also goes for ideas, I suspect. Many years ago, when I was giving a talk, somebody asked me what prompted my ideas, and all I could tell them . . . it was malnutrition.

Benson: *The Spirit* was immensely more successful than the work of other comic creators who have had less business acumen.

Eisner: Not necessarily. After all, the fellows who turned out Superman, it really turned out in the end, had very little business acumen—they ultimately lost their ownership of the property. Actually, they were more successful; the feature itself was more successful than *The Spirit*.

I became an entrepreneur because, as I said, I would generate many ideas and I had to find a market. I had the structure within myself to generate those ideas, but selling is another thing. It's terribly frustrating, as any artist knows, to have somebody look at your idea and say, "I don't think it's any good." Generally the fellow who doesn't think it's any good doesn't seem to have the great intellectual powers that you think he should have. It's hard for an ego to survive a guy with a dead cigar in his face who looks at your effort, belches, and says, "Nah . . . it ain't gonna sell."

At the very least you come away frustrated. Very often, of course, when you don't have access to markets, you have to create them yourself . . . or try to. *The Spirit* did grow out of acumen, a groping for a new market. I got into the comic-book business very early, and I think I was the first to sort of mass-produce comic magazines. I was running a shop in which we made comic-book features pretty much the way Ford turned out cars. So perhaps the reason that the *Register and Tribune* consented to distribute *The Spirit* in the first place was because I had demonstrated an ability as a producer—and after all, turning out a sixteen-pager (which at the time it was) every week for newspaper distribution, with no tolerance for delivery, where you had to make a scheduled delivery each week, did require some kind of respect from the people who were going to handle distribution. I had at least struck a new market . . . a comic book insert for Sunday newspapers . . . that had never been done before.

Benson: You published a couple of books under your own imprint, and they didn't do very well.

Eisner: They sure didn't . . . which will give you an idea of how far a creative man generally goes in marketing his own ideas. I published a thing called *Baseball Comics*, with Rube Rooky, and I also published a thing called *Kewpies*, which we got the rights to. Both of them died—oh, they were absolute disasters. Rube Rooky was a great idea, but it just came along *long* after it had a right to come along. Well, they were two lone books . . . they got lost in the distributor's lists. There's a lot to magazine distribution that does not meet the eye; it's like a big iceberg. Today, as always, the creator and the publisher (who is really a packager) is at the mercy of his distributors. And you can create the finest things in the world . . .

Benson: I'd like to go back to the comments you made at the 1968 Comic Art Convention dinner, at which you and Burne Hogarth were honored. Relating to the discussion you had, I think, is a story that Chuck Jones, the animator, tells about a young fellow who visited Robert Frost. Frost asked him what he did, and the fellow said, "I'm a poet." And Frost said, "That's a gift word, son: you can't call yourself a poet—only others can call you a poet." Jones expanded the thought to animation, and any art form. Would you agree? Would you say it is not important to you (or not something you should concern yourself with) that you be called an artist?

Eisner: I would take the same position. If I recall, the question you posed at the meeting was one I welcomed, because I candidly took great issue with what Burnie Hogarth was saying. As a matter of fact, I was quite warm under the collar because I felt that Hogarth, in sort of a left-handed way, was tearing the rug out from under creative people . . . and it surprised me. I can't believe he could mean that, because he was, after all, making a living from the teaching of artists—he's running a school, he makes his bread from kids like that. To make an issue over whether you are or are not an artist . . . or, "is a cartoonist an artist or not," is rather unimportant, and a teacher shouldn't be talking that way. I can see kids sitting around and discussing that, young kids just starting out—"Are we artists?" or, "Are we craftsmen?" or, "Are we legitimate artists or not?" But for a teacher to do that, it seemed to me an inexcusable thing. I honestly believe that you've got to go out and be what you are, and let the critics label you. Within that frame, however, you must have a goal in mind. You have to want to be something.

Now, I will very candidly tell you, and I'm very firm on this, that I always thought of myself as a craftsman when doing *The Spirit*, and *The Spirit* was really a culmination of all the talent, skill, and imagination I could muster. Prior to that time I was just making a living. *The Spirit* was the first major effort in my life where I was able to do something I wanted to do, and was doing something I thought was meaningful, and at the same time making money on it. They were good years! I felt that I was at the epitome of the medium, and that I was helping the creation of a medium in itself. I had found a new milieu all to myself, and I was helping to make it. Comics before that were pretty pictures in sequence, and I was trying to create a *thing*, an art form. I was conscious of that, and I used to talk about it. I remember when, especially in the days when Feiffer was working for me, we used to have long discussions about it as an art form—not quite the same way it's done today as an art form; with no nostalgia, really groping. "How can we improve this? How can we make this better? How can we do better things?" It was almost a continuing laboratory, and I was very lucky, because there wasn't anybody who could stop me from doing what I wanted. I owned my own feature and I had the respect of my distributor, and there was nobody to stop me. I had only to stay within those bounds of propriety that would enable it to get by the editor of the newspaper. But I also thought of myself as a writer . . . a visual writer, let's put it that way. I never thought of myself as an author in the traditional sense . . . but a combination of the two things—artist-writer. It's very pleasing, I confess, after twenty years, to have people refer to it that way, because it gives me a sense of having accomplished something.

Benson: Would you say, then, that it would be pretty necessary, in order to utilize all the aspects of the art form, for the creator to be both a writer and an artist?

Eisner: I think it's absolutely essential. To achieve the name, or to be worthy of the name, of creator, a man should be both writer and artist. Now, he doesn't have to write with words. After all, [Diego] Rivera and [José Clemente] Orozco were making murals which, as far as I'm concerned, were vast pieces of writing, because the painter had an idea and he was trying to communicate with the people who would ultimately view it. He had something to say. That's the heart of it—having something to say. The man who sits down and takes somebody else's script and merely renders it into pictures is doing something, and I don't withdraw from him what is his due. I can only measure him by the contribution he's made to the script. He is going just so far, but he has a limitation. [Salvador] Dalí is a writer-artist combination. I could name any number of "creators" who write and draw. You don't have to use words, is my point. Of course, in the comic field I consider Harvey Kurtzman one of the great, real geniuses. I'm not talking about the work he's doing now, I'm not talking about the work he did at *Mad*, I'm talking about the stuff he did prior to *Mad*, where he experimented in . . .

Benson: His war comics?

Eisner: No; this is the stuff he did for the *Herald Tribune*. As a matter of fact, very few people remember it. It was incredibly good stuff. But he had something to say—he feels. You know when you talk to him that he has something to say. [Jules] Feiffer always had something to say. He isn't the craftsman, perhaps, that, say, Burnie Hogarth was. I considered Burnie Hogarth a great craftsman, but I don't know of anything that he . . . he may have, I really don't want to put him down. I use him as an example. Another man I admire, whose *craftsmanship* I admire, is Alex Raymond, who did a *certain* amount of writing; but he brought something, he said something—he said, "This is a style, this is the thing I'm going to say." Then there's [Al] Capp, [Milton] Caniff, [George] Herriman . . . many others. I think everybody says something—when a guy draws a dirty picture on the wall he *says* something. But the limits of his contributions are measured only by what the reader gets from what he says.

Benson: Do you know the work of Bernie Krigstein?

Eisner: Yes, to a limited degree. I'm not very familiar with his work. I think he was the one, was he not, who did a sequence where he showed a train killing somebody? It was brought to my attention by somebody in the shop, because it was very similar to something I had tried sometime before. I think he did it with much more craft than I did. He carried it a step further, and I admired it. I don't know much about him. Somebody handed me something he had said about me in an interview—was it your thing? And he seemed to be very unimpressed with what I had done.

Benson: I wasn't able to convince him.

Eisner: Well, no, he's certainly entitled to that opinion, and he may very well be right.

Benson: I spent my vacation watching the Democratic Convention, and seeing Mayor Daley's power plays, shaking his fist, stuffing the galleries with his party regulars, I could only identify him as a character out of *The Spirit*. If there is one theme that runs through *The Spirit* from its start to the last episode in the *Herald Tribune*, it is big city politics. Why is that?

Eisner: Remember that I grew up in the city—I sold newspapers on the street corners in the city. My whole background is a city boy. I went to high school here. All my culture is city culture. I lived in all the nooks and crannies of Manhattan. You know, it was all part of what I had to say. Central City was New York City as far as I was concerned, and the city politics was obviously what I knew and understood. I had no other place . . . this is what I was drawing on, what I had to start with. I grew up in the Depression, so the application of politics was the frame of the Depression. Actually, it wasn't very much different than it is now, except that now there's a different level of protest, but the protests are essentially the same. We had Mayor Daleys then. We couldn't drop out then because economic security was the measure of achievement; but we were protesting. We didn't wear beards, but we ran around and protested, joined causes and dreamed of brave new worlds. The protests were the same—instead of dropping out on pot, we dropped out on liquor, or you dropped out by going out on the road. But it's strangely not a hell of a lot different, and the establishment looked as dastardly then as it looks impossible to me today. Except that now I am a member of the establishment. As a matter of fact, I'm quite content to know that the only comfort we establishment people have is the knowledge that these kids are going to someday *be* the establishment . . . and it will serve them right.

Benson: Mike Barrier explains his interest in the so-called funny-animal comics by arguing that this exaggeration is a necessity in the comics medium, and can be used effectively in funny-animal strips because they're exaggerated to begin with. He says that some serious strips have used this necessary exaggeration and the results are grotesque. An original creator can make this a virtue, but he must use stories where grotesqueness is appropriate. He cited *The Spirit* as a successful example.

Eisner: If you have to break it down to that kind of laboratory definition, he's correct, but in my judgment there really is not much difference between a "serious" or a "comic" strip. I wouldn't think it out of character if Prince Valiant had a humorous character or comic relief. A cartoon, really, or any drawing . . .

Benson: I don't want to interrupt, but I think Barrier is referring more to the dramatic stories that featured "funny animals" such as *Uncle Scrooge* by Carl

Barks. They could use very exaggerated facial expressions, actions, and so on, because of the "funny animal" medium. But you were able to do that, too, with *The Spirit*, in a more realistic vein.

Eisner: The drawing was somewhat realistic, if that's what you're talking about. I employed exaggeration where I felt I needed it, and where I felt I wanted to be serious, I did. But I was never conscious of saying, "Well, I'll exaggerate here and not there." I played it the way you might in music. You got louder when you felt you wanted to emphasize something, and you got quieter when you felt you wanted a downbeat. Use any device the tool allows.

Benson: There is an element of the grotesque in *The Spirit* which naturally lends itself to this kind of exaggeration. If you were telling a drawing-room story it would be very difficult to use exaggeration.

Eisner: Yes, but then again, you select the way any painter would. It becomes very plastic in your hands if you are in command of the technique, and I think that's the essence of it. People have often referred to the stuff I did as grotesque. I wonder exactly what they mean by grotesque. I mean, I understand the definition, but what do *you* mean by grotesque? What do you think they mean by grotesque? I don't mean to turn the tables, but I'd like to know.

Benson: The milieu that *The Spirit* operated within . . .

Eisner: You don't mean distortions, optical distortions?

Benson: The optical distortions which created the mood that the Spirit operated in . . .

Eisner: Well, then yes, I'm guilty. I'm quite grotesque.

Benson: I don't think it's a matter of being guilty. What Barrier is saying is that since the media needs to be distorted, and thus to be grotesque, if you're going to do a realistic story you have to do a story which already has its own elements of grotesqueness in order to utilize the form.

Eisner: I see what you mean. As far as my pattern went, I would say about 25 percent of the time only would I work from a visual concept to story. The rest of the time I would work from an idea. I'd start with a doorknob and build a house with it, generally. I'd come down with a basic idea or thought that I had, or something that I wanted to say, like the story of the atom bomb. When they blew the atom bomb in 1945, I was really caught up like everybody else, frightened and disturbed about the whole thing. I did a story one day about the discovery of fire by two men on a planet. They treated the discovery—these were two prehistoric men—as though it were the discovery of atomic energy. One fellow says to the other, "Why, this is terrible, this could wipe out the entire face of the earth; let's handle this very carefully," and so on. It reflected a very personal thing. I myself was trying to come to grips with this enormous idea, and in writing it I guess it was a sort of exercise in my own mind. But there was a grotesque treatment, obviously, because it was a grotesque subject.

Benson: Where do the Warner pictures come in as an influence?
Eisner: Everybody from Feiffer to others who have written about me in recent years have attributed to various motion picture productions a great influence on me. You've got to remember, as I said, I was a city boy; I grew up on the movies—that was my thing, that's what I lived with. The movies always influenced me. I was seriously interested in the theater at one time, and at one point I wanted to be a stage designer; it was really something I was terribly interested in. Then, for economic reasons, it just didn't seem like a viable thing, but I still retained an interest in the theater.

The early Man Ray films interested me tremendously. I used to go down to the New School and spend hours looking at these old Man Ray experimental films; and it gradually dawned on me that these films were nothing but frames on a piece of celluloid, which is really no different than frames on a piece of paper. Pretty soon, it became to me film on paper, and so obviously the influence was there. But timing, sequences—I think I was influenced by almost any film. I think if anyone asked me what films were the ones that I thought were most exciting, or most interesting, I really couldn't put my finger on it. I suppose people can, later in life, point to an author that influenced them most. One of the artists that influenced me most, I would say, was Lynd Ward, his woodcuts and wood engravings; they were fantastic. And I always felt he was *the* daddy of the pure ultimate visual. And ever since then, and this is now thirty-five years, I've tried to reach that mountaintop, and I've never been able to do it.

Benson: But getting back to film, I would say that the films influenced me tremendously. When I look at your material, I don't see that you're copying any film techniques—you're using your own techniques. But as far as the stories themselves go, there is a certain similarity.
Eisner: Well, my big influence in stories is not so much films, although they got their stories from the same place I did, actually. That influence is the short stories—the O. Henry short stories, the Ambrose Bierce short stories, and so forth. I was an avid short-story reader, and as I got into the business, the

short stories became really useful. I used to seek out short stories wherever I could. I picked up once, in an old book store, a collection of short stories written in Scotland in 1830, in the newspaper called *The Border Papers*, and they'd have short stories every week—it was a weekly newspaper—very much like the short stories of the period when Charles Dickens wrote. I was a great fan of [Ben] Hecht, and I was also a very great fan of O. Henry and the whole gamut which I mentioned before. These had the twist endings, the surprise endings, and so forth. *The Spirit*, as I saw it (and as I saw comic books), was nothing but a series of short stories. They were the pulps in visual form.

Benson: That's interesting. It sort of dovetails with what you once told me before, that *The Spirit* was the precursor of television.

Eisner: The comics filled a gap. I was conscious of it at that time, because all during the time *The Spirit* was being produced and I was in comics actively, creatively, television was just around the corner. And *The Spirit* was a half-hour TV show.

Benson: Do you go to the films now?

Eisner: Yes, I'm still a strong fan. I don't get to films as much as I used to, but I do see . . . I watch a lot of television whenever I can.

Benson: Do you see the European films much?

Eisner: I haven't really kept up with the European wave, largely because my activities now keep me pretty busy going into more pragmatic things.

Benson: Of course you know that all the European directors, especially Alain Resnais, are great comic fans.

Eisner: The ones I have seen employ a great deal of the technique . . . I thought the early Italian films did have . . . there's a change that I've noticed that perhaps is different from the kind of things I was doing, which of course is to be expected. These films seem to employ the visual image for the sake of the visual image—not with any message in mind. It's almost as though somebody had experimented in the laboratory with a whole series of things, and then just simply put them together and said, "Here, look at what I came up with." Occasionally there's a strong message; obviously the Fellini stuff has a strong message . . . the symbolism . . .

Benson: What was the last Fellini film you saw?

Eisner: 8½, which left me gasping because it was really quite a smashing thing. Remember, however, that I grew up in an era where the story and the message was all. And when the message becomes very obscure, then it's rather hard to get.

Benson: Did you know Jack Cole?
Eisner: Yes, very well.

Benson: Did you work with him?
Eisner: When I was in partnership with "Busy" Arnold . . .

Benson: You were partners; that was another thing I was curious about.
Eisner: E. M. Arnold and I—"Busy" Arnold, Everett Arnold, however you want to put it—were partners in a series of comic books. He was a businessman, purely an entrepreneur, and we had this partnership. He also published books on his own, and a couple of the books he published on his own were done by Jack Cole. Jack Cole was not actually working for me directly, although he was working for my partner, and I knew Jack. Plastic Man was something we came up with out of an idea I talked with "Busy" about; I think ultimately Jack did it. I am always, or I was anyway, always generating ideas, and it didn't matter to me where they went or who took them or what. I don't lay a claim to any of these ideas, it's just . . . you know, everybody gets influenced by everybody else. I was influenced by people who were doing backgrounds for me. And I'm sure they were influenced by me.

Benson: You mentioned the story about the atom bomb. You used to have what might be called peace parables. I recall the irony in a Christmas story, and I believe it was before Feiffer was with you, which started with a sign reading, "City of Bethlehem—We Make the Finest Steel for the Finest Guns." Now you're working for the Army . . .
Eisner: . . . and you want me to equate that? OK, I'll evaluate it for you. I haven't changed, one bit. What I'm doing for the Army today is instructional and educational material. We're teaching people how to maintain their equipment. I'm a teacher; I'm turning out instructional material. I don't feel the slightest feeling of guilt, or separation, or any relationship between that and what I might think about war as war, or warmongering as warmongering. Or even, for that matter, whether or not we should be in Vietnam or shouldn't be in Vietnam. As a matter of fact, I spent last summer in Vietnam myself. And I don't think this is the place to discuss it, but I have some strong opinions . . .
Benson: I'd be interested to know what they are.

Eisner: I have very strong opinions about it, and I haven't hesitated to discuss it. I'm not a dove in the sense . . . you see, people like to categorize things very simply. A man stands up and says, "Let's get out of Vietnam," and I'm too old now to jump up on the barricades and wave a flag and say, "Yeah, let's get out of Vietnam." I have to say first of all, "After we do what?" Or, "How do we get out? Which way do we get out? And when, and who?" But as far as my attitude toward war is concerned, and my attitude toward my relationship between the work we're doing now and the war . . . The military instructional material that I've been turning out began in 1950. It's one of the reasons why I left *The Spirit* and got out of entertainment comics—because I have been devoting the last twenty years, really, to developing the comic-strip medium, which I had always experimented with, into a legitimate teaching tool. This is really the thing I'm proud of. I'll teach anything with that tool. I'd teach how to conduct a peace march in that tool, if we had a customer for it, or if I felt it was useful, or if I had a place where it could be distributed. I'll teach . . . do a comic strip on how to burn your draft card, if I felt that was an area . . . fix an engine . . . anything. We have done comics on democracy for Latin America, how to drive a truck for Turks . . . and so forth. But I have no patience with that kind of relationship, because I think it's misleading and unfair. Merely because one works . . . one sells one's product or one's product is bought by the Army, really, is . . . to me it doesn't make any sense. But that's another discussion.

Benson: The *Philadelphia Bulletin* and one or two other papers ran *The Spirit* in tabloid size. I'm curious as to whether you had anything to do with that and whether you liked it.
Eisner: No; strangely enough I hated it. One of the reasons I hated it was because it wasted a lot of space; if I could have used that same tabloid section and told more of a story, I would have liked it.

Benson: Another subject brought up at the Convention dinner was the character Ebony. But I'd like to talk about some of your other Negro characters that seemed to be both realistic portrayals of Negroes at the time and also an attempt to, say, integrate the strip.
Eisner: At the time I was very conscious of this and I tried, where I could, to make what I felt was a departure. You have to keep in mind that for whatever else I did, I was always interested in, and still am interested in, departure. The only kicks I get out of this business is being able to break new ground. Now very often I don't succeed, like any first man into something. But that's really,

as far as I'm concerned, the name of the game—to keep trying something with the skills that you have.

Now, I did create a character called Lt. Grey. Lt. Grey was really what the two *I Spy* characters are today. I had precisely that idea, that I was going to create an intelligent, well-integrated, acceptable Negro who was every bit as good as his counterparts, and who fitted into the stream of things. Now, no one stopped me, but I remember I was also sensitive to interest; I was responsive to the times. Ebony was done with a great deal of love and affection. I want to tell you something I couldn't discuss at the meeting, which I think is fair to discuss here. At one point, I think it was somewhere around 1949, I got, strangely enough, two letters in the same day, one of those rare coincidences. One letter came from the Education Division of the CIO in Philadelphia. It happened to be from a fellow who went to school with me or something, and he wrote a long, bitter letter about how he was shocked, and dismayed, and disappointed that a fine liberal like me had gone down the road of portraying Negroes in this fashion. On the same day, I had this long and wonderful letter from the editor of the Afro-American newspaper in Baltimore congratulating me on the courage that I was displaying in showing a character like that. Now the strange thing about this is that neither of these fellows was quite right. I was neither a defrocked liberal, nor was I setting out to do any more than what I thought was right. I treated Ebony in the scheme of things as it was then. There was a time when both liberal and reactionary thought *Amos 'n' Andy* were just great. They were being very honest about it; I think they thought they were being quite kind. People forget that because we now discover what a terrible thing it was—patronizing Negroes. But anybody who has been part of a minority knows that there was a time when people are patronizing. So when somebody tells Jewish jokes today, I don't bristle nearly as much as I did when I was sixteen years old, so many, many years ago when people told Jewish jokes, because I knew in those days they weren't being very kind. Today no one gets mad; it's part of the changing culture. To me, Ebony was a very human character, and he was very believable . . . I don't hold out and say that I was setting out to be a friend of the Negro, but I at the time, with all the idealism I had then, I felt that he deserved to be treated as a human being, and have emotions. Remember, that was a breakaway in itself. No one ever showed Negroes with any emotions other than weeping over the death of poor little Mandy, and the little white girl. As far as having emotions for reasons of their own, nobody really ever did show that. In comics, only Ham Fisher did anything like it and he stayed with the safe stereotype. We're doing stuff now—one of the things I'm currently engaged in is a whole series of Negro-oriented educational materials, in the comic technique, with all Negro characters. A totally different approach than I took then—but done in the comic style.

Benson: You're quoted in the *Herald Tribune* as saying, "The Spirit was an existentialist—he solved crimes for no reason . . . he was the first middle-class crimefighter." Wouldn't these statements also be true of the Humphrey Bogart archetype?

Eisner: I think you could say "yes." They both had the same reasoning; his motivation was as obscure as the Spirit's motivation. As a matter of fact, one of the things that perhaps crept through *The Spirit* that makes people say to me slyly, digging me in the ribs and looking at me out of narrowed eyes, "You really had tongue-in-cheek all the time, didn't you? It was all a big put on." Well, yes, in a way, because I could never understand why any crime fighter would go out and fight crime. Why the hell a guy should run around with a mask and fight crime was beyond me. Except that I, and there again it was part of my own background, this kind of mystical thinking, in which I've always felt that people do the things they have to do. So man does what he's confronted with. You put a man in front of a wall, he will climb the wall, just the way an ant does. As he builds a society, he builds a wall and then struggles to climb it. The Spirit had all the middle-class motivations, which is that "I've got to have something to do; this is my thing, this is my shtick," and he went out and did it. Of course, the big thing, the big problem each week was to figure out an acceptable reason why he should get involved in this in the first place.

Benson: I was ready to come here and say, looking out of my narrowed eyes, "Everyone says The Spirit was tongue-in-cheek, but you were really serious, weren't you?"

Eisner: Serious only in that when I did *The Spirit*—and this *is* serious—I really wrote my heart out. I really was saying what I wanted to say. If I had been writing at a typewriter, I couldn't have done it with more intensity and honesty. It probably is the most honest work I have done in all my life, and I'm rather proud of the fact that most, *most* of the things I've done in my career were done honestly. Very early in life I reached the point where I could afford to pick and choose the kind of work that I wanted to be involved in. Leaving the comic field and going into the educational field involved a very substantial risk in the beginning. It turned out to be economically very wise. But it was seriously done.

Benson: We seem to have come to the end of the hour; I'm amazed that we've covered so much ground.

Eisner: You had some questions I never expected. You know, every once in a while I try to read these . . . this *Graphic Story Magazine*. I'll tell you, if I were to go back (it isn't a question of going back, it would be going forward), if I had the time to devote myself fully, that would be the direction in which I would probably go.

Benson: Which direction?

Eisner: In the so-called "graphic story," because this has been something that I believe the comic strip technique had all along. But I read this article the other day, in *Graphic Story Magazine* I think; it was a review of Gil Kane's magazine *Savage*. I was sorry they put it down. Sorry Gil's magazine failed . . . I believe he's got the right idea. That thing I did for the *Herald Tribune* was in that track—I got a tremendous charge out of that; it was fun to do. It was a freebie, practically, and I did it with real good fun. But this is probably the way I'd go. But I don't think the media itself, right now, unless I misread the public, can stand an extreme acceleration into that area. It has to come somewhat from the public. I think that the public is a very impatient reader today. You see, if you refine the technique far enough, you'll come to film, and you'll be a film.

Benson: I don't agree with that, because you, I think, refined comic technique farther than anyone else, and it was not film, it was comics.

Eisner: I'm wondering now, I would like to find out myself; because I'd jump into it in ten minutes if I felt that there was a really substantial need for it, or a substantial appreciation. But I suspect, and I found that happening in *The Spirit* toward the last few years I was doing it, that people haven't the patience to read that long, or to devote that much time or that much attention to a lengthy thing. You look at the comic strips in the newspapers; they're all very short and punchy things.

Benson: But comic-book stories have gotten longer. They're twenty pages, and even that's often part of a continued story.

Eisner: Are they popular? I mean, are they well read, are they appreciated for that? Because if that's so, boy, I think that's marvelous, that's the way it should go. But they were talking about doing a whole novel in comic form. The idea of doing a novel in comic form is not new and it's not novel, but it's how you do it. Now, the review of Gil Kane's stuff was rather rough; I think they were pretty hard on him. But I think he left himself open for it. I think he did that thing as though he were doing a comic book for National Comics. He wrapped it up; he was doing it for dough, he was doing it to get it out. He was hoping, I think, that the mere novelty of the approach would carry him home. I think that was his mistake.

Benson: The book was very wordy.
Eisner: There's nothing wrong with words; except the words aren't used properly here.

Benson: Did you read the "Master Tyme" strip in that issue of *Graphic Story Magazine*?
Eisner: Yes. Fascinating stuff; great stuff. There's tremendous talent around, tremendous. It's too bad these kids are going to have a hell of a time finding a mass audience. It's disastrous to new talent, and I don't know how much of an audience there is. They're going through the same agony that kids did earlier, and the man who publishes a 300- or 400,000 edition of a comic and puts them on the newsstand on consignment isn't about to take a chance on a kid like that because he's got too much money invested. So you've either got to prove to this man that he's going to move 300,000 copies of the comic book, or . . .

Benson: . . . or else you have to market it to a smaller audience at a higher price so as to still get a satisfactory return.
Eisner: A smaller audience may not be enough to support the artist. In one of our publishing companies here, we talked about possibly going into this market several times; but we can't find it. How are you going to reach the people who may be interested in the stuff? How many people are interested? We don't know.

Benson: Warren's *Creepy* and *Eerie* seem to stay in business.
Eisner: What are they?

Benson: Horror stories in the *Savage* format. They had some fine material in early issues—people like Alex Toth.
Eisner: Toth is great—Toth is one of the great illustrators around. But do they sell?

Benson: Well enough to continue, and they've been around for four years, but I don't think they're doing great guns.

Eisner: Well, they may just have a piece of market and that's it. No room for anybody else. But as an artist/publisher, I'm fascinated with the market. I'm very interested. I'd go into it in a minute if I could get some lock on it, if I could see the dimensions of it—I just don't know. There may be just simply dozens of readers who are fascinated with this thing, and that's all.

Will Eisner: Before the Comics

JOHN BENSON / 1973

An excerpt from "Art and Commerce: An Oral Reminiscence by Will Eisner," *Panels* No. 1 (Summer 1979), 4–12. Reprinted by permission of John Benson.

I was born in New York City on March 6, 1917. I have absolutely no way of knowing what stars converged at that time, what great earthshaking events occurred. My father was born in a little village just outside of Vienna, so I am Austrian, I guess—although I understand that the municipality kept changing hands over the years, so I might be Hungarian or Polish by extraction. His father was a kerosene miner or something like that. They weren't farmers. My mother was conceived in Romania, born on the boat on the way over here, so she was, I suppose, technically American. I don't know whether the birth occurred in territorial waters or not.

My father actually started life as a painter; he was an artist of sorts. He studied in Vienna, I guess. He said he came to Vienna when he was very young, twelve, thirteen years old, and apprenticed himself to a muralist. There were a number of muralists in Vienna at the time, and they worked in churches, and decorated homes on soft wet plaster. Alfresco was quite a fashion in those days, so wealthy people would hire a muralist to come in and do a whole dining room or a living room. And that was what my father did. Just prior to the outbreak of World War I he came here; he must have been about twenty-five. He was in his early thirties, I guess, when I was born. He died at eighty-three or eighty-four, and when he died I was forty-nine or fifty.

His brother was also an artist. He was one of about eleven children. A number of them died, or were scattered by the holocaust of World War I and wandered all over Europe. When he got to this country he couldn't find work in church murals, but he did paint scenery-backdrops for vaudeville and the Jewish theater. Later, when the work slowed, he became a house painter for a while, and that didn't suit him. He finally became involved in a company in New Jersey that painted metal beds to look like wood. He was very skilled at that, and did that for a while until he became ill. He never really was able to get back, so he finally went into the manufacturing of fur coats and opened up a factory until 1929, when the crash wiped him out.

My father was very old school. He still fancied himself an intellectual back in Vienna in the coffee houses, and I think he would really have loved to have remained with that whole Bohemian group for the rest of his life—but here in America he became a businessman. It became his major effort, at which he never really succeeded in any large scale. He was always involved in some wild scheme or other.

I have a brother, four years younger, and a sister about thirteen years younger. My brother Julian, we call him Pete, worked with me in the publishing business beginning in 1950 and stayed with me twenty-two years. He's not an artist; he's an awfully good production man and has talents in other areas.

Well, my early home life was spent in upper-lower-class poverty. Which was probably lower-middle-class as the sociologists put it. There's upper-upper-lower class, and lower-lower-middle class, and then lower-middle class and middle-class, so somewhere between the middle-class and poor is where I was living, although we regarded ourselves as middle-class. The family had a sense of pride, and we lived well above our means, with as much dignity as we could muster. I think we were quite poor and didn't know it. But we always sort of managed somehow.

My mother was very typical of the girls of that era. She had no formal education. She came over here and as soon as she could stand up straight, I suppose, she was working in a factory: a very typical factory girl of the period. She worked in hat factories until she married my father.

My father was very interested in literature and painting and so forth, but he was not a highly literate man. He had difficulties with the language here, but was in love with the classics. He had the feeling, which I suppose I inherited from him . . . it was that atmosphere in the house. He would buy books. His proudest possession was a one-volume life of Julius Caesar, which was given to him by his night-school teacher. He had gone to night school to learn English when he got here, and he apparently did well and was given this book for a prize. I remember the book because I illustrated it. I decided for a while when I was a kid I was going to do book illustrations. So I made illustrations and leaved them into the book. I did a rather gory illustration of the death of Caesar at the hand of Brutus. I remember it very clearly. It was really a proud possession of his. My father painted—he never could really draw. My father hadn't lost his ability to draw; he never really learned how to draw a figure. He never learned anatomy, really. Most of what he did was by rote, so that his work always had this calendar-painting look. He was very skilled at doing cartouches and decorative things. He knew all the techniques of painting and so forth, but he could never really go beyond that.

For a while I was very interested in painting. I wanted to be a painter, which of course upset my mother terribly because she was the practical one in the family. She was a very pragmatic woman in many ways—totally surprised and really dismayed by art in itself. She felt it was a hobby. She never thought of it as a vocation or as a life work. She was terrified I would go that route, and she and my father were at loggerheads. I remember her accusing him of leading me into it almost as though he were a dope pusher. She'd say, "Don't encourage him; you're going to ruin him. He's going to wind up in some attic somewhere starving to death!" She had a very practical sense and was very contemptuous of any effort made on the line of art for art's sake. If I would show her something I did, she would immediately want to know what the market value of it was. That was her thinking. And yet she was a remarkably astute and clever woman, and had a great deal of heart, and a very decent woman. It was the atmosphere in which she grew up; things were a matter of survival. Economic security was her key. I recall she finally compromised. One day we were sitting talking in the little kitchen, and she said, "If you're going to go into art," and she sighed very heavily as though to say, if I can't stop you, "at least be an art teacher, because I heard from a friend of mine that art teachers get a steady salary. They don't make much, but they get a good income, and they get two months off in the summer—and they get retirement pay." Then she said, "I would be able to face my friends a little bit more. Then I could say, 'Well, you're an art teacher.' That has some dignity to it." That was her fond hope, and she was brokenhearted when I didn't go to Syracuse where there was a scholarship available and I couldn't afford to take it. I just couldn't afford to go to college. They were flat dead broke.

I mean, we talk in this era about being broke, but when you suddenly discover that your parents have something like $75 in the bank, which represented the total amount they were able to salvage out of the collapse of the Bank of the United States. As always, my father seemed to be right in the eye of the disaster. I recall a very sad scene at home one evening when he announced that he had just come from the bank, there was a big line, they had shut the doors, nobody could go in and get their money, and we were dead broke. Zero. We had enough to pay for two, three months' rent, I recall him saying. It was a family question what to do about it. And yet somehow or other we managed to live. I recall in his more affluent times we had a car. He bought a Ford and drove me around through Central Park. I recall he took me past the one traffic light in the city, and told me that someday there would be a lot of these traffic lights, he hoped. Because, he said, that was going to be the thing of the future. He was always fascinated with that kind of thing. He'd clip little filler articles about unique things around the country. In fact, that book I did, *Facts, Statistics and Trivia* was sort of inspired by that idea.

Later, as I grew older, we found our way into a "better neighborhood" . . . peopled by policemen, civil servants, postmen. These were people to envy, in those days, because those were good solid jobs: $25 a week, every week, with a pension sometime in the future. It was security. I recall comparing notes with Jules Feiffer one day, because his background was pretty much like mine. He passed through the same thing, only about fifteen years later. And he said his parents didn't even have the dignity of being poor. I always remembered that remark because it describes what very few people understand. Just as you try to explain to your children about what the Depression was like and it's hard now for anybody to understand. "What do you mean, there were no jobs? I mean, you could always go out and sweep floors, somebody would pay something." There were just no jobs! Seeing people in Chesterfield coats with velvet collars and a nice bowler hat, good shoes, standing in Wall Street with an orange box selling apples at five cents each. These were weird, almost theatrical scenes. People who had a car in the yard, a very good car, which they couldn't drive because they didn't have money for gasoline. They couldn't sell it. Anyway, they didn't want to give it up. Some kind of times. They helped shape your outlook. But in the main, I can say that I lived within a family that had some feeling of dignity.

Finally, just before entering high school, or the early part of high school, I was selling newspapers down on a Wall Street corner. So you might say I began my career in newspaper marketing and distribution. As the Depression continued, I maintained myself in high school selling art work, posters, and stuff like that on the side to make a few dollars, and selling newspapers in the afternoon. I went to elementary schools, in various places, Brooklyn and the Bronx. Very early in elementary school, when I was seven or eight, I became very interested in art. I spent a lot of time drawing. I recall my father telling me that he was very pleased at my showing talent, and got very interested in it. I showed a greater interest in art than I did at academic subjects. I was good at writing; I remember my teachers telling me that. I recall my father finding some art school in an effort to help me along, which had a system of teaching art by strapping your arm to a kind of machine that would guide your hand. My father was always intrigued with that kind of instant educational thing. I suppose I got from him a love for all kinds of machinery.

I was very friendly with a boy named Fred, whose last name I don't remember, when I was about eight years old. He had a brother who was working in the early Max Fleischer Studios as a cartoonist. Animation had been proliferating. We went up to visit a studio once, and I decided at that time that that was going to be my career. And I recall doing a lot of drawing, drawing on the streets and sidewalks. I was amused when I went to Denmark a couple of years ago to discover that students were making great chalk drawings on the sidewalks, and it was regarded as a rather new thing. But it wasn't new with kids in New York.

I went to DeWitt Clinton High School, and my interest in art and writing of course sharpened there. It had a good teaching staff. I got into DeWitt Clinton in the black depths of the Depression, between 1932 and 1936, I've forgotten the exact dates now. It was a very good school in those days. It had a huge mix, a lot of black students, and a huge mix of economic levels, which was unique then. There were so-called "wealthy kids," as well as very poor ghetto kids. It started as Boys' High and became DeWitt Clinton later, so it had a lot of kids from Hell's Kitchen and so on. They had a very good art department, and they had a good newspaper program and a unique journalism class run by a teacher who is still alive and with whom I keep in very active touch still—a fellow by the name of Ray Phillipson who is very beloved by all of us. In fact, he influenced a great many people who became successful in the publishing field.

I became interested in theater. I got involved with Adolph Green, doing class shows and so forth, and I thought very seriously for a while of becoming a set designer. I had a whole range of experiences. I was very active in school politics. I was active on the newspaper. I started a comic strip in the school newspaper, my first comic strip. Bob Kane was a fellow student. Bob and I became very close friends for a while, and we also knew each other after we finished school. When I opened up the studios he did a feature for me, about a cat or something. Oh yes, *Peter Pupp* it was called.

While I was at DeWitt Clinton I used to take on summer scholarships. A lot of the art schools in the area, like the Art Students League and there was a school of commercial art somewhere, they'd offer scholarships to the better students in the high schools in an effort to bring a whole bunch of paying students with them, because things were so bad in those days. Generally the kid who was good enough to win the scholarship would have a little entourage of followers who were perhaps more affluent and could pay the tuition, so he would pay for himself by bringing in the three or four other kids. That's how I got my art education, actually. The Art Students League was probably the most fruitful of all for me. The thing that really I attribute most of my drawing ability to is the period I studied with George Bridgeman, who was a great anatomist. And I studied painting with Robert Brackman. So actually the greatest part of my formal art education came from the Art Students League. And a lot of it, too, was from hundreds of little places that were set up by the WPA at the time. They'd offer courses and you'd take them because they were free. They were federally funded. But a large portion of my education, like everybody else, was self-education. We would spend a lot of time sketching and drawing and reading and looking. We saw a great deal of movies. Movies then became a drug for all of us. So Saturday afternoon was spent in going to the movies, movies, movies. And pulps! I was an avid pulp reader.

My interest in the theater didn't materialize. That fell apart on the guillotine of economic decisions. There was a fellow named Dunkel I was at DeWitt Clinton with, and his father had a firm that made all the scenery for the Metropolitan Opera. I was very excited about that, because what I really wanted to do was stage sets. I thought that was the greatest. I used to make sketches, and we made models, and I did very avant-garde stuff. Then he came and said we could get a job; his father had worked it so we could go with a road show and do stage sets, that is, paint the scenery and so forth, and maybe occasionally design something. I was all excited and went home, and my mother was dead against it . . . great Victorian thinking. Oh, she had an aunt or a sister who was a showgirl, and that was a terrible life, and this would lead to all kinds of terrible things for her boy. Not only that, but I had to stay around and make some money, and what they offered to pay us on the road show was just nothing; just room and board—there'd be no money going home and I had to do something more gainful. So that fell apart.

I think by then I was beginning to see that what turned me on, really, was the idea of print. I still like it. Of all the media, print has always been the most attractive to me. There's a permanence to it. There's an intimacy in reading that to me transcends motion pictures. People ask me, "With your technical approach to things, why didn't you go into motion pictures? Why haven't you been in animation?" The reason is that film never seemed to me to be satisfying, and that's probably why I didn't pursue it heavily. I have had several opportunities to go into film, I've always been on the border of it. But working with live actors is something . . . I suppose there isn't that kind of instant response that print gives me. When copies get printed, it's there, it exists, and you can look at it any time you want.

I did some acting too for a while—again in high school. High school was tremendous; to me it was everything. The four years at DeWitt Clinton gave me probably all that I could have gotten anywhere. I suppose had I gone on to college I might have gotten a different dimension. I might have been somebody totally different. But those formative years were very satisfying; I had an opportunity to try almost everything. For example, a fellow student, Ken Ginniger (who later became a publisher with Prentice Hall), and I started our own underground journal; the first publishing venture I ever went into, a literary journal called *The Hound and Horn*, or, I think it was *Lion and Unicorn*. I've forgotten. Something like that. It was very snooty. We were all into T. S. Eliot, and that was the thing . . . We got a printer somewhere down on Varick Street. See, paperbacks in those days were a very snooty format. The French, ever since Emile Zola's day, had paperbacks. Generally they were the printer's remainders, and he would simply wrap brown paper around them. In fact, that was the way a lot of the French books were sold, because that was the only way of getting them to students cheaply. So we put out this thing, which had poetry and writings, and some erotic writing and so forth—or what was considered at that time erotic writing. We needed illustrations, and since I was the art director and co-publisher I discovered very quickly that making metal plates—in those days there was no offset to speak of, it was all letterpress—was very costly. That led me into wood engraving. You could buy wood blocks at that time which were type-high; their height was equal to the height of the type. So I cut wood engravings for the illustrations for the book, and that printer printed them along with the typeset material. I learned a lot about wood engraving. In fact, I still have some of the old tools. I had for many years the old blocks. I saved them because . . . every time I hit a new medium I decided that was for me and I was going to go on. That's why today I'm very tolerant and pleased to see a student really get "worked up" about a newly discovered area. I advise students not to worry about being trapped by a given medium. There are so many other factors and events rubbing on a human being that generally speaking unless he makes a mighty mind-closing effort he or she will not remain "trapped" for long.

I would go down to the New School in the evenings. It had just opened up and it was then a very avant-garde school. (It's much more conservative today.) There was a painting class or lecture series being given by the muralist

Thomas Hart Benton. He was very new and very avant garde at the time. The situation or the mix then in the so-called underground in the new art was not a heck of a lot different than it is today. They're really the same people, and the conversation's the same. It's not quite as political as it was, that's the big difference. In those days there was a lot of political experimentation. Communism was a new concept. Fascism. Technocracy. Socialism. Neo-socialism. All kinds of things. You could be a communist one day, and a fascist or a technocrat the following day. You could get involved in all these unique political systems. People were dreaming of brave new worlds, and artists kept thinking that under a socialist or communist government they wouldn't have to worry about making a living. We could paint, do what we wanted. Nobody really could conceive of the idea that if somebody set up a social system that would free the painter to paint he'd have to paint what they told him to paint, or he'd be an anti-establishment. But these things formed part of our mix; each time, they left a little residue, a little spot of paint on you.

In about 1936 I left school and got my first job, with the *New York American* down on South Street, working from nine at night to five in the morning in the advertising department. I was writing copy for small one-inch, two-inch ads, and laying them out. If there was an illustration I'd do the illustration and perhaps do some lettering—although I was an atrocious letterer. I love lettering, but I'm very dependent on people who assist me on lettering. I have come to regard lettering as absolutely integral to the main art itself. I do a lot more of it now because of this.

After a short while I left to freelance, because I felt I wasn't doing enough art there. Some printer gave me a job as his "art department," and I was very impressed with that. I could freelance, I had a few accounts, and I would help in the afternoon washing up the press, which helped pay for the space. And then he would turn over to me some of his accounts that needed artwork. My first account was a funeral parlor. I did letterheads and ads for him. Another job I got I think was my first comic. I sold my first commercial comic—and maybe it was the first one anybody did—to Grease Solvent, which was a gritty soap compound for printers and people who work with oils and grease. I got it through the printer; it was his account. I think it was a four-page comic on yellow paper, because that was their package color, which told the advantages of using Grease Solvent for washing your hands. Meanwhile I tried selling cartoons. There was a whole group of guys selling cartoons to *Liberty*, *Judge* and the old *Life*, and they'd go up to the Wednesday sessions where the editors selected cartoons. I was never successful. Bob Kane was, but they would never buy any of my stuff. I tried various places; I even made a stab at fashion illustration, which I bombed out on. They kept saying my stuff looked like comics. And they were right.

Then I stumbled onto a magazine called *Wow!*, one of the first attempts at comics . . .

This transcript was recorded on December 27, 1973, and is an excerpt from a much longer feature titled "Art & Commerce: An Oral Reminiscence by Will Eisner" that appeared in Panels 1, Summer 1979. Panels *was published and edited by John Benson, and this first issue was devoted to Eisner.*

An Interview with Will Eisner

DAVE SIM / 1974

From *Comic Art News and Reviews*, July 1974, 2–5. Reprinted by permission of
Dave Sim and John Balge.

Sim: How do you see the development of comic art in recent years?

Eisner: I think it is undergoing an exciting imaginative change. I think we're
at the threshold of a big directional change in comic book art. I'm very excited
by the new, more intelligent, more intellectual talent that is coming along. I
think the biggest single thing that is happening in comics is that it's moving
toward intellectualism. I think this is an exciting thing and I think as technology increases the physical format of comics is changing. And the audience is
increasing. As the audience becomes more demanding and more intelligent, I
think comics will become that way too. I wish I was twenty years old. I'm trying now to be part of it all because I think it's great.

Sim: Do you think the underground market has potential?

Eisner: I think it will always be worthwhile and potential in one form or
another. I consider *The Spirit* an underground feature. I consider myself an
overaged underground type.

Sim: What package have you preferred to present *The Spirit* in?

Eisner: Well, I would say presenting *The Spirit* as part of a newspaper supplement. In recent years, the most exciting to me has been the underground
comic (Denis Kitchen) experience where I did some covers. Really, as far as
the Warren books are concerned, momentarily they are all reprints. In some
cases I'm redoing portions, but it's the most promising package yet.

Sim: Of black-and-white or colour, which do you prefer to work in?

Eisner: I like to work in black-and-white, that's my medium. I think in terms of colour. I like to work in washes, but it's not practical and my work comes out weak as a result. I prefer colour although black-and-white has a lot for me. I'm used to black-and-white done in a manner which can be supportive of colour.

Sim: How essential is the format of the comic book to its appeal?

Eisner: I think that the comic book technique is a series of pictures with specific reading sequence. And *that* is essential to its presentation. Whether they are framed by a thick panel or no panel at all is really unimportant. It is a combination of words and pictures which tell a story. And as long as that's present, whether they are enclosed in a box called a panel or whether there are three of them on a page or four of them on a page is unimportant. They are a very important continuing medium—motion pictures on paper.

Sim: How conscious have you been of reader reaction to *The Spirit*?

Eisner: It went up and down. Newspaper comic artists don't and didn't get as much mail as one thinks they did. And those fans who do write either write very flatteringly, are friends in the first place, or they are enemies and they write you nasty letters. Or you get letters from people who write about something they feel good about, like the woman who wrote and said "God bless you" after I did a Christmas story. You do develop a consciousness, but you continue to write to an audience that you've created yourself, so you have a vision of the kind of audience you are talking to. You can't work without an audience or the concept of an audience. That's very important. In my case, I knew my audience to be a certain kind of person—a young college person, perhaps a little more well read than the average comic book reader. I didn't have an age fix. I couldn't have said it was an eight-year-old or a ten-year-old. I had some feedback, but not a lot. In fact, I tried to avoid getting too hung up on the feedback because you tend to write for the few who keep writing letters and that's not the whole audience. I was always conscious that I was writing to a broad audience that read newspapers in the 1940s and early 1950s. You knew that a Sunday newspaper was read by the entire family. Therefore you had the son or daughter who was going to college, the little eight-year-old kid who was in elementary school, and the father and mother. So you had a broad audience and I did try to straddle them all. And the range of stories was an obvious evidence that I was trying to reach them all. But basically the stories were aimed at my same level because that's where I was talking at.

Sim: The Spirit often lashes out when there is no need to. Why is he so violent?

Eisner: Well, I've never seen him as lashing out when there was no need. I attribute his violent nature to the fact that we are telling stories about violence. Violence is very attractive. Violence and adventure is what it's all about. I don't see him as a violent person who will lash out illogically. In fact, I see The Spirit as a very logical, realistic person. I think he is a very middle class kind of person. Oh, he's capable of rising to anger over injustice. This would represent a basic characteristic in both The Spirit and any other kind of comic character. There isn't time for him to wreak retribution on his enemies by more subtle means. I don't know that the reader would stand still for subtle retribution. I think the reader wants to see a violent outburst. I think they want to see things settled by a gunfight. I just don't see him as violent. I see him as a very human, real kind of character. I think we are basically primitive people who understand the importance of violence. And violence is always there in one form or another, in word or deed. It is always part of our efforts at survival.

Sim: Do you get rid of any pent-up emotion through *The Spirit*?

Eisner: That's a question like, "Do you beat your wife?" We're writing fantasies. If you are serious about what you do, as I've always seemed to have been, you insert those actions which have always been part of you. After I finish a story, I don't lie there and say, "Well, I really did it!" It's a story that I like to tell, that I want to tell. I'm a storyteller. I'm no different from anybody who likes to tell a good story and tell it well. I tell it in words and pictures. I think the flights of technique and skill that I can exhibit are like that of an athlete who's going to do four handstands on one finger or something of that nature. That I think is a better equation, a better example of what I do, than saying I approach *The Spirit* all pent-up with these terrible violent things which I HAVE TO GET OUT! I HAVE TO TELL THE WORLD! No, that's not entirely me.

Sim: Was the humour in *The Spirit* consciously injected or did it develop naturally?

Eisner: If you mean by that did I say, "I better put some humour in here," or "I have a drawer full of jokes for this page," no. I was writing the story. My definition of humour is an incongruity that is bizarre and that suddenly occurs. Where I saw The Spirit doing something bizarre or incongruous, I injected the humour. Where I wanted to be serious, I was very serious. I tried very hard to be serious. My sense of humour is my own. It's very much mine and I couldn't very well be Bob Hope or Jack Benny or Lenny Bruce any more that they could be me. So, yes I did inject humour because I felt it should be in there. Sometimes I would sit down with a funny idea and put humour in the story all the way through. Sometimes a note of pathos would creep in and I would treat it as such.

Sim: What advantages are there in drawing the stories you write?

Eisner: I think that stories I write must be drawn by me. I am a firm believer in writing and drawing your own stuff and I tell that to my students. Although I can recognize the practical necessity of having an artist *and* a writer working as a team because they can turn out twice as much work. There are some writers who can't draw and there are some artists who feel that they can't write. I don't quite go along with that. I believe that a good example of great comic artist-writer combinations of my time was Jules Feiffer whose draughtsmanship was not as good as Jack Kirby or somebody of that caliber. But what he has to say is terribly important. And he graphically portrays what he has to say with skill adequate to the task. It's important to both write and draw. I think that drawing is an extension of the writing and the words are an extension of the drawing. There's no clear separation. So, in answer to your question, I think it's very important to draw my own stuff, even down to designing the chairs and tables if necessary.

Sim: Are there disadvantages?

Eisner: Time. If comics become a more important media and if comic artists are paid adequately, then they will be able to devote, let's say, a month of their life to a single story, instead of having to turn out that same story in a week in order to meet the page rate. Comic artists are still being paid by the page rather than by a given story and they're still using comics as a means of making a living. You might very well have asked that question of a painter. If he wants to make a hundred thousand a year and gets a thousand dollars a painting, he has to turn out a hundred paintings. It's the same with comic artists. A lot of great talent is being destroyed in this business largely because they have to make a living at the same time. A lot of great talent is made because of that. There are two sides to the coin. A lot of the great talent emerged out of the fact that they had to turn out four or five hundred drawings (pages) a year in order to earn enough money. And in that process they trained themselves as a great athlete might. I don't mean to say that this is bad or good. It's just a fact of life and it'll change when a man can spend a lot of time. European artists today are turning out fewer stories than Americans. They get enough money out of it because they get high rates and they survive and they turn out a marvelous piece of art. There's a lot that contributes. There's distribution; there's media; there's audience; there's publications in which you appear; there's what you're saying. There's a whole wealth of things that go into it. The European artists are not really interested in storytelling. Gil Kane's right. I discussed this with him just a couple of months ago and he mentioned it and I agreed with him. He's a very astute observer of our art form.

Sim: How important is storytelling?

Eisner: Very important! I think that this is a communication art and a drawing should communicate a message. A large part of that problem is caused by the fans, the readers, particularly fans, or what we call comic freaks, who become very excited about flights of tour de force in comic technique. This somehow transmits itself to the artist who then thinks, "Well, that's something I'm going to do." It's like the entertainer who jumps through a hoop backwards and the audience applauds. He tells himself to do it again, only this time through four hoops. And all of a sudden that's all he has to do to get applause which is often the *only* applause he hears. It's a very easy thing to get caught up in just the craftsmanship side. It's a very involving thing, craftsmanship. You get lost in it. It's much harder to tell a story. Some people have no story to tell. Lou Fine was a very intelligent man. He was well read, an intellect, but he couldn't really care less about telling a story. He didn't want to tell a story. All he wanted to do was devote his time to rendering beautiful drawings. He had to tell a story, ultimately, later when it was forced on him. But telling a story, saying something with your art, is very important. A piece of graffiti on a wall has more message to me than some gallery art that I've seen. The Spanish artists are tremendous. They are enormous. But they are émigrés from the field of illustration and painting where there's no market for them. So they've come here. It's not the first time it happened. It happened when I started. A lot of the early artists who worked with me were painters who had nowhere else to work, so they would do comics. I think the message is important and the story is important. This is a storytelling media, or a story telling art form. Period.

Sim: Are many artists passed over by fans who don't understand their work?

Eisner: I think that happens in any medium. There are a lot of people around who are going to be discovered six or ten or twenty years from now who are working their hearts out. A guy who comes to mind is Klaus Nordling, a guy who still works with me, did "Lady Luck," but never really achieved the fame and prominence that he should have. And he could write and draw. For some reason or other, no one appreciated him, in many cases because they didn't get to see him. That's why the undergrounds are so marvelous. I wish the underground was around when I was a kid. What a great opportunity . . . to get out a magazine with a small circulation—a chance to be published! If he has anything at all, no matter how embryonic, the hungry underground will exhibit him! You get him an audience . . . small, yes, but an *audience!* I'm publishing a magazine with the work from kids in my class at the School for Visual Arts. This is the first time in their lives they'll see their work in print. What an exciting thing to have someone see your work! This is what it's all about.

Sim: What kind of stories appeal to today's audiences?

Eisner: Right now it appears that "sensory" material is most popular. The reader seems to want to "feel" with his nerve ends not with his intellect. The stories that appealed to the 1940s people were what I call the morality stories. They accepted certain standards that were valid then, such as "Crime does not pay." This generation does not believe that crime does not pay and will not accept it. Secondly, we accepted in the 1940s and 1950s the description of crime as being a very simplistic kind of thing. The definition of crime has changed. We now know that if a man is found standing over a person who he has just assaulted, the public, the arbiters of what is evil, are willing to ask themselves, "Now wait a minute. What made this man do this? Why did he do it?" Crime is not as clear cut any longer. Crimes change as society changes. At one time miscegenation was a crime. Now it's not a crime. My grandparents might have regarded it as a heinous crime against society. Homosexuality was regarded as a crime only until yesterday. So "what-is-crime" changes. What I called a crime in 1940 is perhaps no longer a crime. Of course, there are basic crimes around which we live, like man hurting man. That's an interesting area which I would like to explore at great length in some new stories. I was just talking to Jim Warren about that just a while ago when he asked me, "What would you do if you did new stuff?"

Sim: Do you foresee any problems in working for Warren?

Eisner: The reason I entrusted this feature to Jim Warren is because I believe the standards are very high and they're compatible to mine. In many ways I think they are higher than any of the other publishers in the business, largely because he has a small house and he must fight to survive. Largely, his survival depends on his ability to put out a good quality magazine. I find him very quality oriented and I think that there is a mutual respect between us. I think he is a very able publisher and he has a creative background. I don't think he'll betray my trust. The standards and tastes are entirely mine. I accept the responsibility for them. Everything that's done has to have my approval. He consented to that without any question, which shows, as far as I'm concerned, a great deal of trust in me on his part.

Sim: Do you look forward to doing all new material in the future?

Eisner: I think that it will be some time before I have to. I'd like to see if *The Spirit* has acceptance as a new feature, as a new, NOW feature. If it does, I will throw myself back into it. Meanwhile, I'm doing a lot of new stuff in the way of books and other materials. I think the next four or five issues will tell me what kind of an audience I will have. If I find I have an audience, I'd get back into it. To answer your question, I wouldn't hesitate to create new material if the audience asks for it.

An Interview with Will Eisner

JERRY DEFUCCIO / 1976

From Robert M. Overstreet, *The Comic Book Price Guide 1976–1977* (Cleveland, TN: Robert M. Overstreet, 1976), pp. 33–37. Reprinted by permission of Gemstone Publishing, Inc. All rights reserved.

Jerry DeFuccio: Will, what was the creative atmosphere in which *The Spirit* evolved? You know, gestation time, false starts, trying it out on your associates . . . ?

Will Eisner: *The Spirit* was created in haste, to satisfy the need to provide a weekly comic book section for newspapers. The package, at the time, was the novelty, not the features. The Register & Tribune Syndicate and Busy Arnold had the idea, precipitated by newspaper (Sunday) requests, and came to me. I had, by then, something of a reputation in comic books. Also, I was an "independent" with a track record for production dependability. Little did they know I was a "closet classicist" who dreamt of doing big things with sequential literature. I tried several ideas in rough . . . tried the names on Arnold . . . decided on a detective thrust . . . fought Arnold to keep from doing . . . or making him a superhero. Settled for a mask in lieu of costume. Started Thursday night . . . by Saturday night and four phone calls to several bars, I got it in shape.

DeFuccio: Your writing in *The Spirit* is full of the exhilaration of sounds that move: "Down from the mountains of madness, through the gorges of greed, flows the river of crime . . . !"

I think that's called personification, right? How do you judge when a sequence is "writing itself," to your complete satisfaction. And how often has a sequence taken a fortuitous turn that you hadn't even planned?

Eisner: I write in onomatopoeia, which relies on instinct rather than just the conscious mind. Most of my writing is done by sound and visual. I think of words and narrative as the "sound track." As with all art, "serendipity" is a part of the process. I generally start with a premise . . . a doorknob if you will and I proceed to build a house around it.

DeFuccio: It's unusual for a comics artist-writer to own his character. How come you own *The Spirit*?
Eisner: Stubbornness . . . paranoia . . . faith in my future . . . willingness to blow the deal.

DeFuccio: Did you own it from the start, Will?
Eisner: Yes, Jerry! It was a condition of my deal with Arnold. I compromised by allowing him to be my partner, with copyright in his name. After the war (II) I bought him out of even that.

DeFuccio: While the weekly *Spirit* booklets thrived for a dozen years, the daily strip folded after three or so. How come?
Eisner: I was drafted after one and a half years. Anyhow, I somehow was unable to squeeze myself into four panels. I needed a few more years to learn how. Also, 1942 was a lousy time to start a new strip.

DeFuccio: What sort of circulation did the strip have, how many papers?
Eisner: Four or five. Don't remember.

DeFuccio: How many papers used *The Spirit* Sunday booklets?
Eisner: Twenty Sunday papers. Five million circulation.

DeFuccio: Were the booklets printed by Arnold?
Eisner: They were printed by Greater Buffalo Press.

DeFuccio: Sounds like a pretty confident name for a Press! How were they distributed?
Eisner: They were ready prints. Each paper ordered a quantity and had its logo imprinted. They were delivered by truck.

DeFuccio: How far ahead did you work, Will?
Eisner: Three months.

DeFuccio: How did a client paper pay? A flat fee or so much per book?
Eisner: Per copy.

DeFuccio: There was a drastic change in the look of both the booklet and the strip after you entered the service. Was this done with your approval?
Eisner: Reluctantly, Jerry! All good talent, except for Lou Fine, was drafted. After a while I couldn't even write stories because I was in uniform and into Army guides, manuals, visuals . . .

DeFuccio: I remember seeing *Army Motors* and *Firepower*, very well done, Will! Joe Dope, terror of the Motor Pool. So, Arnold handled *The Spirit* in your absence . . . ?
Eisner: That's right.

DeFuccio: Let's take it from the antipasto, Will. Were you already working professionally in comics, before graduating from DeWitt Clinton High School? The earliest Henle and Centaur comics show that your style and idiom developed early in your career.
Eisner: I did my first commercial comic while in Clinton. A flyer for Gre-Solvent, all in comics on yellow paper. I was into comics early in high school. The only market then was newspaper syndicates.

DeFuccio: What was your connection with Editors Press Service, Will?
Eisner: Eisner & Iger sold its first output through them. Young Eisner had the idea that "original comics" were the coming thing. There were not enough famous syndicated features around. I convinced Jerry Iger to come in with me on the premise. He knew of Editors Press's shortage of material for foreign sales. So our first customer was the Joshua Powers organization . . . Editors Press.

DeFuccio: Characters such as Sheena, Hawks of the Sea . . . ?
Eisner: Yes, they first appeared in an overseas publication called *Wags*.

DeFuccio: *Jumbo Comics* seemed to reuse some of this material. Whose idea was it to do the magazine tab size? Was it, like earlier attempts at "big mags" by Delacorte and Major Nicholson, unsuccessful in the larger format?
Eisner: It was T. T. Scott's idea . . . based on an attempt to get better newsstand display. Also, it was on colored stock in black and white.

DeFuccio: What about the Eisner-Iger Syndicate, reborn as Phoenix? What sort of strips did you do? Where did they appear?
Eisner: We syndicated newly created strips to small weeklies . . . with space

for tie-in ads (local) . . . good idea, but our salesmen were crooks . . . we had three of them.

DeFuccio: Was your first professional comic book work in *Wow*?
Eisner: Yes . . . *Wow, What a Magazine* . . .

DeFuccio: What about *Circus* . . . ?
Eisner: That was done for Monte Bourjailly, the former editor of United Feature Syndicate. *Circus* was an ill-fated "classy" comic book.

DeFuccio: Where was your full-complement comic books studio located?
Eisner: We had fifteen people at 202 East 42nd Street . . . ran it like a Ford Motor Company. We had to . . . we were selling pages at $7.00 and $5.00 each.

DeFuccio: Bob Kane worked for you . . . ?
Eisner: Yes, he did Peter Pupp and Spark Stevens of the Navy, Jest Laffs . . . and lots of fillers . . . then he went to Detective Comics for more money.

DeFuccio: *Mad*'s Dave Berg is especially rhapsodic about the days he spent in your studio, doing *Death Patrol* and *Uncle Sam*. He says that working conditions were ideal and his co-workers were happy and attuned. Was your studio somewhat of a "classroom," too? Did you create new characters and features solely on your own or with the individual artists who were going to draw them . . . ?
Eisner: Dave is right . . . it was a golden time!! We worked buttock to buttock and communicated like cellblock inmates. My style was to at first rough out an idea . . . sometimes drawing the first page. It was very much like a school-workshop format. Lots of looking over the shoulder . . . suggesting changes. Talking, talking, talking . . . and sharing. Getting and giving! I was squad leader . . . so, it started with me in the beginning. We learned from each other!

DeFuccio: You developed many fine "thinking artists" who conceive crystalline continuity and dramatic story-telling, under your guidance and direction, Will. Aside from the "neophytes," you had such old-timers as Alex Blum and Henry Fletcher and the ubiquitous Henry C. Kiefer working for you. The notion of ingrained former pulp artists and magazine illustrators re-tooling to adjust to the comics boom is tantalizing. Was it tougher converting them than working with the fresh-outlook "youngsters" . . . ?
Eisner: Not really, Jerry. It's hard to evaluate them as a group. I was recruiting

wherever I could. I sought talent in the highly crowded illustration field. I was more interested in the man than in his portfolio. It was different then . . . not many comic book artists around. As a general rule, the easiest way to avoid "hacks" is to recruit outside the field.

DeFuccio: In a burgeoning industry bankrolled by people who were hardly intrepid or imaginative, printers, accountants and garment businessmen, what were the advantages of your partnership with Everett "Busy" Arnold of Quality Comics . . . ? In our correspondence, Busy impressed me as not so much of a creative factor but more like a resident live wire or cheerleader. Perhaps, regarding his artists and writers much like the athletes he rounded up for his alma mater, Brown University.

Eisner: Exactly. Busy was to me what he was best . . . a salesman. What a productive artist needs most is a salesman. You don't make contacts . . . you don't call on newspapers . . . you don't know what's "happening out there" . . . or what editors are buying and paying . . . sitting at the drawing board in the studio.

DeFuccio: Speaking of publishers, I've always been friendly with your present publisher, Jim Warren. Jim likes to ask me if I'm still with *Mad*, whenever he meets me with a date. But Jim has rendered a great service to *Spirit* enthusiasts and new readers by reviving this material in solid magazine form. My *Spirit* sections from the *Newark Star Ledger* days are rapidly decomposing . . .

Eisner: Jim and I are very much in accord. I really admire him and respect his thinking on the magazine.

DeFuccio: The Flame isn't far behind The Spirit as one of my favorites. I always thought of him as a sleek, sophisticated fire genie. You and Lou Fine gave an exceptionally delicate touch to that character. Can you rekindle any sidelights on The Flame?

Eisner: Lou and I were very close professionally. I admired his Herculean draftsmanship and he respected what I wanted to do with story. He didn't like to write . . . at first . . . but Mama Mia, that guy could draw! Lou was a very sensitive person. The sleekness and sophistication was part of the shop atmosphere. "Hack" in our shop was a dirty word.

DeFuccio: As mentor of so many distinctive talents, I'm sure you were particularly fond and proud of Jack Cole. That man put the splash in splash panel!

And he had little subplots going on in the backgrounds. How did you two devise *Plastic Man* for *Police Comics* . . . ?

Eisner: My memory is vague on that. Jack really worked for Busy Arnold's books. Busy and I were beginning to get competitive. Busy hired Jack . . . Jack (a genius in his own right) came up with *Plastic Man*. He probably reacted to Busy's pressure for another Superman, like I did. *Plastic Man* was, at first, a put on. Jack would fight back that way. Don't give me too much credit for Jack.

DeFuccio: Your lead feature in *Wonder Comics* No. 1 (May 1939), Wonder Man, lasted but one issue, causing a lot of conjecture in my prep school. I remember him fondly because of his non-macho name . . . Fred Carson. He acquired his extraordinary powers through a ring given him by a mystic in a quickie opening panel ceremony, amidst rampant flames. I'm going to my prep school reunion, soon, and I'd like to be able to tell them why Wonder Man got the axe . . .

Eisner: Wonder Man was an outright imitation of Superman, perpetuated by Victor Fox, Publisher. I didn't know it but Victor Fox, my customer, specified the dimensions to Iger who was the company salesman. I remember raising the issue with Iger who, as senior partner, cautioned me against interfering with a client's right to get anything he's willing to pay for. When Fox was sued by Donnenfeld for plagiarism, I testified against Fox . . . which resulted in Eisner & Iger suffering its first major financial loss . . . about $3000 . . . which Fox refused to pay us because of "our betrayal." Fox lost the suit . . . was enjoined to "cease and desist." Young cartoonist learns about the world of business. It was a foundation case because later actions between Superman and Captain Marvel had stems that led to or emanated from this case.

DeFuccio: Did you ever raid another outfit to get a talent, Will?

Eisner: The talent was a terrified boy named Alex Kotzky . . . yes, he does Apartment 3-G today! Chuck Cuidera smuggled him up to the studio one day during the noon-hour. I looked at his work! Dave Berg and Bob Powell and Chuck Mazoujian looked at his work . . . a genius. Fantastic inker. I said, okay, we'll call you. Kotzky nearly fainted. Cuidera said, "We can't do that! You gotta hire him." "Okay," I said, "You're hired! Come in next week." "No," says our Italian madman . . . "he's gotta start now . . . NOW!!" "Why . . . ?," I say. "Because Chesler won't let him out of the shop . . . he's a prisoner. They make him eat lunch in the office. They won't let him talk to anyone," says Cuidera.

"Okay . . . start now," I shrug! "I can't," says Kotzky very quietly. Cuidera says his coat and lunch and portfolio and pencils and pens are back there and if he goes back . . . CLANG!! They'll shut him in! So Cuidera goes back to steal Alex's belongings.

DeFuccio: Will, I understand a *Spirit* two-hour TV movie is in the works. Billy Friedkin of *The French Connection* and *The Exorcist* at the helm. Any new developments on the production as *Comic Book Price Guide* No. 6 goes on press . . . ?

Eisner: It is in the works, Jerry. A story is being thrashed out. I'll be a consultant and maybe involved in the graphics. Not ready to report . . . airing is due November 1976 . . . NBC.

DeFuccio: Say, Will, you look a lot like Commissioner Dolan . . . !

Eisner: My students, whom I teach at the school of Visual Arts, told me that. I told them I used to be Denny Colt . . .

Will Eisner Interview

CAT YRONWODE / 1978

From *The Comics Journal*, No. 46 (May 1979), 35–49, and No. 47 (July 1979), 41–48.
Reprinted by permission of catherine yronwode.

yronwode: Since you are best known to comic book readers as the creator of
The Spirit, suppose we start with a history of that era—how did you come to
create that character?

Eisner: It was in 1940, late '39, to be exact—the Register and Tribune Syndicate asked me to produce a newspaper insert for them, called a ready-print,
which would be in comic book format. Now that was the mission. They left
for me a certain amount of freedom to develop the characters that I wanted
to do, to develop the material I thought would be appropriate. By "freedom"
I mean that they had no prerequisites or requirements in the way of stories
or ideas, other than that they said they wanted stuff that was in the genre of
comic books. You must understand that the years between 1936 and 1940 saw
the rise of comic books as a popular reading force and the newspapers, ever
alert to trends, sought to latch on.

There was a very commercial interest in the comic book insert—in fact, at
the same time, King Features started a competitive one. Theirs only ran a few
months, but couldn't make it.

So, as I said, I had freedom and I developed three features. It was a sixteen-
page book, eight pages of the feature that I would personally produce and
then two four-page features—*Mr. Mystic* and perhaps *Lady Luck*. *Mr. Mystic* I
assigned to Bob Powell, now deceased, and *Lady Luck* was assigned to Chuck
Mazoujian, who could really draw—he was a very good artist—but the writing was done either by me or by another writer—a freelancer outside the
shop. Klaus Nordling took it over from Mazoujian and John Celardo in about
1947 . . . I think.

yronwode: How many people were working with you at that time?

Eisner: About four or five. You see, I had left Eisner and Iger in order to do *The Spirit*; I sold Jerry Iger my 50 percent stock interest in the Eisner and Iger Corporation, and with it went all the customers and all the properties, including Sheena, which I had created, and a whole bunch of other features. But I took with me some of the good artists like Lou Fine, Bob Powell, Chuck Mazoujian, and a couple of others, in order to create a staff that would be able to produce not only *The Spirit* but whatever other comics we were involved with in partnership with "Busy" Arnold, who headed the Quality Comic Group. These comic books were, I believe, *Hit Comics*, *Police Comics*, and *Military Comics*. For these I created *Uncle Sam*, *Blackhawks*, and others. As far as the creation of *The Spirit* itself, I had the idea that I would like to do a kind of detective feature. This was for me an enormous opportunity. I wouldn't have left Eisner and Iger, which was a profitable operation, to take the risk of doing *The Spirit*, which could easily have been cancelled within six months, leaving me totally out of work or out of business, unless I felt that this was something I couldn't let go by—so it was not only a tremendous financial gamble but also a career risk. I had to believe at the time that I could make what I called "the big time." After all, newspapers were the major leagues then, at least as far as cartoonists were concerned.

yronwode: As for the character of The Spirit himself—at that time, super-powered characters were proliferating wildly and detective stories were actually being phased out . . .

Eisner: Well, what I was *really* interested in was developing the kind of character who could be a vehicle for the kind of stories I wanted to do. I had always wanted to do short stories. I always regarded comics as a legitimate medium, my medium. Creating a detective character would, as far as I was concerned, provide me with the most viable vehicle for the kind of stories I could best tell. The syndicate people weren't in full agreement with me. They wanted to have some kind of mysterioso character that emulated the so-called super-heroes, so in my first discussion with "Busy" Arnold, his thinking centered around a superhero kind of character—a costumed character; we didn't use the word "superhero" in those days, nobody talked about it that way—he and the syndicate sort of anticipated a costumed character and I argued vehemently against it because I had my bellyful of creating costumed heroes at Eisner and Iger—and I didn't want a freak character at all, so actually one evening, around three in the morning, I was still working, trying to find it—I only had about a week and a half or two weeks in which to produce the first issue, the whole deal was done in quite a rush—and I came up with an outlaw hero, suitable I felt for an adult audience. When "Busy" Arnold called, he suggested a kind of ghost or some kind of metaphysical character. He said, "How about a thing called The Ghost?" and I said, "Naw, that's not any good" and he said, "Well, then call it The Spirit; there's nothing like that around." I said, "Well, I don't know what you mean," and he said, "Well, you can figure *that* out—I just like the words 'The Spirit.'" He was calling from a bar somewhere, I think . . . and anyway, the more I thought about it the more I realized I didn't care about the name. I had the character fairly well framed in my mind, and what he would do, and I felt that there ought to be a pretty urban kind of heroic character which would be a good vehicle for stories. And that's how it started. You know—one thing led to another.

I must add here that I was aware that I was about to write for a different audience than comic books. I wanted it to be varied and adult.

yronwode: In the early pre-War stories, The Spirit seems to me more of a cardboard "heroic" character: he has the Spiritmobile—he's a superhero without super powers, like The Batman. Later, after the War, you got much deeper into the short story form, telling stories in which the Spirit is not always even the major protagonist.

Eisner: That's right, that's right. In the earliest installments I was groping. But the hero was secondary to me—he was really a vehicle for telling a short story. You must understand that artists and writers grow—and prior to the War I had spent most of my early life working and drawing within the walls of the studio—a pretty cloistered life. I had really not seen much of the world before that. I started selling very early, so to speak, and I had no time to travel around or ride the rails like some of the other artists and cartoonists did, so I had no chance really to get to see much of the world outside of New York. So a lot of my life was a fantasy life prior to '41 when the War came on. I got into the army then and I had a chance to really see what was on the other side of the mountain, so to speak. All that did really, strangely enough, was to reinforce the determination that I had to go beyond "cardboard characters," as you called them. I knew I was dealing in a medium capable of more.

The earliest *Spirits* were a response to the mission I had been given, which was to create an adventure story. You must understand that I had very little time to really develop a rapport with the audience; compared to most new comic strips, it was nothing. It was 1940 that I started and suddenly in late '41—thirteen months later—I was notified that I was being drafted, and then I had about another half year which the government gave me to clean up my affairs before going off to help save America from the Nazis. So I really had very little time to mature a relationship with my audience.

yronwode: The people who are drawing and writing comics today, the so-called third generation, were raised on comics. They learn by imitating other comics artists and writers until they find their own styles—if they ever do. People such as you, who were working during the beginning of the field, didn't have that influence. You couldn't swipe Jack Kirby because . . .
Eisner: . . . There was no Jack Kirby to swipe.

yronwode: You were working with Jack.
Eisner: Yeah, Jack was working in my studio. Under a different name. [Laughter] He later became Jack Kirby.

yronwode: . . . So your art has been variously described as cinematographic and your writing as short stories. Were you influenced by film and literature?
Eisner: That's absolutely true. Both films and short stories—particularly the highly specialized short story writers like O. Henry and Bierce, de Maupassant—there was a whole period in the '30s during which the short story was an artform unto itself. Today, people are still writing short stories, but it doesn't command the writing market as it did once before.

I had only two . . . well, actually three major influences: the motion pictures I saw—and I saw lots of 'em—short stories I read, which nurtured my own imagination, and my own life experience, which figured heavily in the things I did. It's very easy to see the influence of where I lived on the kinds of layouts and artwork I did.

yronwode: What films or filmmakers would you say . . .
Eisner: Well, it's sort of hard to . . .

yronwode: Your work has been compared to Fritz Lang . . .
Eisner: Yes, Feiffer's said that . . . people say that . . .

yronwode: . . . and Orson Welles . . .
Eisner: I saw every one of those—the early experimental Man Ray films and others. I felt a very strong kinship to Orson Welles in those days. The old Fritz Lang movies were around. I saw every movie I could. I didn't catalogue them by director—because in those days, with the exception of Orson Welles, I was

not as conscious of directors as I am now. Movies were like our television—we consumed 'em at about the same rate of speed that you consume television today. Movies became part of one's life experience. This is something which perhaps sociologists should someday explore—Jules Feiffer touched on it in his writings and I think he's aware of it because he grew up in somewhat the same environment that I did. Movies were part of our life experiences just as television is for the people who stay home and watch it every day of the week. To many people, moving picture characters and television characters are *real people*—when the actors die, they get very upset.

Well, movies were part of my life and so they had an influence. As far as ideas and so forth, movies were *their* medium and comics was my medium. I saw comics as an art form, legitimate within itself, and just as movies borrow from comics and are influenced by comics, so I was influenced by movies. And the theatre, by the way. I had a *strong* interest in theatre and I often tell my students (at the School of Visual Arts) to see in terms of lighting and stage sets. Theatre was very strong; my father did stage sets when he first came to this country—that is, scenery and backdrop paintings. Among my first experiences is the memory of visiting Second Avenue Jewish theatres where I could see the men working on backdrops. I have a feeling for theatrics. I did some in high school too—some stage design. In fact I did a play with Adolph Green where I did all the stage sets in a very modern form and he did the music and the words.

yronwode: What was the date on this?
Eisner: About 1934, I believe.

yronwode: What led you to comics then?
Eisner: Well, I was always interested in comics ever since I was a kid. As far as comic *books* are concerned, that's something else—I'll get to that in a moment—but as far as comics themselves, that was something I always wanted—actually, I wanted to be many things but I found that my ability seemed to tend toward storytelling in this medium.

yronwode: What comics did you like as a kid?
Eisner: There were lots of comic strips. Of course one of the comic strips I was influenced by was *Popeye*. That will probably surprise you.

yronwode: Really?!
Eisner: You know, a year ago I guess, somebody wrote a book showing all the

early comic artwork of comic artists and I unearthed some stuff I did when I was fifteen or sixteen and it looks just like *Popeye*—a *cold* imitation of Segar's work. I was terribly influenced by that. I was *very* fond of Alex Raymond's work, and Caniff's *Terry and the Pirates*.

Fortunately, when I was a kid, strips proliferated in this city. We had tremendous numbers of 'em so I was exposed to a wide range. There was *Krazy Kat*—Herriman influenced me *tremendously*. I remember the tremendous impact his crazy backgrounds had on me. I recognized it as art, and that is exactly what it was. I don't think *he* even thought of it as art to the extent that *I* did.

And then I studied painting with Robert Brachman. I tried to be a magazine illustrator—I did pulp illustrations for a while—but mostly people would look at my work and say, "Geez, you're a great cartoonist," so gradually it became very clear that that was a way to get out of the ghetto, a chance for the upward mobility, by becoming a famous cartoonist. So I wanted to be a cartoonist for a long time, even as a kid.

yronwode: Just for the record—what was your first published work?
Eisner: I think my first published work was in high school, but then my first professional work was in *Wow!*, which was published by a fellow named Henle and the editor was Jerry Iger who I approached when *Wow!* collapsed and asked to become my partner in what I felt was the wave of the future—the development of original cartoons—comics—for the faltering pulps.

yronwode: What exactly did Jerry Iger do in your partnership?
Eisner: Well, Jerry was older than I and he knew more about the field and the markets, so his function was selling and doing lettering. He *had* a couple of comic strips of his own—*Bobby* and I think *Peewee*—which were forerunners of *Peanuts*—in that style or genre. I was doing production and he was doing sales. He was a *very* good salesman. He also did some lettering when we were a very small company—he could letter better than I did and he knew where the market was—but he cared little about story or drama as I knew it. I learned about business from him.

yronwode: Your studio has had a wide reputation as the hothouse . . .
Eisner: . . . or sweatshop [laughter] . . .

yronwode: . . . where hundreds of famous cartoonists were first employed. There is a *Spirit* section called "Lurid Love" in which you did a little joke on

that—there's an advertisement for the Will Eisner School of Cartooning: "'I make $13.00 a week,' says famous cartoonist Will Eisner."
Eisner: [Chuckles] Yeah . . .

yronwode: A lot of well-known people have worked for you, including Jules Feiffer and Wally Wood . . .
Eisner: I'd like to change the word from "worked *for* me" to "worked *with* me" because, while I obviously was exploiting their talents to get rich and grinding them down and squeezing every little bit of their life-blood out of them [laughter]—nonetheless we had—and I think they will agree—a kind of a creative relationship between us that in hindsight was more than just employer and employee. Because I was their age or of their general background, we had a kind of rapport.

yronwode: In general, what were the duties of these people?
Eisner: It's hard to say where their input began and ended. I tried to run a production shop. One of the reasons for the success of Eisner and Iger was that I ran it like a mass-production operation. We were getting $5.00 a page when we started and we came out with a net profit of about $1.50. So one had to get large volume production. Mine was the function of the major creative force in the shop and the staff would work on features created initially by me or written by somebody under my direction. We had one internal writer later on, when we got affluent.

yronwode: Who was that?
Eisner: A girl named Tony Blum. She was the staff writer at Eisner and Iger. She started there about 1938; I don't know what became of her afterward.

yronwode: You created most of the characters . . .
Eisner: What I would do was design and develop and do the first sort of rough drawing or the first final finished drawing. For example, in Sheena I did the cover after I had created the character and the first one was, I think, done by Mort Meskin—he actually executed it. Later Bob Powell did it. We had pencillers and inkers, just the way they do 'em today. In the case of Jack Kirby—he would both pencil *and* ink. He was incredibly fast.

yronwode: Could you name some things he did then?
Eisner: He did a thing called *The Count of Monte Cristo*, which we sold overseas. We began Eisner and Iger selling comic strips overseas—comic book

stuff—because they had no original comic book material around at the time and this is what I saw as having tremendous potential in the future—and it turns out that I was right. Because actually there just were not enough daily newspaper strips to reprint . . . which was how comic books started.

Lou Fine was another one of the men in the shop—a real solid draftsman, a great artist, one of the greatest in the business, I think, and a very sensitive and intelligent man—but he was not a story writer. He didn't like to write stories. He would do the superheroes and was very good at superheroes, and he came over with me when I left. Bob Powell wrote: He wasn't too interested in writing initially, but later he did his own writing when he took over Sheena. We had house names under which I would either write or develop the characters. Sheena—I think that was under "W. Morgan Thomas." Then there was "Spencer Steele"—there was a whole bunch of names. House names were traditionally the way publishers protected themselves against defecting artists. There was a lot of talent-raiding in those days.

yronwode: Jules Feiffer came to work for you after the Eisner and Iger period, didn't he?

Eisner: Feiffer walked into my studio after the War. I had an office on Wall Street as I recall. I forget the year it was, but it couldn't have been earlier than '46 or '47. Feiffer walked in and asked me for a job and said he'd work at any price, which immediately attracted me. He began working as just a studio man—he would do erasing, cleanup, and whatever else he could do. Gradually it became very clear that he could write better than he could draw and preferred it indeed—so he wound up doing balloons. First he was doing balloons based on stories that I would create. I would start a story off and say, "Now here I want the Spirit to do the following things—you do the balloons, Jules." Gradually he would take over and would do stories entirely on his own, generally based on ideas we'd talked about. I'd come in generally with the first page, then he would pick it up and carry it on from there on.

yronwode: What about Wally Wood—when did he come to work for you?

Eisner: Wally Wood never actually worked on staff, you know, from nine to five. He was freelancing. He came in much later, sometime around 1949–1950. I knew him and I needed some help because about that time, when I'd started American Visuals Corporation, business was booming and I was facing the possibility of having to either give up *The Spirit* physically myself or hire a ghost. Wood came along and I talked him into doing a series of *Spirit* stories. I think he did something like four or five *Spirit* stories, a whole series on the moon.

yronwode: "Denny Colt in Outer Space."
Eisner: Yes. I designed the series to accommodate Wood's style. They looked like Wally Wood doing *The Spirit*. It was viable because it enabled me to let Wood work without having to alter his style so drastically that it would look like me. One of the problems I was having then was that I couldn't find people who would emulate my style sufficiently. *The Spirit* just wasn't Mickey Mouse, you know.

yronwode: Did Wood ever work on any other *Spirit* stories aside from "Denny Colt in Outer Space"?
Eisner: No. That was the only series he did. He came and went. We have had other contacts, but not on *The Spirit*.

yronwode: How about Jerry Grandenetti?
Eisner: I found Grandenetti as the result of a search for a good background man. Grandenetti was either recommended to me or I found him through an advertisement, I forget which. I had the idea that what I needed was somebody who was working as an architect's assistant, you know, doing renderings, and Jerry was working in an architectural firm at the time, doing actual rendering, I believe. He came in and his stuff was just great—he liked the idea of comics—I don't know how much he knew about comics then, but he learned quickly and he did a fine job. I would only have to rough in a building and give the general effect I wanted and he would then finish it off—he had a nice strong line. Gradually he got stronger and stronger and then—as others, he wanted to do his own features—shortly after that, he went.

yronwode: When did he work for you?
Eisner: He came in . . . probably '48 . . . '47 . . . and left about '49, I think.

yronwode: Did he do any figures or was it mostly architecture?
Eisner: Very little on figures until much later when I got stuck, and then he would ink over some of the penciled figures.

yronwode: Another person whose name is mentioned in the fake advertisement in the "Lurid Love" story is Abe Kanegson. He was your letterer, right?
Eisner: He was the best letterer I ever had. He worked with me from 1947 to about 1950. I don't know what happened to him after that but I miss him sorely. He brought far more to *The Spirit* than many of the background people ever did—he was very responsive to ideas and he added a creative dimension

to comics which I always thought was very important. He's the only one who ever really *understood*. I had other letterers before he came in but he helped me reach out. Sure, I had certain standards I wanted him to follow—for instance, I did Old English before he came in, but he would take that Old English and really *do* it—his skill was enormous—but even more, he understood the function and rule of lettering in comics. He regarded it as something important. Everybody before him regarded it as a chore.

yronwode: You did the lettering on the splash pages, though—the "Spirit" logos.

Eisner: I did that. Abe did the balloons and the running text, but the creative lettering, wherever it was part of the artwork, I did that. His greatest work was done on the *Spirit* stories that were done in rhyme—like the Christmas *Spirits* and the "Tragedy of Merry Andrew."

yronwode: Why did he quit?

Eisner: I don't remember. It wasn't in anger. I guess he just wanted to move on or something. I don't know.

yronwode: After Kanegson left, the lettering style changed abruptly—it became very "normal"—and then in '51 someone else took it over in a pretty good fake Kanegson style. Who were those other letterers?

Eisner: Whatever freelancer I could get. Ben Oda did some lettering then. Unfortunately, you see, letterers in this business never had a real chance to make a creative contribution for two reasons. First, economically it didn't pay them—at $3.00 a page they've really got to grind it out in order to make a living—and second, a lot of cartoonists don't regard the balloons, the lettering itself, as anything other than a major nuisance. The letterer is probably lower down on the totem pole than the eraser. I think that's a shame because I think the lettering is very important.

Incidentally, in *A Contract with God* I did all my own lettering because I regarded it as integral to the art. I should add that you'll find more creativity in lettering among the "gag" or humor comics than in the so-called realistic strips. Walt Kelly's *Pogo* had very creative lettering. European comics . . . Nikita Mandryka for one . . . use lettering creatively. It's hard to make sweeping, absolute generalizations here . . . but I think in general my point of view will hold out.

yronwode: More recently, Mike Ploog has worked with you . . .

Eisner: Yeah, well, Mike came in working for me in 1967. I was looking for someone who could work on the *P.S.* magazine which I did for the Army, and Mike sent me his material or somebody sent it to me, I don't remember which, and I found myself in California, talking Mike into coming to work for us, which he did. We had a very happy relationship for maybe two or three years, four years.

yronwode: His style is closer to yours than some of the other associates you've had through the years.
Eisner: Yeah—it was a happy coincidence. His style was his own long before he came to work for me. I don't think I altered his style necessarily. I may have influenced his way of *thinking*, perhaps. We had a very good relationship. It never was—unlike what you hear in circles of fandom where everyone's analyzing who influenced whom. It was never an issue of discussion. The studio had a style—and a direction—and we adhered to it. I was also influenced by people who worked in my studio. We learned from each other.

yronwode: But the basic style was yours.
Eisner: Yes. I established the philosophy which they adhered to. I set the standards. You just can't help that when you run a studio.

yronwode: For *The Spirit*, did you usually write out a full script first and then do layouts and pencils—or did you just devise the rough plot and layouts and come back and add the dialogue later like they do now at Marvel?
Eisner: We always wrote the dialogue on the pencil roughs first—all the lettering was done first. Rarely did I do the lettering after the artwork, occasionally, when we were in a hurry, but rarely. The plot was laid out as thumbnails, generally on a few sheets of paper, then it was laid out roughly on the illustration boards, and then it was written in. I'd write the lettering in, and it was inked—or I'd go over Jules's writing and tighten it up, and it was inked— then I'd pencil it, and sometimes we'd have the backgrounds done or I'd ink the figures right away, heads and a few bodies—it depended—some stories I did totally myself and on some I wouldn't touch it. Sometimes I had the time and sometimes I didn't have the time. There was no set formula. I did— always—the heads.

yronwode: Just for the record, can you name one story you did completely by yourself with no assistance?
Eisner: Well, there were a whole lot of them. I can't remember them, I can

only tell when I see them. I can now look at them and point out the ones I did or didn't do. But most of the stories between late '46 and late '49—I did most of those stories. Some of the backgrounds were done by somebody else, but I did most of the art on those.

yronwode: Who did the coloring?

Eisner: I would do the color guides. Jules Feiffer would do a lot of the coloring. That's why I was so amused when he said (in *The Great Comic Book Heroes*) that The Spirit never had any socks. [Laughter] We had a problem—we never knew what color the socks were. You see, if you made the socks red that would look too ridiculous, but red or yellow would be the only colors that did not clash with or disappear with the brown shoes or the blue pants. He couldn't have *blue* socks 'cause that would look like an extension of his pants and he couldn't have *black* ones 'cause that would look real weird, and he couldn't have *yellow* socks 'cause it would look like an error and so we would invariably try to fudge it and of course the engraver would just color 'em flesh . . . [Laughter] . . . so he would never have socks! I didn't realize this until Feiffer pointed it out many years later when he said, "Do you realize The Spirit never has any socks?" I said, "You're crazy!" and he showed me a couple of panels— and by God, he's right! Also, by the way, Feiffer signed the artwork; that was his job: to sign "Will Eisner" on it. [Laughter]

[At this point an off-the-record discussion of the many different "Eisner" signatures took place. The conclusion was reached that it's an easy one to forge, as the interviewer proved. Eisner blithely dismissed the theory that the several variant forms are useful clues to the identity of certain assistants by stating that the anomalous ones were simply "sloppily done."]

yronwode: Okay—let's talk about your work for the Army—the technical manuals. This is back-tracking now to the time of the War . . .

Eisner: When I was drafted, kicking and screaming all the way, into the service in 1941—late '41, early '42—I was assigned to the camp newspaper in Aberdeen and there was also a big training program there, so I got involved in the use of comics for training. Then suddenly the Chief of Ordinance got into the whole business of preventive maintenance. I was applying for a commission at the time—I finally became a warrant officer, which involved taking a test—that way you didn't have to go through Officers' Candidate School. Anyway, Washington wanted someone down there right away and so

I went—and en route, I stopped at the Hollabird Depot in Baltimore, where a mimeographed sheet called *Army Motors* was being distributed. Together with the people there, because I had nothing to do, I helped develop its format. I began doing cartoons—and we began fashioning a magazine that had the ability to talk to the G.I.'s in their language. So I began to use comics as a teaching tool and when I got to Washington, they assigned me to the business of teaching—or selling—preventive maintenance. Preventive maintenance required voluntary cooperation on the part of the readers—the G.I.s. The military was faced with the problem of getting voluntary performance from its troops, so I proposed that one teaching tool that would be very viable would be comics—and they allowed me to try it. Meanwhile, the *Army Motors* idea became popular and the magazine became an enormously successful publication—I did a comic strip in it called *Joe Dope*, which I created. So I spent my four years in the War in the Pentagon building working as the editor of a magazine called *Firepower*, which was an ordinance man's journal, and involved with *Army Motors*, developing cartoons, and using comic strips to teach.

yronwode: Did you do most of the artwork yourself?
Eisner: Yes—I did all the general illustrations—that is, cartoons—in that book. I continued to work on it after the War. In 1950 *P.S.* magazine began as a successor to *Army Motors* and I did that too.

yronwode: Did you know that those are now being sold in some comic book shops?
Eisner: The old *P.S.* magazines? God, that's fantastic. Well, they're very hard to come by because they were government property—although they distributed over a million of 'em. That's incredible . . . A lot of the artwork has probably disappeared in the government warehouses.

yronwode: Of course you continued to work on *P.S.* after the War and, once *The Spirit* ended in 1952, the general public didn't get to see much of your work for the next fifteen or twenty years . . .
Eisner: I was mostly running a business, an educational company. My time was spent in the development of ideas for the commercial application of comics. I've always been interested in the furtherance of the uses of comics. There are two levels—two broad areas—for comics. One is entertainment and the other is instructional. I've always seen it like that. So, for a while after I left

the entertainment field—the comic done purely as entertainment or literature—and involved myself in the use of the comic as a teaching tool, an informational tool. What I'm doing now is returning to the entertainment side, coming back to comics as a literary form.

yronwode: In the late 1960s *The Spirit* was revived, first by Harvey and then in black and white format by Denis Kitchen . . .
Eisner: Denis asked me back then if he could try running *The Spirit* in the so-called underground market. I really didn't think *The Spirit* had any viability and I was surprised that anybody was interested in it—so I paid very little attention to it. He couldn't afford to run it in color, so I said to go ahead and run it in black and white. I just handed him some proofs and I paid very little attention to it except to do the covers for him. I had a lot of fun with that because it was the first work of that kind I had done in twenty years.

yronwode: And then you went to Warren with it—and the stories were given a new look with wash toning . . .
Eisner: With the success of the two from Denis, a couple of houses became interested. I ran into Jim Warren one day and we talked about the use of *The Spirit* as a magazine. He first wanted to do it as a feature in one of his *Eerie* or *Creepy* books and I said no—I didn't want that—he could either do it by itself, as a book, or not at all. So he decided to do it as a book. Stan Lee said he was interested in it too—he was always a good friend and he's always understood what I was doing. At DC, Infantino was interested in it—so I had to make a choice. With Warren, *The Spirit* would have the best chance because Warren is a smaller house, Jim is a very involved publisher and would really treat it with care; it would be 20 percent of his stable. So, I gave it to Warren. It was there that we began to experiment with the wash overlays. We did *some* color—the color inserts—but to my amazement, *The Spirit* seemed to look better to me in black and white than it did in color! A lot of people don't agree—*The Spirit* was originally designed for color—but I found myself liking the work better in black and white. It seemed to have more of the mood and expression, everything I wanted to convey—and suddenly, color seemed superfluous.

yronwode: I agree—I've been collecting the original Sunday sections too, but I like them much better in black and white because there is that mood. In fact, I really actually prefer the stark blacks without the wash tones that appeared in the Kitchen issues—that "original artwork" look . . .
Eisner: . . . Is that why you like those better? Well, from the point of view

of the story I like the use of wash. I keep *trying* to use wash and I keep being defeated because I find that it seems to be a kind of an overkill. As a matter of fact, in my new book, *A Contract with God*, you will find that there's no wash—but as I'd originally planned it, I had done some one hundred pages of overlays in wash and color and I scrapped them about halfway through the book because I realized that they were killing the effect. So apparently my *line* seems to be able to stand up without the wash, although it adds a secondary tone, a realism. I can also do lighting effects more easily with wash than I can with line and it does create a mood—that secondary tone seems necessary to me now. But I like black and white and I think I can do well with it.

yronwode: You don't see color as an essential art of comics . . .

Eisner: No, I don't think color is essential. Color can kill certain effects. I see the entertainment side of comics divided again into two kinds—there's the comic that's a sensory experience, a visually sensual experience, and there's the comic that tells a story utilizing pictures as a language. In those a very delicate balance exists between story, or text . . . and the art. To me, comic or sequential art is a language and the use of color is like setting print in 24-point type as opposed to doing it in 10-point type—I don't think it will enhance the value of the story, although it may add another dimension. And then, very often, enormously powerful, full-color art swamps the story. About the only ones whose work seems to be able to survive a thing like that are men like Richard Corben and Jean Giraud, or Moebius as he's called. Both men, particularly Giraud, seem to be able to do a feature whose color is compatible with the story. Occasionally Corben will overwhelm the reader with a powerful work of full-color art that really knocks you off your chair—and you almost forget what the story's about. Well, anyway, that's how *I* see it. I think the story is paramount.

yronwode: Seeing *The Spirit* in black and white always reminds me of those black and white movies that were made around the same time—Clark Gable and Jean Harlow in *China Seas* or *Red Dust*, or Humphrey Bogart and Lauren Bacall in *Dead Reckoning*, that sort of thing—whereas Corben and his use of color is like a science fiction movie full of special effects . . .

Eisner: Corben is the twenty-first century and Will Eisner [laughter] is the '30s and early '40s? Well, that's how you see it anyway. I don't know how representative your way of thinking is—but I have to work in terms of what I'm trying to do—and at this time I have no intention of trying to be anything but a story teller. I see comics as a form of literature for the future.

yronwode: Kitchen Sink is again publishing *The Spirit*, this time using wash tones, like Warren did.

Eisner: That's right, Denis is doing it again.

yronwode: One thing I've noticed, in both the Warren and the Kitchen *Spirit* is that you have redrawn a lot of the artwork to a greater or lesser extent . . .

Eisner: Well, not a *lot*—certain panels—there are certain things I have redrawn.

yronwode: Why? Is it just your perfectionist attitude or . . .

Eisner: Just think of how lucky I am. How many people have had the chance to do it over again? [Laughter] Oh, I'm a perfectionist, too!

yronwode: Could you be a little more specific about why you go to the trouble of redrawing the stories?

Eisner: There are two reasons why I might redraw a panel. One is that the original art is lost or the proof is so bad that it's just not reproducible. The second reason I might do it is where the artwork is so awful that I would like another chance to do it right. That's all.

yronwode: You see your own work as *that* awful?

Eisner: Well, sometimes. Most of the time it was other people's inking. Very often I would have a story which I pencilled and somebody else inked it and completely distorted it. At the time I had to let it go through because there was a rush and we had to make a deadline. Sometimes I'd only have time to fix up a few heads or the figures—we were always in a rush. Now I have a chance to look at it and I say, "Oh my gosh!"—and I'd like to be able to fix it up—so that's why I'll do it. In the process of redrawing, of course, I use the opportunity to make a few changes or make adjustments. In the story about silence, the one called "Sound," I rewrote it a little bit.

yronwode: And "Gerhard Shnobble" . . .

Eisner: Yeah—I did major surgery on "Gerhard Shnobble." Someday I'd really even like to redo that whole story *again*. That was a very important story to me.

yronwode: That story contains a photo-montage—and, well, I didn't see these *Spirit* stories until much later. I mean, I was raised on Mighty Marvel— so anyway, in retrospect, I find it very amusing to remember that back in the mid-'6os Stan Lee "introduced" the photo-montage to comics. I remember all the big to-do about this stunning innovation—and in one month there, I think three or four Marvel mags featured 'em; it was supposed to be the greatest new thing . . .

Eisner: [Chuckle] Yeah—in 1949 it was the greatest new thing . . .

yronwode: . . . that had ever happened to comics.

Eisner: . . . that had ever happened to comics. Right. Yeah, well, I was always looking for new things to do, to stretch the medium, so to speak, and one day I had this great idea—I took this newspaper print, which had a 60-line screen, laid it right down, photostatted it and reproduced from it—and thought to myself, "what a great new idea this is!" But frankly, I'm sure somebody must have done it before me—they *must* have. No ideas like that are "original."

yronwode: How many more *Spirit* stories are there available for reprinting?

Eisner: As far as I'm concerned, I don't think there are more than another forty stories that have not yet been published which are worthy of the visibility. There were about 250 stories of course, and only about 170 have been reprinted—but if the magazine gets enormously popular—who knows?

yronwode: When these stories run out, will you consider writing new *Spirit* stories?

Eisner: I'll consider anything! [Laughter] But no, I can't say now what I'll do—that's like asking a candidate whether he's gonna run for office next year. I think a lot would depend on what the situation was at the time and also how successful I am with the things I'm doing *now*. I feel I'm creating new things—hopefully the new material I'm creating will be of interest. I think *The Spirit* . . . I don't know . . . is it the *character* the people are so interested in—the character of the Spirit, the idea of a masked crimefighter—or is it the *stories*?

yronwode: I don't know, I don't know why . . . it isn't entirely the idea of a crimefighter, that's for sure—and it isn't always the stories, because sometimes the stories themselves seem to detract from the mood. It's something about the atmosphere, the rain, the chase, The Spirit in the night. The Spirit—it means "soul"—I see him as the inner soul of some idealized masculine image. But then, I'm a woman—I mean, I know men who like the Spirit too. He's like The Batman only he's not a psychopath—he's like Captain America only he doesn't wear a stupid costume. He has a sense of humor but he's not a fool. And mostly he walks around in a fantastically romantic atmosphere—the criminal women, the life below the streets, the docks—ah, you know.

Anyway, I'm supposed to be asking *you* the questions here . . . so how about a couple of trivia questions before we go on? I've noticed an *incredible* number of left-handed people in *The Spirit*—sometimes up to 75 percent of the attackers in a group criminal scene will be holding their weapons in their left hands, the Spirit himself consistently picks up the telephone with his left hand and so forth. Is this intentional on your part or is it the result of unconscious panel composition?

Eisner: *Holy smoke!* I never *heard* of this before! I'll have to check back. *Good grief! I'm* right handed—I can't do anything except scratch my head with my left hand! I'm not even conscious of this—now you have me there. If that's so, it's probably the result of the fact that I was very conscious of composition and I compose a scene very much the way you would a group of actors on a stage—and if I have to take the liberties with the hands I will—that's *fascinating*—I must look into this . . .

yronwode: Okay . . . well, what's the tune to "Every Little Bug Has a Honey to Hug"?

Eisner: [Laughter] You wanna hear that? [Laughter] You know, at the last convention I was at, down in Orlando [Florida], people had the sheet music on it!

yronwode: Was it published as such?

Eisner: Yes, it was published as sheet music by Miller Music Company and it was probably the world's greatest disaster because I don't think *anybody* ever played it. I never heard it played—I've *forgotten* the melody [laughter], I really have forgotten the melody—but I know it was a little jazzy thing. It was written by a fellow named Bill Harr—I wrote the words.

yronwode: When?

Eisner: Oh, about '48, '49, somewhere in there.

yronwode: No, it appears earlier than that—in 1946 there's a *Spirit* story about Dulcet Tone . . .

Eisner: Yeah—'46, '47—but it was not before the War because Bill Harr was one of the reporters on my paper, *Firepower*, and I discovered one day that he could write music. He came up to New York after the War and said he was going to go into music writing and he said, "Let's do a song together," and so we did and there it was.

yronwode: Do you play the piano?
Eisner: No, no—I just wrote the words. I'm great singing in a shower, very operatic in the shower and I studied . . . I once played the violin [laughter].

yronwode: All right, and now for something completely different [laughter] . . . I'm sorry about those questions—that's just the kind of stuff I think about sometimes . . .
Eisner: Oh, that's quite all right . . . those are very unusual questions.

yronwode: You've got some new projects in the works; one of these is being published by Kitchen Sink in *The Spirit* magazine . . .
Eisner: The thing for Kitchen Sink is an idea—to see if I can develop it into a new dimension of a novel in comic book format within the framework of the paperback size. I've always been fascinated with this. I think comics—well, let's say I think that's where comics have to go.

yronwode: Paperbacks rather than the large "coffee table" size?
Eisner: It's not *size* so much—there's a lot of things happening right now. Comic books, the old ten-cent comic book, are of course changing, and the old standards are disappearing. We know where some of it is going—some of it's becoming *Heavy Metal*, some of it's fractioning off into things like *Howard the Duck* and that kind of stuff. There have been a few attempts made, several times, in fact, to bring off a paperback—which is the logical successor, in my opinion, to the comic book format. So far, paperbacks have never done well with comics in them, with the exception of those which have been reprints from cartoons or magazines like *Mad* . . .

yronwode: There were those EC and Warren reprint books too . . .
Eisner: I don't know how well those have done—but most of the distributors tell me that they haven't sold all that well.

yronwode: Do you think that's because of the small size? People are used to having comics a certain size . . .
Eisner: Well, I think there are many reasons. People think of comics as kid stuff and also they are used to seeing comics in a larger format—but more important than that, people regard paperbacks as an inexpensive reprint or

a bargain, if you will. From a big novel which they would normally pay $10.00 for, they can get a paperback for $1.95. So it's a reprint, they think. Secondly, there's a phenomenon that occurs in the bookstore—people pick up a paperback and if it's filled with cartoons or with a cartoon story that doesn't seem to have the kind of permanence of a collection, say, of *Peanuts*—and those sell very well in paperback—or a reprint from *Mad* Magazine, which contains classic jokes by some of the best talent there is—they tend to read it in the store and put it down and not buy it. Most of the booksellers that I've talked to tell me that. At this point there has been no real market developed for comic books in paperback format. Several people have tried—Gil Kane, with his *Blackmark*, Warren's *Vampirella*, and so forth—and now they're attempting to do classic stories in the paperback format. I believe that we just haven't found the right formula yet. It's there. So one of the things I'm going to do now is attempt a series of stories in *The Spirit* Magazine which will be a pull-out section—you can pull it out and fold it up and you get a paperback. Since I can't sit down and write and draw a two-hundred-page story in one issue, I'm going to do it in serial form which will be gathered together maybe and be cut to one big novel.

yronwode: What's the name of this?
Eisner: It's called *Life on Another Planet*. It does not deal with mutants or people living in other galaxies—we never get into another planet. It's going to explore a very realistic, serious theme, one which has occupied my thinking for a long time, which is what would happen on *this* planet, on planet Earth, if we were to discover that there is intelligence on another planet only ten years away. The idea is very exciting to me—the possibilities are tremendous—and while it doesn't have a lot of visual potential—that is, I won't be dealing with mutants, aliens, and clones, with spaceships flying around and blasting each other into nothingness—I *will* be more concerned with character study and so forth. The first chapter goes rather slowly because I tried to get a great deal of the story into it all at the same time and I'm trying to develop a character, a man called Cim Blud—an astrophysicist turned detective. He'll be a space detective—the first space-sleuth.

yronwode: [Laughter] Is this an extension of "Denny Colt in Outer Space"?
Eisner: I would suppose, yeah, it's Denny Colt without a mask, I guess.

yronwode: Does he have gloves?
Eisner: [Laughter] No—no gloves, no mask. He wears a hat and has a hawkish

nose. Actually, I haven't really centered on him—I'm gonna' let it happen, just do it and let it happen. For me this is the real fun and excitement. Aside from the preliminary plans I did for Denny Colt, most of the characters I've created just happened, they arose in answer to a given problem. I don't know what the second chapter is going to be yet, but I'll do that very shortly. The first chapter [appeared] in *The Spirit* #19.

yronwode: And then there's the book . . .

Eisner: Ah yes, that's the other project. I worked on that for two years and it's also out now—the book is called *A Contract with God*. This is what I've devoted my major serious efforts of the last few years to. It's something that I've wanted to do for a long time. In the foreword of the book I explain why I did it and how it came to be, so there's really no sense in repeating that— hopefully people will buy the book and read the foreword and then they'll know what my reasons were. For the purpose of this interview I must say that I am still the same Will Eisner of 1942–43, trying to expand the horizons of my medium, my medium being a sequence of pictures on paper. I believe that sequential art is the oldest communicating art form, I think it has the validity of any other art form—and while it may not have the breadth and dimension of motion pictures and it may not have the ability to cover abstracts the way lines of words do, and it may not be able to do a *lot* of things—it has served humanity since early man because it has the ability to transmit a story. So I am at work now, hopefully not singlehandedly—I'd like to be joined by other artists—in an effort to produce literature in sequential art form, or what you would call "comic art." I've been struggling with the word "comic book" for thirty years now . . .

yronwode: It's a bad word . . .

Eisner: It's a *terrible* word—but every time I try to change it, I find that people force me back into it. I had finally settled on the term "graphic novel" thinking that would be an adequate euphemism, but the class I teach is called "sequential art"—and of course that's what it is—a sequence of pictures arranged to tell a story.

yronwode: You say you're the same Will Eisner and that's exactly what I thought of when I read *A Contract with God*—in some ways it strikes me as the story of what was going on in the streets on which The Spirit wasn't chasing criminals. The atmosphere is the same—the tenements, the rain, the poverty, and without the use of crime per se—without the almost metaphoric use of crime as a vehicle for social commentary which you developed in *The Spirit*—the themes are even more clearly expressed. *A Contract with God* deals with the ideas you would bring out in the more "realistic" Spirit stories— like the ones about Bleak and Sparrow or the ones which follow some little man as he becomes trapped in societal forces beyond his control. And of course, in the introduction you state that the work is in some ways autobiographical . . .

Eisner: *A Contract with God* is drawn from life. Keep in mind that all the work I've done is done within the frame of what I knew about. I'm not writing fantasy. If I were writing about life on Mars, that would be something else again. But here I'm writing, as I did in *The Spirit*, about an area which I knew first-hand. Over 90 percent of the artwork—and perhaps I shouldn't say this because it might defeat the impression which the artwork should have—but over 90 percent of it was done from memory. I *know* buildings by heart. I *know* how an elevated structure works. I *know* what a fire hydrant looks like—I know it by *feel*. When I was selling newspapers in New York, I used to *sit* on a fire hydrant [laughter]—I know it from the seat of my pants. The city is my territory as much as another artist might know the West. Remington knew the rivers and the streams and the Indians and the horses of the Far West as well as any man did—and he drew it that way.

So anyway, *A Contract with God* talks about an era which I think has been somewhat overlooked. This is the '30s, in the Bronx during and after the Depression period—1932, '35, all the way up to '38. That period was a very exciting time from the point of view that it was a time which produced a lot of very important people—the Danny Kayes, the important people in American literature. *Marty*, by Paddy Chayefsky, was of that era—and I know that era very well. At any rate, I've always believed, as any teacher of writing will tell you, that you should write about the things you know about—and I do know about that era. The city is what I know. My drawings are affected by my life in the city. My lighting is a result of living in a city where lights always came from single sources, from above or from below. My perspective was learned looking out the window of a five-story tenement building. Everything you see in the city as a little boy is in sharp perspective, going up or down.

yronwode: And your well-known use of stark artificial lighting . . .
Eisner: . . . and the artificial lighting. Sunlight only came down through the openings of buildings above you. Had I been born in Montana, in the wide open spaces, my thinking might have been different.

yronwode: I certainly haven't seen you draw many trees.

Eisner: Well, there weren't very many trees to draw. But I do love trees now, of course, and I do think of trees—but I think of them as gnarled human beings. I think of trees as humans.

yronwode: The style of inking you use in *A Contract with God* is quite different from what you did in *The Spirit*—you're not using the coarse brush that you used to use—there's a lot of fine pen lines. In fact, and this is sort of off-the-wall, I don't know if you're into Winsor McCay at all . . .

Eisner: Of course I know his stuff very well.

yronwode: . . . Well, he started off with a relatively simple inking style in *Little Nemo* in 1905, but when he got older and began to do those editorial cartoons during the last ten years of his life, he got into an *extremely* fine crosshatching style—he avoided solid blacks altogether at that point . . .

Eisner: Yeah, sure—we all seem to go that route. Michelangelo too—in his later years he began to have a looser approach to his carving. The unfinished statues that you find in Florence are an example of that. And Milton Caniff— look at the change in his work over the years. As one gets older, as one matures, the tight line, the finely constructed line, loses its value. Perhaps one gets more interested in the theme than in the technique.

People don't remain the same, they change over the years. The only features that never altered their structural line are features like *Mickey Mouse*. Even Al Capp changed—although he never loosened up to the point of sketchiness. When you have a strip that's very very personal to the artist, a strip which isn't drawn by formula, you'll find that the art will change. Usually it will tend to get looser. There's a lack of patience with having to retain that heavy line. In *The Spirit* that heavy, very controlled line was an effort to retain color, color which had to be applied after all by someone else. We had to give them what we used to call "trap areas." Now that's not necessary—the technology has advanced, color can be applied in other ways. Besides, I *like* that loose line— and I think it looks nicer . . . more expressive.

yronwode: In all the work you've ever done, you've struck what I see as an uneasy balance between tragedy and humor. In *A Contract with God* this balance is again expressed, to even greater levels of extremity than you did in *The Spirit*. Also, and I've glossed over this, you've put out a lot of straight humorous books through the years, the *Gleeful Guides*, *Star Jaws*, and the like . . .

Eisner: *Why* did I do that? Is that what you're asking?

yronwode: Not exactly. I think to phrase it *that* way would be to let you know my preferences in too partisan a way. Let's just say that I want a little glimpse into your mind. I want to know what you see as the cutting edge between humor and tragedy and I want to know why you seek that balance, why you carry it to those extremes. On one page innocent victims may be littering the landscape and on another page you may be parodying a singing commercial. You take it from extremes of really gut-wrenching despair on the one hand and then you turn around and just yuk it up.

Eisner: Aren't those two things really the very essence of life? Really—between extreme tragedy and extreme humor—what *is* there? I suppose I never think about it that way until I'm interviewed, I've never really sat down and analyzed it, but I think satire is a form of rage, an expression perhaps of anger. There is kindly humor and there's bitter tragedy. There is a relationship between the two in my mind—I can't keep them separate. Every time I do a very tragic scene, I can see a humorous scene within the same frame and it can be *converted*. A man walking down the street and falling into a manhole can be a very tragic thing—or it could be very funny. So much depends on what else is involved. I see humor as an incongruity. There are lots of definitions of what humor is—some think it's man's inhumanity to man, some think people laugh because they're glad it isn't happening to them, some people laugh because of happiness, or kindness, or even fear—but I see humor as a kind of incongruity. There are a lot of things which do seem peculiar to me and funny to me. I think it requires perspective to see humor as well as tragedy. When you step back, almost the way a painter does in front of a canvas, to look at the humor of something or the tragedy of something, you see it in a kind of clear focus. I don't think you see it if you're up close. If I'm walking down the street and someone drops water on me, it depends on how I see it at that moment whether it's a funny thing or a tragic thing. A good example of that very often is to look out the window, down on the street in New York, and see all the people milling about—and suddenly it seems to you that you're watching a whole scene or act of some kind—and it could be tragic, or it could be serious, it could be very funny. Walk down 42nd Street some time and you can find anything you want—tragedy or whatever. I can't go beyond that with philosophy—but I enjoy humor, I enjoy *doing* humor, and I don't think it's less worthy of me than doing the stories I did in *A Contract with God* . . .

yronwode: . . . which is by no means a humorous quartet of stories.

Eisner: No. Well, *A Contract with God* is a group of stories about the '30s in the Bronx. It's all built around a tenement which I named 55 Dropsie Avenue for want of a better name. I think there was a Cropsie Avenue in the Bronx and I took it from that. The tenement is as typical as I could get it—and I built all the stories around that one old structure because in one tenement you could have as many stories as there were families—and that's another fact which has always intrigued me.

yronwode: The last of the four stories, "Cookalein," seems to be highly auto-biographical—there's a character named Willie in it . . .
Eisner: *Really?!* How *clever* of you! [Laughter]

yronwode: [Laughter] Yeah.
Eisner: Every one of the people in those stories is either me or someone I knew, or parts of them and me—but like any other writer of stories I suppose I—well look, in *Death of a Salesman*, Willie Loman was Arthur Miller's father. A lot of these characters were people I've known intimately, or me, or people like me. How can you *not* be autobiographical if you're writing about something that you've seen. In the character Willie—well, I was called Willie when I was a kid, so I guess you might say it was autobiographical, yeah. I *did* go to the country, to a cookelein like Willie does—and I *did* see many of the things that he sees there. And I must say that it took a lot of determination, a kind of courage, to write that story.

yronwode: I was personally very affected by that last story—it has a universal quality, at least it reflects some events in my life . . . all of them do, but the last three stories hit me closer than the first one did.
Eisner: That's very interesting because the first story, "A Contract with God," rather than "Cookalein," was the one I treated as seriously as I could. Well, they're all serious stories as far as I'm concerned—there is humor in them but they were all very seriously done. It will be interesting to me to hear the reactions from people who have never lived in this area of New York, or during that era of time—to see whether they find any relevancy to it at all.

yronwode: Right—that's why the first story doesn't affect me as much, even though it is a very well told story—it relies too much on the idiosyncrasies of Judaism for its punchline, if you can call it that—whereas "The Street Singer," "The Super," and "Cookalein" deal with some of the common horrors and joys in almost anyone's life. The *setting* is ethnic but the emotions are universal.
Eisner: That's an interesting reaction. You see, when I did it, I wasn't certain that the subject matter of the plots would be of any interest to anybody

beyond Hoboken. In the case of "The Super," I feel you have to have lived in a tenement at about that period—or maybe even today—to understand the role of a superintendent and what was happening to him here. It wasn't attempted as a child molestation exercise—that was just incidental to the story—it could have been anybody else—but it was the relationship of the super to the whole rest of the tenement that I wanted to explore.

yronwode: Speaking of child molestation, there's a lot more overt sexuality in this book than in anything else you've ever done . . .

Eisner: Yes. I realize that. I found it difficult to keep it out. Even though my women at least have always had strong sexual overtones, I struggled with the problem of inserting it—I didn't *want* to get into the sex thing but no way I could avoid it.

yronwode: In three of the stories it's actually the major turning point of the plot.

Eisner: Well, how could I avoid it? In "The Street Singer" that scene is essential to the kind of man he is. At one point in early roughs I had eliminated the scene in which he has sex with the old singer, largely because—well, I guess I was almost embarrassed by doing it—it was an intimate thing. But it was the only way I could show this man's relative impotence—really, that sex act had to show her strength. She was using sex as a kind of power. So I redrew those panels three or four times—I enlarged 'em and I reduced 'em, then I had just one scene, then I had two—and it didn't seem honest—so finally I decided I was just gonna let it hang out and *do* it. In the case of "Cookalein," the discovery of sex was what it was all about—going to the country. In a sense that was what it was all about. Now that's my statement—maybe other people will not agree. The relationships in tight families stem from a kind of sex relationship. In the case of the first story, "A Contract with God," there was no sex because there was no need for it to tell the story. Sure, he had a mistress—but there was no need to demonstrate any sex between them. I don't like putting intimate sex into a comic book, visualizing it unless there's a reason for it—unless it belongs. When it's absolutely essential I will put it in, regardless of how explicit it gets.

yronwode: *The Spirit* always seemed to contain more sex in it than other comics of its era . . .

Eisner: I don't think so, no. We-e-e-ell, yes—but only because of the girls— only because the girls were very suggestively sexy. They exuded a kind of sex in their physical presence. But I don't believe I actually ever *showed* anything . . . But P'gell was always a very sex-oriented girl.

yronwode: [Displaying a copy of the first Kitchen Sink *Spirit*] This . . .
Eisner: But that cover was done *years* later!

yronwode: I know, I know . . . But this little scene amazed me because P'gell says, "I never made it with The Spirit—wanna sell him?" and I couldn't *believe* that she had never made it with The Spirit—I always thought they had! I mean, to find out that they *hadn't* really shocked me!
Eisner: [Laughter] The Spirit was the epitome of the 1932–33 male movie star who was very attractive but really was innately very shy with women.

yronwode: In this new book as well as in *The Spirit*—and I'm referring here to most of the male characters in *The Spirit*—the men are seen as victims of the women for the most part. The women are stronger, more aggressive— they make sexual advances to the men . . .
Eisner: In *A Contract with God*?

yronwode: The little girl in "The Super" . . .
Eisner: Yeah, well in that . . . yeah . . .
yronwode: . . . The woman, Maralyn, who comes to Willie in the night . . .
Eisner: Yeah, but *that* . . . well, yeah . . .

yronwode: The old singer . . . and of course women are always coming on to The Spirit—everyone from P'gell down to Ellen Dolan . . .
Eisner: Do you think that possibly there's some significance—that maybe it's a clue to my own attitude toward sex?

yronwode: Well, that's for you to say, isn't it? But I do think it's interesting because several people have accused you in print of having a "sexist" attitude toward women.
Eisner: Well, I was brought up as a male chauvinist.

yronwode: By that do you mean that you think that men are innately superior to women?
Eisner: No. When I say I'm a male chauvinist I say it with some tongue in cheek because it's now a trigger word. But remember that I was brought up to believe that manhood was somehow synonymous with sexual prowess and

wealth. It was the man who *did* things and the women who were dependent wholly on men. This was my early indoctrination.

yronwode: But you rarely do a story about women like *that*. The women you draw are . . .
Eisner: They're strong—because it's women like *that* that I admire. Obviously everybody "does" women that they admire—Frank Frazetta does big busted, solid fleshed women and Rich Corben does big busted . . .

yronwode: . . . bigger *busted* . . .
Eisner: . . . solid fleshed women. I go for the skinny, neurotic [laughter] *sexy* woman who's got an intellectual problem. I don't know—incidentally, I didn't marry such a woman—I married someone entirely different from P'gell.

yronwode: Was she like Ellen?
Eisner: No, not at all—as a matter of fact she's not like any one of my heroines. But in the case of *The Spirit* I was drawing the kind of women that I thought were attractive to see.

yronwode: A lot of them are based on movie stars.
Eisner: Yeah—Lauren Bacall was a *tremendous* influence on me—I was *fascinated* with her and very attracted to her kind of woman. There was a whole series of women like Lauren Bacall and Katherine Hepburn in the movies at that time, during the Bogart era.

yronwode: The other day I saw a publicity still of Bette Davis and she was posed *exactly* like—she looked like that *Spirit* splash page of Olga Bustle in "Outcast" . . .
Eisner: Well, that was not Bette Davis—that was—what's her name—a girl named Jane Russell. She advertises bras now on television. She was a Howard Hughes discovery with an enormous bust that absolutely defied the law of gravity.

yronwode: Well, having disposed of sexism and sex . . .
Eisner: Have we? [Laughter]
yronwode: [Laughter] No . . .
Eisner: I hope not!

yronwode: [Giggles]
Eisner: What more can we say about sex? I mean, I just admit that it deserves

a long discussion. I just want to point out, before we let it go, that I am conscious of the fact that I'm not associated with it in the mind of the public—I mean, I've never before shown any explicit sex acts in anything I've ever drawn—especially in *The Spirit*—even though they might be suggestive, they only kiss . . .

yronwode: They certainly are suggestive kisses though . . .
Eisner: They're very sexy and very suggestive . . .

yronwode: They're more sexy than a Jack Kirby kiss . . .
Eisner: Oh yes . . . oh yes. I hope Jack Kirby will not take offense at that.

yronwode: [Laughter]
Eisner: I've never kissed Jack Kirby, by the way.

yronwode: [Hysteria deleted] None of your work has ever been subject to the Comics Code and it doesn't look like any of it ever will be . . .
Eisner: That's right—I have no contact with it in any way . . .

yronwode: Do you think it's unnecessarily restrictive?
Eisner: Well, actually I don't know how restrictive it is—I've not seen their editing. The administrators of the Comics Code are very conscientious people—I know the people who are involved with it. The Code was formed to provide the comics field with freedom from legal restrictions which would have been imposed on them had the Code not appeared. So really I see them not as an enemy but as a policeman who stands in front of your house to keep you from being attacked. He's there and he gets in the way and he's a nuisance—but he's a necessary evil.

yronwode: Do you think that comics should be censored in this way?
Eisner: I don't believe in censorship. I don't think there is such a thing as pornography. I think there is *obscenity*—one man killing another man is obscenity. We see it on television all the time and I can't say in my mind that it's all right to show one man stabbing another man or shooting another man or causing the death of somebody while at the same time not allowing a sex act to be shown.

yronwode: In *The Spirit* you certainly gave violence equal time and emphasis with sex.
Eisner: Yes, it was very violent . . .

yronwode: Those scenes where *The Spirit* gets beaten up by a criminal and he's lying there bleeding and then you turn the page and the guy comes back and kicks him in the head—those are very violent scenes. They wouldn't print things like that now under the Code.

Eisner: I think they wouldn't have printed them *then* either, if there had been a Comics Code. But the Code only came in in the 1950s.

yronwode: And do you think that scenes like that like could damage youngsters' minds?

Eisner: No, I don't agree with Dr. Wertham. Well, actually I believe that *all* literature "damages" the mind in that it *influences* the mind. I think you can't say that comics depicting violence and mayhem should not be shown to children because once you start doing that you're setting up a literary and intellectual diet for somebody. And who can set up a diet for society? I don't believe that censorship can be administered—countries have tried it over and over again and it just doesn't function well. I'm against it, against any form of censorship other than the restrictions imposed by the creators' own taste, or sense of responsibility to moral values.

yronwode: One of the things you've been repeatedly criticized for is the matter of "racism" in the case of The Spirit's sidekick, Ebony White . . .

Eisner: Oh yes. Well here we go again. [Sigh] We might as well get it over with. We might as well talk about it because people have been talking about it for twenty-five years. The Warren magazines had a whole exchange of letters on the subject which I read with great interest—people wrote in and argued with each other over Ebony. Look, let's just say—I don't know whether this is gonna' finally knock it in the head and kill it—I *did* Ebony, I'm *glad* I did Ebony, I'm not *ashamed* of having done Ebony, I *don't* think I was racist, I *know* I wasn't racist, I was *not* doing Ebony in the same spirit that a Nazi propagandist might have drawn hook-nosed fellows with curly hair and Semitic features in anti-Semitic literature, I drew Ebony as he was because he was a creature or pattern of the *time*. If Ebony was appearing today he would still be valid because television today is *filled* with Ebonies, with caricatures of blacks. I realize that Ebony was a stereotype because I drew him in caricature—but how else could I have treated a black boy in that era, at that time? Yes, I was drawing humor out of the incongruities, but so did Harry Hershfield before me in drawing *Abe Kabibble*, so did Al Capp in *Li'l Abner* with the hillbillies—they drew humor out of certain types, certain language characteristics. *Happy Hooligan* was another that drew humor out of the alien or foreign characteristics.

So did *The Katzenjammer Kids* with their German accents. It was a different period, another time. And in conclusion I would like to say [Laughter] . . . in conclusion let me just say that at the time I had as many approvals as I had disapprovals. I tried later to pick on other, less vocal minorities—like Eskimos.

yronwode: Toward the end of *The Spirit*'s run, Sammy is introduced and he gradually more or less replaces Ebony. Was this done in answer to criticism?
Eisner: No, I was just looking for new characters, that's all. No one ever threatened to bomb me or drop the feature. I feel I treated Ebony with great care and great honesty. And by the way, nobody ever seems to mention *this* when they bring up Ebony—but I had a Lt. Grey in *The Spirit* who was a black detective and who spoke with no trace of a southern drawl. He was very realistic. At any rate I gave Ebony all the warmth and the feeling and the humor that I thought he had to have. He was a little body-servantish perhaps, but that was the real part of the way it was at the time.

yronwode: You've always kept the copyrights on your things . . .
Eisner: Yes, the only ones I let go were Sheena and those—but that's because they were properties of a company which I sold. From then on I owned everything.

yronwode: If they make a movie out of *Sheena*, as has been rumored, will you or Jerry Iger get any credit or money?
Eisner: I don't know if Iger will get anything or not. Since I did create the feature while I was part of Eisner and Iger they may, out of generosity, put my name on it.

yronwode: I don't know if you're aware of the things going on at Marvel and DC now—the "work for hire" dispute . . .
Eisner: I'm aware of it, yeah.

yronwode: Do you think that the artists and writers—the creators—should have the rights or do you think that they're just "suppliers" to the company?
Eisner: The artists and writers should have rights and the publishers should have rights. There's two sides to that issue. It isn't even a question of what rights they *should* have—it's a matter of what agreements they choose to make if and when they negotiate. But let's look at the publisher's side too—when a publisher buys artwork from people—especially when one person's doing the pencilling and another one's doing the inking and another one's doing the

story—whose is the final product? Another question: if the publisher accords an artist control over the property—then who answers for libel actions? Also, how should they deal with an artist or writer hired to simply execute a feature which has existed before the artist hired on? Historically, comic book publishers regarded the sole ownership of any feature in their comic books as solely theirs. It's not a question of right and wrong—as long as the artist and writer know they're selling out. I was denied many markets because I would not deal on a sell-out basis. I paid for the ownership in that way. I really don't think we can adequately discuss this subject in the abstract.

Let's leave it this way . . . the creator has an inalienable right to own what he creates . . . unless he chooses to sell it.

yronwode: Who are your current favorite comics artists?

Eisner: I like Rich Corben—I recently wrote a foreword for a book in which I expressed my feeling about his work, complimenting him. I think Moebius is one of the world's foremost comic book artists today. There's a whole bunch of them. I think Art Spiegelman is tremendous and Crumb—unfortunately he's not doing enough, but I would love to see Crumb continue. I haven't really followed what's being done at Marvel and DC very closely. It's hard for me to follow anyone there because I don't know *who's* doing *what*. You see, I don't separate drawing from writing the way they do, so it's very hard for me to evaluate their work.

yronwode: And now for the obligatory last question: Why does The Spirit wear his gloves all the time, even when he's asleep?

Eisner: That's a very good question. I'm glad you asked that question—and good night!

A Talk with Will Eisner

TED WHITE, MITCH BERGER, AND MIKE BARSON / 1983

From *Heavy Metal*, 7 (November 1983), 45–47. Reprinted by permission of Heavy Metal.

Will Eisner may not be a genius, but in the history of comics, he'll do until the real thing comes along. People think they are doing Eisner a favor by comparing *The Spirit* to *Citizen Kane*, but *The Spirit* came out every week for thirteen years, and *Citizen Kane*, wonderful as it was, was just one movie.

The fact is, even without *The Spirit* in his resumé, Will Eisner could lay claim to being the most important artist/writer/editor/creator/packager of the Golden Age of Comics. Blackhawk, Sheena, Uncle Sam—Eisner created and developed them all, along with Doll Man, Espionage, Hawks of the Seas, and a dozen others he professes to have forgotten. And this was before World War II.

There are many creators and many great creations: Segar and *Thimble Theater*; Barks and Uncle Scrooge; Kelly and Pogo; Kurtzman and *Mad*; Herriman and Krazy Kat; Cole and Plastic Man; Caniff and Terry; Kane and Batman; Gould and Dick Tracy. But of all of these, only Barks and his Donald Duck/ Uncle Scrooge stories can really rank with the constant inventiveness, humor, and impact of *The Spirit*. Eisner did things with storylines, visuals, and characterization that had never been done before in one strip. Parody, tragedy, humor, suspense, action, slapstick, sorrow—*The Spirit* had them all. Not every week perhaps, and not always at optimum effect . . . but Eisner had the nerves of a riverboat gambler, and there was nothing he was afraid to try. Most of the time, he had the skill to carry it off. And when he failed—well, a lot of comic artists and writers wish they could achieve in their work what passed for failure in *The Spirit*.

But talking about this is boring. *The Spirit* has to be read, and read again, to appreciate the enormity of Eisner's achievement. Luckily for us all, the stories from the forties and fifties are being made available in a variety of inexpensive formats.

As Jim Steranko once described *The Spirit*, "Never has so much happened, to so many, in so few pages." And expanding on that—never have so many unique things happened, to so many fascinating characters, with such effective results. And even that's not enough.

Only the stories are enough. Will Eisner has told hundreds of them, and he has more to tell. And that's a very, very good thing to know.

—Mike Barson

HM: I guess we should begin at the beginning, back before *The Spirit* had been created.

Eisner: About two years after I got out of high school, around 1938, I started a little company called Eisner and Iger in New York. We had one of the first bullpens of comic artists, with people like Bob Kane (*Batman*), who was doing a feature called *Peter Pupp* for us, and Jack Kurtzburg, who later became known as Jack Kirby. Actually, we also called him Jack Curtis and Jack Kurdery on his stories—we had *lots* of house names. I myself was doing five features under five different names.

HM: Such as?

Eisner: One was Willis R. Rensie—that's "Eisner" backwards—another was W. Morgan Thomas, another, Spencer Steele—that's a marvelous name, isn't it? I always wanted to be named Spencer Steele. That was when I still had hair, of course.

HM: I used to see those names on *Jumbo* and *Jungle* comics, and they didn't seem real.

Eisner: It was all part of the fantasy world of comics. Eisner & Iger started with $15.00—I financed the operation, so my name came first—and pretty soon we were flourishing. The idea of doing original art for comic books was a new one, but it was obvious to me that the newspaper syndicate stuff, that comic books were reprinting, was going to run out eventually, and that original material would be needed.

HM: So tell us what it was like for twenty-two-year-old Will Eisner walking from syndicate to syndicate, trying to peddle his character, the Spirit.

Eisner: I didn't go to them; they came to *me*. Eisner & Iger was making a lot of money—we were producing the entire Fiction House line, and that was just one account—and we had in short order developed a reputation for reliability. Now, around 1940 the Sunday newspapers were beginning to feel the competition from the superhero comic books, just as today video games are cutting into the sales of comic books. The syndicates wanted to get a comic book produced to insert into their Sunday papers. The Register-Tribune syndicate, under Henry Martin and with comic book publisher "Busy" Arnold [né Everett M., who had founded the Centaur line of comics in 1938] called me. They needed a combination of quality and reliability—you just don't miss deadlines in the newspaper business. What they wanted was a caped character like Superman, which was their concept of a comic book hero.

HM: But you dissuaded them from that concept.

Eisner: When they asked for a caped character, I said, "No!" flat out, it wasn't what I wanted to do. I realized that this was an opportunity for me—I was just twenty-two, and newspaper strips meant the big time for a cartoonist—but it was also a risk, and I was no novice. Nevertheless, I sold my half interest in the company to Jerry Iger, who thought the whole idea was awfully risky, but wished me well. In hindsight I still get chills; a sensible, practical person wouldn't have taken such a chance.

Anyway, there were many arguments with the syndicate concerning the character and personality the strip was to have. The final decision came when one dark and rainy night at around 2 AM—I used to work all hours back then—I got a call from "Busy" Arnold. He was in a bar; I could hear a jukebox in the background as he talked. It was like a scene out of *The Spirit*; I was looking out over East Forty-second Street, and the rain was pouring down. "You got the character yet?" he asked me. I told him I had a detective character for them. He said, "Okay, we'll buy it." But then they found out that my detective was dressed normally, and what they wanted was a caped, Batman-type character. So we argued about whether I would put a costume on my character. Finally I gave in. "Oh, good," "Busy" said, "so what's the costume?" I told him, "He's got a mask." "Well," "Busy" said, "at least put gloves on him." So, the Spirit got a mask and some gloves, and I threw in a hat, which happened to be the same kind of hat "Busy" always wore. It was a private joke, and I don't think "Busy" ever caught on.

HM: You did great things with that hat.

Eisner: Yeah, but I kept trying to get rid of that *mask*. I'd put the Spirit in dark glasses, I'd do all kinds of things. But the syndicate was satisfied, because the product *looked* like the comic books of the day, therefore it *was* comics. But I was able to satisfy my creative instincts, right down to changing the logo every week, which was unheard of back then. Those were halcyon days for me.

HM: Until you heard from Uncle Sam.

Eisner: Apparently the army needed me badly. So I went—kicking and screaming all the way. But those four years in the Pentagon building opened my eyes to a whole new potential for comics. Other people had been doing *The Spirit* while I was away, and it looked as though it was on its last legs. I took it over again, because I didn't want it to die.

HM: It was under Lou Fine's direction while you were away, wasn't it?

Eisner: Yes, but Lou had never had any interest in the writing end of the business. He had a brilliant technique, the best of anyone working then, and when I did the writing he was free to spend his time rendering a magnificent piece of art. There are writers who are capable of inspiring an artist, bringing things out of him that he might not have known were there. There has to be a kind of emotional welding between the two where trust takes place. That's why we worked so well together. But doing any comic strip secondhand is a problem. Except for the ownership of the concept, I felt *The Spirit* had ceased to be mine while I was away. But when I came back and took it over again, I felt I was really ready to *do* something with it.

HM: How do you feel today about getting so much mileage out of something you did thirty-five years ago?

Eisner: It serves me right! Well, it's hard not to answer immodestly.

HM: Go ahead, be immodest!

Eisner: Seriously? Okay, I'll tell you that I'm well aware that I am a singularly fortunate man to command any kind of following for a feature I put to bed so many years ago.

HM: How did the decision to put it to bed come about?

Eisner: After the war, I had started a company called American Visuals Corporation, which was devoted to the commercial and instructional application of comics. During the war, I had come to the realization that comics were a far more sophisticated teaching tool than I had ever thought before. I saw how they could be used for training and other special purposes by businesses. I put on a staff of salesmen and had them approach the big concerns. Our first customer was General Motors. Pretty soon American Visuals was going like gangbusters. It was at that point, around 1952, that my availability and devotion to *The Spirit* began to diminish.

HM: You felt there was nothing more to do with *The Spirit*?

Eisner: I felt there was a whole new world to conquer. *The Spirit* was nice and safe, but at that point there was nowhere to go with it. I wanted to leave while the show was still a success. Had I waited another year or two, I probably would have started getting cancellations. I had been relying more and more on assistants, and readers were noticing the changes of style. We just couldn't keep up the quality. I finally had to make a decision—the same kind of decision I made when I left Eisner and Iger.

HM: What happened to the *Spirit* movie we kept hearing about?

Eisner: Oh, every five years or so someone comes in to take an option on doing it as a movie. The last one came very close. Bill Friedkin [*The Exorcist*] was very serious and gave it a good try. He bought scripts from three writers, Harlan Ellison, Pete Hamill, and Jules Feiffer, before he finally just threw his hands up.

HM: I would have thought Jules Feiffer . . .

Eisner: I would have thought so, too. And add Will Eisner to that list. We just couldn't give Friedkin what he wanted. But now it's really being done, by Gary Kurtz, *Star Wars*' producer, as a full-length, animated film.

HM: Have you worked closely on this version?

Eisner: I've been involved in many of the story conferences—it's based partly on some of my old stories—and I've made model sheets. I have veto power over the art prior to the beginning of principal photography. A lot of the pre-production work is completed, although we don't know yet who the distributor will be.

HM: That's good news. Still, I've always dreamt of a live-action, black-and-white version that looked like a 1948 movie.

Eisner: Maybe someday.

HM: Your work on *The Spirit* involves all the aspects of directing a film. A lot of artists aren't able to do that, to impose their vision . . .

Eisner: Some do. But many comic book artists are really illustrators. An illustration is a moment in time, selected and carefully rendered to reinforce text. A visual, a good visual, is complete without any words. Comics, I believe, should be a *series* of visuals.

HM: The "camera angles" you choose for your compositions provide the point of view and mood that you're trying to establish.
Eisner: The "camera angle" is not selected casually. It's chosen *because* of something. Cinema is really nothing but comics put into motion. I learned about lighting from the theater. During my high school days, I became seriously interested in stagecraft. As a matter of fact, once I was a set designer for a high school show that Adolph Green put on. To this day, I refer to the panel as a stage. But with comics, there's a certain innate visual sense that comes across, which really has nothing to do with film. Film, to the audience, is a transient thing; with a comic, the audience can look at what's happening for as long as they desire.

HM: How did the resurgence of interest in *The Spirit* during the sixties happen? I don't recall that sort of grassroots movement ever happening, before or since, for a comic book character.
Eisner: In 1966 Leon Harvey, the publisher of Harvey Comics, called me. He had the idea that there was a superhero revival, and he wanted to reprint *The Spirit*. I think he misread the market—it was the Stan Lee–type of superhero stuff that was hot then. Anyway, we put out two issues, then gave it up. But a few years later I ran into Denis Kitchen at a comic's convention in New York, and Denis said he'd like to try a reprint. I said, "Sure, go ahead." To my amazement they sold enormously well. A bit after that, I was talking to Jim Warren at some convention in Canada where I'd been asked to speak, and he expressed an interest in publishing a *Spirit* book. Around this time, Stan Lee had also indicated some interest, but I made the decision to let Warren do it because he was very serious about it, and I felt he would do it with soul. And he did. Eventually he had to give it up because of the distribution and returns problems he was having, but now with Denis doing the magazine, I think we've got those problems licked.

HM: Doing *A Contract with God* was quite a gamble, since no market for graphic novels had been established at that time.
Eisner: I suppose the decision started with my teaching at the School of

Visual Arts. In the process of teaching, you get to test your own concepts; you look at the professional world with a different perception. I began to discover that there were some things to do that hadn't yet been done in the world of comics.

I wanted to do something that I had just been talking about for a long, long time; I wanted to take sequential art another step forward by doing a graphic novel. I had no economic hope, no publisher, but I sat down and did *A Contract with God*. You reach a point in your life when you say, "If I don't do it now, I ain't ever going to do it."

HM: It's a very personal book; it must have been very hard to put all that on paper.
Eisner: It was. "To stand," as we used to say in the army, "naked on the drill field." When you do adventure stories, you can hide behind the hero's costume, and say, "This isn't *me*, folks!" I became terribly embarrassed while doing *Contract* . . . I had trouble rereading what I had written. Being honest is like being pregnant—there's no such thing as being "a little bit" honest. Once you start, there's no turning back.

HM: It received, deservedly, very good reviews. Were you satisfied with it?
Eisner: It was my first effort at a serious work, and I realized later that I could have turned what I was attempting up a notch—gone a bit further. Maybe unconsciously I had held back a little. So with *Life on Another Planet* I tried to carry the experiment to the next level, to merge sequential art and the classic novel.

HM: This is the serial that you ran in the *Spirit* magazine recently?
Eisner: Yes. This fall it is being published as a full-color hardcover both in the U.S. and in Europe; it will be released as *Signal from Space* in France. Andre Le Blanc, one of my assistants from the old days, rendered the color. I revised the first three chapters from the magazine for the book version. It has a subject that hasn't been dealt with before in comics, and it's presented much like a "straight" novel.

HM: Is another graphic novel on the drawing board?
Eisner: Next year Lyle Stuart will be publishing *The Big City*, which is a portrait of New York from a worm's-eye view. It's a series of vignettes of life in the city as experienced by the people who've always lived there. I look at the

fire hydrants, the stoops, the street noise—*Metal Hurlant* has published the "Street Music" chapter with a record that is meant to be played as you read the story.

HM: Will *Big City* be in black and white?
Eisner: Yes. I'm hoping that this will be the book that gets me into the "establishment" bookstores. *Contract* got shuttled all over the place; they didn't know whether to put it in "Religion," in "Humor," or some other section of the store.

HM: And then?
Eisner: I'm looking towards sort of a sequel to *Contract*, set in 1934. There are a lot more stories about that tenement on 55 Dropsie Avenue that need to be told.

HM: The *Spirit* magazine will itself be seeing some major changes soon, from what I understand.
Eisner: True. Denis is splitting it into two separate magazines. One will be called *The Spirit*—the numbering will begin again at one—and will be full-color, comic-book size, printed on Baxter paper. This will run my postwar *Spirit* stories in chronological order, four to an issue. The full-color, gray tones, and flat color we're using will take the quality another light year forward. Mike Newhall will be coloring this book, which will be bimonthly.

The other magazine will "humbly" be titled *Will Eisner's Quarterly*. It will be in black and white except for a color insert of a full prewar *Spirit* section—including *Mr. Mystic* and *Lady Luck*—in sequence from 1940 onwards. Denis wants this magazine to be the platform for launching my new projects, and running things like "Shop Talk." [Eisner's interviews with other artists.] As it was, the magazine just couldn't contain all the elements we had going. The opportunity to run the *Spirit* stories in order, the way they were meant to be read, and to have a creative outlet for new work, was too good to pass up.

HM: Listening to you detail all your plans, I have a hard time remembering that I'm talking to a "relic" from the 1930s!
Eisner: Well, hang on, because I'm just now reaching my stride.

Will Eisner

DALE LUCIANO / 1985

From *The Comics Journal*, No. 100 (July 1985), 83–89, 185–186. Reprinted by permission of Dale Luciano.

Dale Luciano: Since you've traveled in Europe and America in connection with your work, you would seem not only to have a good overview of the entire history of comics—

Will Eisner: [Laughter] Well, you might be right about that . . . Certainly I'm old enough!

Luciano: —and also the recent history of the direct-sales marketing system. Where do you think things are right now?

Eisner: Well, there's really some good news and some bad news. Actually, although this is nothing new, we're in a moment of crisis. We've just come through a year in which, to my dismay and concern, a great number of the smaller, midsize, and little publishers ran into marketing trouble in the comic-book stores. These are the small, independent comic-book publishers, who for the past fifteen years have been the great hope of the newly emerging, young comic-book artists, who have provided the platform for new ideas and advances in the medium, are having difficult times. They're being really muscled around by the flow of tremendous volume of titles pouring out of the larger distributors . . . As a result, a lot of the independents are having a tough time staying alive financially. I hear collection problems and display problems are worse than ever.

From all that I've heard, sales of the smaller, new *experimental* books seem to have dropped off in the last six months. The store owners I've spoken with tell me they have difficulty moving new and unknown titles. A lot of their young readers come in now looking for books that have *collector* value, rather than *reader* value. Also, the price of comic books has gone up so high that a kid—a "kid" meaning a fourteen-, fifteen-, or sixteen-year-old—can hardly afford to accumulate three, four, or five titles, on one visit to a bookstore.

Another confounding factor, in terms of the overall picture, is that the *content* of the magazines seems to be dividing into categories. In the current crop of comic books, there's a real schism between what I call the "mutant" story and the genuine adventure kind of story that seems to be having a difficult time making it. Young readers are buying them on the basis of what I call *the sensory experience.* They're looking for fantastic, "blow-your-mind" kind of art. They'll buy the books without having any idea what the story content is! They just flip through the pages in the book store to see if it has a lot of "picture value," almost completely disregarding story values. That's not to say this hasn't always been present to some extent in the comic field, but it's certainly a very important factor in what's currently happening.

Looking on the brighter side, the comic book field *is* moving forward in terms of how the artist is regarded. Better rates are being paid, and both artists and writers in the field are today able to support themselves and really, truly make a living from comics. Today some of them even own the properties they create and are doing very well financially. Therefore, the field has become more inviting to people who would normally have gone into other fields in the past. They're now willing to come into the field. I'm talking about the American scene, of course.

What's *still* missing on the American scene is, however, the *acceptance* or the *status* of the comic-book artist. In Europe, the comic-book artist still enjoys a status far in excess of that of a comic-book artist in America. The European artist finds himself accepted in the company of painters and illustrators and writers and so forth, where in this country, there's still a great difference in status between even a comic *book* artist and a comic *strip* artist . . .

Luciano: Have you found that to be a changing at all?
Eisner: To a degree, yes. Yes, I do feel it's changing here. It's certainly a helluva lot better than it was when *I* started! It's certainly a helluva lot better than it was in the '50s. Each year it's better. But, you know, asking a question like that is a little like asking a black man, "Well, do you find less prejudice in this country now after twenty years of Civil Rights?"

Luciano: [Laughter]
Eisner: So the answer to the question has to be, yes, of course, on a professional level, comic-book artists now have things they never had before. They have fan recognition, for one. They develop followings. Today we have artists

like Frank Miller who have a following, who can *command a position with a publisher*. The comic-book artists' names are now prominently featured as part of a book's appeal. (As a matter of fact, even the sweep-up man in most of the shops now gets a mention on the page!) Comic-book artists now have a recognition that serves them in the art world. Many artists are now doing covers: Frazetta's doing pulp covers, book jackets, record jackets. Rich Corben, who for me represents the archetype of the cartoonist who fought his way up the ladder, literally on the strength of pure skill, and made it into the establishment, is now doing paperback covers and has just finished a record jacket. *And* he's now commanding very fancy prices which permits him to move into the so-called "better" illustration field, moving "Uptown" in other words. Most comic-book artists still dream of that upward mobility *out* of comics.

Luciano: If we could get back to the problem of the direct-sales distribution system for a moment, I'd like to aim this question squarely at your own books. What impact does the product glut have on *The Spirit* reprint book and *Will Eisner's Quarterly*?

Eisner: Well, it does have an impact, but I'm actually in a totally different world than most other comics. I'm so to speak in a different orbit. And I knew this when I started out years ago. Let's talk about *The Spirit*. *The Spirit* is a reprint of work written years ago. It must compete with current production. It has a category all its own and must find its own place on the store racks. A second point is that *The Spirit* never had, even from the day it was created, the same audience that today buys *X-Men* or *DN Agents* or books of that kind. And the readers for those books represent the large bulk of the comic book-buying market. By the very nature of the material, the *Spirit* reader has to be a more sophisticated reader who is, unfortunately, a minority among those that come into the specialty stores.

This doesn't mean I'm not satisfied. Remarkably to me, *The Spirit* has enjoyed a very, very solid, almost fanatical following. There's a *Spirit* cult out there, I'm told. Yet in all the sales charts I've seen, *The Spirit* has never equaled the sales of, say, *American Flagg!* or, again, *X-Men* or things like that. Now the impact of that recent product glut I talked about *obviously* has an effect on things like *The Spirit* because the retail merchant, who is very concerned with moving copies, knows he's dealing with a product that satisfies only a small segment of his customer list. Therefore he won't stock heavily and probably won't promote it too aggressively. It depends a lot on location. For example, *The Spirit* does very well at the Forbidden Planet store in New York City, but it may not do as well down here in Florida in a little bookstore on one of the avenues.

Let me provide another answer to your question in regard to the material I'm doing in *Will Eisner's Quarterly*. I'm not for the bulk of comic book buyers, who buy *X-Men* and books of that kind. In fact, everything I've done in the last ten years has been addressed—rather pretentiously, I admit—to the *adult* reader. And I don't mean *adult* reader in the sense of explicit sex. I mean *adult reader* in the sense of somebody looking for good story content, who's willing to go along with me and is capable of looking at something that deals with real life. Hopefully mine are books young people can buy for their parents.

Luciano: How is something like *Signal from Space* received differently in Europe than in the United States?

Eisner: Well, *Signal from Space* is a socio-political comment wrapped in a spy-adventure yarn. It deals with an adult premise in diverse situations. It is "realistic" science fiction. I believe it has experienced a good reception in the European marketplace because the European market represents a more diversified audience than we have in this country. These seem to be a larger group of adult readers with the life experience that is capable of understanding storytelling that relates to real experience. Here, superheroes still dominate the output. I'm not dealing with two mutants killing each other, I'm dealing with real life, people involved with life itself. This requires a common experience between me and the reader. When I write I intend to share an experience. I'm telling a story that deals with an aspect of life. A case in point is a book I did recently, *Life Force*. This is a reportage that deals with the history of my experience, or experience that I've seen, or felt, or been aware of, during the '30s. It deals with *life* during 1934. It's reportage, in the pure sense. As most storytelling is.

The point is that the publishers in Europe seem to be willing to respond to a marketplace that accepts the comic-book medium as a valid, legitimate literacy form. A very important thing when you consider it. It has an effect on the kind of work I'm doing, and provides me with the marketplace that I'm working for. Here in the United States, the marketplace is more severely divided, even though it has a vast young audience, a preponderance of young readers whose interests are in fantasy art, and whose interests are in science fiction, mutants, for example, that is *Teen Titans* and *X-Men*, things of that sort, and whose life experience, as readers, is not really conducive to a concern with man against the system or against life itself. They're concerned largely with fantasy or escape. Their interest seems to be largely in the, what I call sensory experience, and, they are also influenced, the young readers, largely by motion pictures. Which have in the past been influenced by comics, so you have a kind of dog chewing on a dog's tail, the thing is going back and forth. European readers are terribly interested in New York life. One of the most successful comic strips coming out of France right now is done by this Italian boy named Gaetano Liberatore, doing *Ranxerox*, which is a violent, *violent*, sex-laden strip. Beautifully drawn, magnificently executed. It deals with, really, punk life, and, really, very distasteful to adult readers in this country who are concerned with that kind of living as being part of the inner city in L.A. So we have a different kind of interest. Another strip that's doing very well in Europe, that originated in Spain, and originally the first issue was done by Alex Toth, is a thing called *Torpedo* which, fantastically, concerns itself with a hitman in the '30s, a ganster and bootlegger era, who's really a terrible person, a killer, and who is the hero of the strip. Anti-hero if you will. But there's a great interest in inner-city living, and in the American scene. There still exists in Europe an interest in the Western scene in this country, which we no longer have. So you really have two basically different, broad markets.

Luciano: Well, it's my general impression when you take something like *Will Eisner's Quarterly*, or something like *Love and Rockets*, that even though these books may appeal to a minority audience in comparison with some of the mainstream books, nonetheless, they have an influence by their very presence. I assume that they've built up an audience, a following, over a period of time. But one of the things that impresses me, having only followed the field for six or seven years, is the appearance of these books, and the influence that their presence has in terms of revealing to readers that these alternatives exist.

Eisner: Well, yeah. Hopefully, that's the case. As a matter of fact, I'm hanging my entire career on that thing, on that one hope. And that is that, hopefully, there's going to be a growing acceptance of this kind of material within the frame of the so-called comic medium. Now, right now, there's a hard-core audience that I write to. Readers who are looking beyond only either sex or some kind of violent experience, or pure fantasy art. So that, you're quite right, it's there all right, and I hope it will grow and expand.

Luciano: Well, you're a unique figure in the history of comics, not only because of the *Spirit*. When I first became interested in the field, as an observer and a critic, one of the first things that appeared was *A Contract with God*.

It seems that that virtually came out of nowhere, a kind of complete, full-blown, autobiographical, visual novel, dealing with one's recollections of a certain period in a certain *milieu*. At least from my point of view, there wasn't anything quite like that, and it must have taken a certain amount of daring to conceive and work out that project.

Eisner: Well, it was a, there's no question about it, it was a gamble. It was a risk for me, because I had no client or customer for it, but it, it took me a year and a half to do, but it represented something that I always believed had to be done if the art form was valid as I believed it to be. I had been working within that field generally and within that frame generally over the years, even in the days of the *Spirit*. The *Spirit* stories always came out of some kind of personal experience.

Luciano: Yes.

Eisner: The stories of the '30s, if you go back and look at them, while the Spirit was a masked hero and kind of a spoof on superheroes, although in those days we called them "costumed characters." The stories were able to stand on their own. Many of the stories could exist without the Spirit. The story of Gerhard Shnobble was a story that could have been told without the Spirit. So my interest always was, from the very earliest days, in extending the medium as far as I possibly could. After all, from the very beginning, for me, comics, or the comic medium, this precious combination of words and pictures, was my art-form; it was my medium. As a writer of words only, I would probably not make it, as a person who devotes himself totally to pictures, I would probably not make it, the combination of the two was the area where I knew I could excel. And I gradually began to realize, as I went on, that it was indeed a valid medium, and it needed no apology. It is a unique kind of literary form. I keep using "literary" for want of a better word, but sequential has in itself all of the structure of literature, if you will. It deals with words, it deals with pictures, it has construction, plot can be fabricated with it, it has a large vocabulary of its own, it is in itself a language, and it was, in my opinion, capable of dealing with subject matter far more advanced and far more sophisticated than the very simple little fantasy stories that are offered in the comic-book stores.

Luciano: *A Contract with God* was the first major work of yours I'd seen, and that seems to have led to the development of other periodicals in your work with *Life Force* and the continuation of that story. How was *A Contract with God* received?

Eisner: Well, first, I had really no hope for any market place for it. There was no comic-book house that I could think of who would want it. And I produced it, really, after I had sold my publishing company and decided I would go back to writing and drawing, and I produced the whole thing in total pencilled form. And presented it in dummy form to Oscar Dystel, who was then president of Bantam Books. He liked it and gave me a very good reception, but told me that he couldn't sell more than a few copies of it, because he felt there was a limited audience for that thing, and he said he wouldn't know where to place it in the bookstores. It had no . . . place. And he suggested that I find a small publisher, which I did. Promptly published it, and then went out of business. Kind of the kiss of death. But, the book itself appeared in the form that I wanted it to appear, and that is in the traditional textbook form, the normal textbook form, 6" x 9" in one color.

Luciano: Beautiful production.
Eisner: Nicely produced, and it was distributed to the traditional bookshops. As a matter of fact, Brentanno's on Fifth Avenue carried it for a week or two, and did very well with it as long as they had it displayed by itself in front of the store. The minute they took it out of that front-store display and tried to put it on shelves, they ran into trouble, because they had no place to put it. The manager at Brentanno's told me that they had put it onto the shelf marked religious books, and, of course, nobody bought it there, and then he took it out of that and put it in with comic books, next to the *Origin of Marvel* and it didn't go there, because it didn't fit. So it had no place. Subsequently, it turned, well, financially and critically. By the way, Kitchen Sink will publish a new edition soon.

Luciano: Well, I'm happy to hear that.
Eisner: Well, it's been translated into six languages, sold close to 50,000 copies, and has gotten excellent reviews. And it has really led, hopefully, to the wider use of graphic novels. Now, I don't claim to have invented graphic novels, and as a matter of fact, in the book itself, I pay tribute to Lynd Ward, the famous wood-engraver, who originally, in the '30s produced a number of books—all art by woodcut, without any words. I felt that he demonstrated that there was room for a "graphic novel," as I called it at the time, and I put it on the cover. Subsequently, the word "graphic novel" has been used pretty widely, and I'm very pleased in that, because I feel that somehow or other, the concept has found acceptance. Now, as to the subject matter of the book, I chose a subject matter I was familiar with, which was life in the Bronx in

the late '30s. This is an area that I knew from my youth, and I was able to talk about it with some authority. A lot of it is autobiographical, a lot of it is experiences that I had, that I saw other people have. Now, not everything in there is totally about myself, and it was fabricated as a four-part novel within the frame of 55 Dropsie Avenue, a tenement. Originally, the superintendent was the connector between all the four stories. Subsequently, before I published it, I dropped that idea, just to do four short stories, but all taking place in that segment of the Bronx and related. The book I did later, *Signal from Space* or *Life on Another Planet*, was really an attempt on my part to prove that one could do, and I put this in italics, *a proper novel*, with all the structures that a novel has, the thread of a theme, the main thrust of an idea, the continuity of characters throughout, the development of a single plot into a drama. That book was my attempt to prove that a serious subject, and a seriously fabricated novel could be attempted in this medium. Now, whether I succeeded or not, I don't know, but I felt I did. The story itself was lighter than the stuff I've undertaken since then. And it was a science-fiction story that takes place in real life, so to speak. I have no apologies for it, I think it was, I did as well as I could, as a matter of fact, I rather liked it when I finished it. I thought the artwork was good, but as always, six months after I've completed a work, I always feel, "God! If I had to do it over again, how much better I could have done it."

Luciano: Yeah, I noticed in the *Signal from Space* edition that you had reworked a lot of it.
Eisner: I reworked, yes, I always do that, I'm cranky with my own work. I'm never satisfied with work after I've completed it. Fortunately, I always have another project awaiting so I just move on. Next, I did a thing called *Big City*, which was a portrait of the city. Again, it was an attempt at doing something different with sequential art. And I used the artform and the series of vignettes about the city, all built around the same opening scene, but each chapter concerned itself with an element of the city which formed a total portrait, from the ground up, so to speak. Walls, windows, things that we live with in the city. The city is a marvelous fountainhead for story material, no question about it.

Following that came *Life Force*. *Life Force* is reportage. It's billed by Kitchen Sink as a sequel to *Contract with God*, simply because it takes place in the same area and at the same time. But there I attempted a kind of quasi-historical work, where I reproduced articles that appeared in newspapers at the time and built my stories around that façade, using the newspaper articles to give moment to the stories, to give a historical reference, and at the same time build a story around a man who was looking for the meaning of life. In the case of *A Contract with God*, it was one where the first story dealt with a man's struggle with his relationship with God. Somehow or other God sometimes does not fulfill on his bargains that are part of the contract that we create. We're always creating a contract with the deity. In the case of *Life Force*, it was really an observation that man continues to move on as a result of some inner force that keeps him going despite all the things that happen to him. And I compare it to the cockroach who keeps going and going on without any perceived reason. So those three novels each deal with a subject area that requires a little life experience to appreciate.

Luciano: It must be difficult for you to look at some of the mainstream comics and the new generation of artists coming along, most of whose experience with life seems to be limited to the tube and super-hero comics.
Eisner: Well, exactly. The reason a large body of our comics are at least poor in depth, is that the people who are producing the comics today, writers and the young artists, are emanating out of a limited life experience, gleaned largely out of the tube, television, and a great deal of youth. Which itself is no crime. We've all suffered from youth.

Luciano: [Laughter]
Eisner: I've been a victim of it. But the artists, their literary nutrition, their cultural nutrition does not come from real experience, it comes from motion pictures and the artificial experience, the passive experience that is provided them by television and movies. In the early days of comics, the artists all brought to comics a background based in the classics, reading, and in their own life. People like Frazetta, and people like Gil Kane, and even men like Jack Kirby, all brought a kind of personal testimony to the field based on their own real experience. They had no comic books that they grew up with. Today you're having a kind of incestuous situation where comic artists are really young people who grew up on comics and are simply giving back to comics all that they've gotten out of comics during their growth. It's not their fault they're unable to bring anything new to it, because they haven't lived there. They're not doing stories about their life in a steel town, or in a steel mill, or their life on the road. The early underground comics at least had a valid contribution, which attracted me, because you were dealing with people who were involved in the drug scene, and who were involved with the so-called "protest period." And they had things to say, even though they were saying

things to themselves, and sometimes what they said was obscure, but they nonetheless had something to say, which gave this tremendous vitality to the so-called underground comics. Which has now almost disappeared from the scene.

Luciano: Yes, yes. And yet an artist like Robert Crumb has earned a place in history. Donald Feine, the professor who put the book together on Crumb's work, has called him "perhaps the most autobiographical of American cartoonists," drawing out of his own experience of things.
Eisner: Well, that's it. Right there is the reason that he has been so successful. I mean creatively successful.

Luciano: Yes!
Eisner: Financially, I don't know, but creatively successful, because he is contributing something of himself. He has something to say. He makes some very powerful statements. I think one of the great masterpieces of the field is his "Yeti." The story of this monstrous human, this huge, female monster that a man takes up with, and finally, it ends tragically because society won't accept it. Crumb is making a very, very powerful statement there. So Crumb is not to be underestimated. He started out as a head writing to heads, I think, then. But he had a lot more to say, and the man feels and talks. He's making a contribution. Every bit as valid as the people who've come before him, like Charles Dickens. The other people who've had . . .

Luciano: Yes, Feine compared him to Dostoevsky.
Eisner: Well, yes, yes. There's the same writing agony in his work that you feel when you read Dostoevsky. And he has a kind of a bitter sense of humor. His artwork fools you because it has the style of what I've always called "bigfoot art," but he's no less a consummate artist. Anybody who's see his poster on the history of America, that wonderful thing he did showing the small crossroads growing into a city, has go to be struck by his craftsmanship. He's a great artist. He's good. His style is just bigfoot, that's all. I like it, I love his work. I read it all.

Luciano: Well, it's interesting that talking to you, and talking about Crumb, two authentic artists. You are continually placed in the position of feeling alienated from any tradition. You have to define yourself as an alternative in relation to mainstream. Maybe that's the lot of the artist in this culture, always to be struggling against the prevailing pop tradition.

Eisner: Well, as Willy Loman said, "it comes with the territory." This is what it's all about. Unless you're struggling against something, you're not bringing anything to it. If you're just drawing what everybody else is drawing, you're not contributing to anything, you're just refining what they're doing. This is where your worth is measured, right there. Just how much have you brought to a given field, how much have you changed it? This is really the measure of what you've done. How you've influenced other artists, that is also a measure, too. But sometimes you influence other artists by skill and razzle-dazzle. For years, there were a bunch of imitators running around, of Milton Caniff looka-likes for a while. But, reflecting on the fact that he made a very substantial contribution in style of art, but style of art is easy to emulate. The thinking process is the thing that, is the real measure of an artist's contribution. He made an enormous contribution.

Luciano: One thing I've noticed about your work that I've wanted to ask you about: You are consciously working to simplify your style, aren't you?

Eisner: Yeah. Well, that's very much a part of what I perceive I'm doing. I'm writing a story with words and images. The story is the main thrust, and if the artwork doesn't serve the story, it doesn't tell what the story is trying to tell, then I modify the artwork. Very often, as in the case of bright colors, or in the case of, a better example, in the case of an orchestra that's playing awfully loud so you can't hear the singing. I find myself having to discipline myself, to modify the art, modify the pyrotechnics of the artwork to satisfy the story. For example, I'm working on a scene right now, where a man who's in the process of retiring comes face to face with the fact that his daugh-ter and son-in-law want his inheritance, and the expressions on his face and his movements when he finds out that this daughter really only wants this money from him are really the most important thing. Now, for me to take that scene from a worm's-eye view, or a bird's-eye view, or with some tricky counter-lighting, is not in service to that particular panel or that story at that moment. It would be far better for me to have a flat, straight view, a flat shot, with the concentration totally on the position of his body, the posture of his head, his arms, the cant of his neck, the tilt of his eyebrows, and the feeling that I want him to convey to the reader. That means that I will have to limit my artwork to serve that particular purpose. Perhaps the artwork comes out looking a little bit more simple than it would have appeared if it were just done for the purpose of excitement and action. And this is part of what I find very, very hard to do today. I'm as much an artistic ham as the next artist, and I like to show off my ability of doing figures flying through space, or popping out of panels and so forth, and trying tricky shots, tricky lighting. But, I have to control it. The priorities are with the story as far as my work is concerned, and not with the art itself. I'm also always a little uncomfortable when fans or other artists say, "Gee, I *love* your artwork in this last book." I love to hear it, but deep down inside me is a stifled cry that says, [in a desperate, begging voice] "please, compliment my story, how did you like my story?" The artwork is very important, but this is part, by the way, of the cross, of the burden that a lot of comic-book artists must live with, and they recognize that their recognition, their acceptance comes from their artwork, and very often they naturally have to pander to it, they naturally respond to it. They're also working in a medium where the publishers want the pages to have excitement. The what-sells factor. And the tendency is to jazz up a page with all kinds of odd-shaped panels and all sorts of experimental compositions in an effort to attract the reader. And after you've gotten the reader to look at the page, there is nothing to say, and then the reader just goes on from picture to picture, and once you've provided the reader, as I said earlier, is essentially a *visual trip*, a sensory experience. It always surprises me to see people paying a dollar and a half to two dollars for a book that looks very good, and taking a risk that after they buy it that the story won't be worth the money they pay.

Luciano: [Laughs]. Yeah, comics are getting awfully expensive.
Eisner: And, I don't know whether they're enriching the lives of the people who buy them in any way, or adding to their own experience. I don't know what contribution they make other than providing a momentary trip, or in some cases, pure titillation.

Luciano: Are you concerned that, unlike the past, there may not have been a new generation of comic-book readers among young children? There doesn't seem to be. I know Marvel has just come out with their line of Star Comics, which I haven't really looked at, but . . .
Eisner: Well, I've heard that voiced, the concern that, "Look, we're not creating any new comic-book readers." Well, I'm not too worried about that. I am convinced that comics or the sequential art form, on paper, the graphic form, will not disappear, television and video tapes to the contrary, notwithstanding. A comic-book, a written, a basic piece of reading, a graphic novel can be carried from place to place. And you can read it again and again at your own leisure, you don't need any machinery to show it to you, or a television set which you can view it with, and secondly you can read as slowly as you wish, you can go back and savor it, you can look at it again and again, you can put it

on the shelf and take it off and study it. There's a kind of *privacy*, too, in looking at pictures that motion pictures doesn't have.

Luciano: You know, that's interesting. That's one thing that nobody has ever written about in the *Journal* or any other thing I've ever ever read, but it's not a passive experience.
Eisner: That's right.

Luciano: The artist is giving you something, but you must bring something to it.
Eisner: Absolutely, absolutely. If I show two panels, with one fellow in one panel raising a wooden mallet, and in the next panel walking away with a man lying on the ground, that reader has to supply what happens in between. Where does he supply that from? Where does he get that information? Well, he gets it from his own life experience, he knows that raising a mallet over a guy's head, and walking away with the man lying down, there had to be something that went on in between, and what went on in between was the mallet striking the man's head and knocking him down. So the reader is supplying something. He's also supplying sound and motion, which comics do not have. Comics are bereft of dimensions, they're bereft of sound, they're bereft of motion and they're bereft of smell, for that matter.

Luciano: That's one thing that I think is unique about your work, that you have used the medium in ways that are unique to the medium. Which I think is one of the critical elements of judging great art in a particular medium that cannot be accomplished in any other medium. Mainstream super-hero comics are sometimes a little pallid in comparison with what they're doing in films now, but I see things in your work that could not really be done in any other medium is precisely the way that you do them.
Eisner: Well, I'm delighted to hear it, and I probably couldn't agree with you more.

Luciano: [Laughter]
Eisner: I'll accept your judgment without any protest.

Luciano: [Laughter]
Eisner: No, I believe it's part of my nature to constantly experiment, and to push the dimensions of the medium onwards. And this comes out of my dissatisfaction with my work of yesterday, and my desire to go the distance with

the medium, so to speak. The goals are still really, open to the horizon. I think that almost any writer or artist worth his salt, is constantly at war with the restrictions of his medium, he constantly feels imprisoned by that medium. I know I do. I constantly feel imprisoned by that page. I'm consciously moving to strike out. There are people whose temperament flies in face of that imprisonment, resulting in some strikingly marvelous things. Jack Kirby comes to mind as the man who has an intense force and drive, he always had when I knew him, when he was working in my shop as a youngster, and who's constantly pushing to make his characters jump off the page. Which resulted in his ability to take standard anatomy, distort it sufficiently to retain the reality of the anatomical construction, but at the same time force a certain amount of power and movement into the work, that lifted the work right off the page and created a kind of excitement. This has to come, as I said before, from a man who is dissatisfied with the restrictions that are imposed by the medium itself, or the limitations, if you will. So, out of that imprisonment, a lot of people develop new and unusual things. By the way, I think we should move on from talking about my work to the field itself, which was the main thrust of your first question, which is, "What's happening in the field, where it's going."

Luciano: Well, we know there's a crisis. You said there always is a crisis.

Eisner: As I said earlier, I view the comics field as very much like looking up into a cloudy sky, where the clouds are constantly changing. Nothing remains fixed. The audience's continually dissatisfied, new tastes arise, and new people arise to satisfy those tastes, new technology. One of the things that should be factored into any discussion like this is the impact of technology. In 1941, and in 1939–1940, comic books were unique because they were colored, but they were crudely produced, they were produced with zipatone separations on metal plates that were fabricated out of mattes. Today, you've got marvelous off-set presswork on wonderfully good paper, with colors produced by scanning process, so that an artist today can do a full-color painting. Look at the Spanish work. Look at the work of Fernando Fernández in Spain who turns out beautiful watercolor paintings of a quality that equals anything ever produced for the best book illustrations published in this country, or any country. The man's a consummate artist, a great illustrator, a great painter, he works in watercolors that are just absolutely beautiful. His work is reproduced in the scanning method, he's getting full reproduction. This is comics. Sure, there's a balloon over the character's head, but this is comics like we've never seen, it's a dimension that artists didn't have earlier. This has an effect, also, on the skills of the artists, it makes a demand on the artist, working in this field, greater skill in their painting, in their drawing, and provides the reader with a standard that the next artist coming along has to live up to. Which is really one of the major effects of the European influence on the whole comics field. There were two major influences on the comics field, in my experience. One was the Spanish artists, or what I call the "Spanish Invasion," because they, in the late '60s, literally invaded this country with fantastically good artwork, far better in classic draftsmanship than anything that the other comic book houses were buying here. Warren was quick to recognize this, picked these people up very quickly. And, I might say, at prices less than he was paying the Americans. Which I think might very well have been part of the stimulation. But they created a standard, the standard for realistic drawing rose 150 to 200 percent. Then, along came the French, who raised the *intellectual* level of comic art by producing things like *Pilote*, there was a fellow named Gérard Lauzier who produced political material, Claire Bretécher, a brilliant woman cartoonist, Moebius who changed the standards of the field, who produced a kind of intellectualism in science-fiction, had an impact on our motion picture industry here. Philippe Druillet with his fantastic art. There's a whole bunch of great intellectual fermentation going on in France that spilled over here. That created new standards. So those two countries had a tremendous impact on the overall field. And I think what happened that caused the division in this country between the pedestrian comic-book, the one that deals with mutants, and hybrid human beings who walk around doing impossible things, and those of us, like Art Spiegelman and a few others who are stretching out and trying to reach the audience that the French had ready-made for them. The audience there were adults who worked in banks, college students, college professors, ordinary businessmen, average middle-class *bourgeoisie*, who had no embarrassment at picking up a comic book and reading it in the subway as they went home.

Luciano: There's another question that I'd like to ask. I used to be more involved with film. And I know a similar process took place with the French film critics, mostly operating out of a journal called *Cahiers du Cinéma*. François Truffaut, for example, was a critic for them originally, and the general thought is that the French critics were the ones who taught the American audience to appreciate their own films. What do you think the future function of criticism can be?

Eisner: Well, I'm glad you asked me that, because that's a point that deserves to be explored. I feel that the real hope of the future of comics in this country lies in the hands of two people: the artists themselves, essentially, and the critics. The people who are now producing very thoughtful, intelligent, well-informed and very literate, I mean *literate* in the truest sense, critical pieces in *The Comics Journal* and in *The Comics Buyer's Guide* and other journals that are coming out now. For the first time in the last five to eight years, I'm seeing critical considerations of comic books that are produced by people who are really intelligent and who by taking the comic medium to task are creating standards for it. These are the people who create the standard. These are the people who establish the values. And whether you agree or not, the fact that the critic takes a piece of work and applies to it a measuring stick that is equivalent to the kind of measuring stick that he would apply to any other serious piece of work is in itself a contribution. The other person involved in forwarding this artform is the artist himself, who seeks to live up to and meet the standards that are being talked about, I'm talking about the literary standards. The publisher is a servant to the artist and the marketplace. The publisher is there with the prime purpose of providing the marketplace with material as he perceives the need of the market or the size of the market. He's there to fulfill a need. That's the only formula for success for publishers. Very few publishers around today, like the late Alfred Knopf, who would nurture an artist, bring him along, guide him, carry him when he's just starting out, struggling through the years. There aren't many such publishers. Among the underground publishers, the Denis Kitchens and the Dean Mullaneys and, well, even Gary Groth and the Fantagraphics line, who are trying to do that now, but they can't because they're small, and in a market place like this, if they do too much of that, they're not going to survive. But, as far as forwarding the artform itself, and having an effect on the future, the future lies in my opinion in the hands of the critics, who are writing seriously about this work, and the artists themselves. As for the audience . . . my advice to my peers is, don't believe your fan mail, because it can destroy you.

Luciano: [laughs].
Eisner: All you have to get is a letter saying, "Gee, you know, that shot looking up through a keyhole was absolutely terrific!" For the next six months, you're doing shots through keyholes. Just to hear a little bit more of the *applause*. After all, that's what it's all about!

Mastering the Form: An Interview with Will Eisner

BEN SCHWARTZ / 1988

From *Daily Bruin*, University of California, Los Angeles, January 19, 1988, pp. 18, 20, and 23. Reprinted by permission of the *Daily Bruin*, UCLA.

Although we rarely take it seriously, cartooning is an integral part of our culture. We see it every day in newspapers, TV, short and feature films, comic books, and even instruction booklets from Sony Walkman radios to sophisticated military equipment. In our society, cartooning is unquestionably a vital means of communication. When done right, it combines the precision of language with the broad emotional impact of well-crafted images.

As will be shown in this series of interviews, cartooning is a complex blend of technical mastery and aesthetic principle. Yet how often do we think of the men and women who create these images? What are their beliefs, politics, and attitudes? And is the cartoon, from comic-books to Bugs Bunny shorts, a viable place in which to express these views?

With this series of interviews, with comic-book artists Jack Kirby and Will Eisner, daily newspaper strip cartoonist Milton Caniff, and animation director Chuck Jones, these become important questions. Each of these men has devoted his life to telling stories through cartooning. Each has used their medium to reflect what they know and feel—and in the process, elevated their medium with higher standards of excellence.

There is perhaps no better place to start this series than with cartoonist Will Eisner. Born in 1917, Eisner has been writing and drawing comic books since the late '30s. By the age of twenty, Eisner displayed a wonderfully innovative and mature graphic style in such comics as *Hawks of the Seas*, *Wow! What a Magazine!*, and *Jumbo*. In 1940, Eisner began an ambitious project which many critics consider his masterwork, *The Spirit*—a weekly comic magazine distributed as a comics supplement in Sunday newspapers.

The Spirit concerned the adventures of Denny Colt, a man thought killed by gangsters who returns to fight crime as the masked Spirit. Yet, from the beginning, Eisner expanded his stories beyond the simple boundaries of superhero comics. Hence, instead of just a masked crimefighter, Eisner's Spirit became a prism for the artist to explore his feelings and reflections on life. In story after story, Eisner used the genre of cartooning and the figure of the Spirit to explore human nature—its ironies, injustices, and at times, its humorous side.

An example of Eisner's thematic concerns can be found in the odd story of Gerhard Shnobble. Instead of being about the Spirit, who only plays a minor part here, the story revolves around Shnobble and his special talent; he can fly. The irony of this situation, however, is that no one has ever seen him fly. And just at that moment when he wants to share his gift with the world—to gain recognition for a thankless life—Schnobble is killed.

In *The Spirit* #35, Kitchen Sink Press's monthly reprinting of Spirit stories, Eisner said, "There is something that has always angered me about life. Sometimes, when a friend of mine dies, I take an assay of his life. Very often I think, here this guy did many good things and no one will ever know. Many of us go through life doing great, even heroic things, and no one is going to know about it."

It was during this period that Eisner discovered a very important quality about himself and the way he liked to tell stories. At the time, the most popular comics in the papers were the daily strips such as *Little Orphan Annie*, *Terry & the Pirates*, and *Dick Tracy*. The daily strips told on-going stories that might last for months, told in one daily segment at a time. But Eisner was more interested in exploring the comic-book form, that is, telling one complete story, from beginning to end, in one sitting.

Says Eisner, "I could never work successfully in a daily strip. A daily strip is too confining to me. I've described it this way so often it has now become a cliché, but I find it's like trying to conduct an orchestra in a telephone booth. I have an almost neurotic need to do something different each time, to have a conclusion to what I did yesterday and start something new. The excitement for me, the fun for me is to solve a problem. For example, to come up with a subject and try to present it interestingly. But I need to tell the whole story in one fell swoop."

For Eisner, cartooning became a form of visual literature. In his textbook on the subject, *Comics & Sequential Art*, Eisner diagrams how the arranged panels of a cartoon sequence relate to a written sequence. For Eisner, the images used to relate the sequence of action are chosen the way a writer chooses to structure a sentence, taking into account how the images, their placement, and their sequential order will affect the reader. Says Eisner, "The effect is the result of my effort to control the reader's attention and the reader's emotion, and try to relate to the reader's visual and spatial comprehension."

After Eisner stopped work on *The Spirit* in 1952, he founded American Visuals, a company which created comics for industrial use in manuals, advertising, and safety guides. Although Eisner wouldn't return to "entertainment" or fictional comics until 1974, his Spirit stories continued to fascinate readers and were popularly revived in the early '70s. Eisner, however, wasn't interested in new Spirit stories and began utilizing the form to tell a different kind of story. Instead of city crime, detectives, and masked heroes, Eisner told stories from his past: New York tenement life during the Great Depression.

In 1978, Eisner published *A Contract with God*, a narrative composed of four short stories about Eisner's past. Unlike his *Spirit* stories, these stories dealt directly with issues of mortality, sex, injustice, and the human spirit. "In these stories particularly," says Eisner, I was writing about things I feel strongly about, personal statements. I think most of us have something to say. We make philosophical statements based on our experiences and our perception of it. We are the result of things that have happened to us.

"I'm also involved," adds Eisner, "more than just pure philosophizing, with exploring the potential of this medium. Remember, with *A Contract with God*, I attempted for the first time to utilize this medium to deal with a serious theme, as in *Signal from Space*. I did a whole novel in an effort to prove that this medium can produce a work in the standard classical structure of a pure novel."

Eisner followed that work with some of the strongest of his career. One story that particularly stands out is *The Dreamer*, an autobiographical piece in which Eisner recalled his first days in the then infant comic-book industry of the '30s.

Here, Eisner disposed of the usual, tightly framed panel, and played with the whole page as panel. Instead of following from panel to panel, our eye travels from image to image, giving segments of *The Dreamer* the dreamlike quality of memories.

"I've been working at that breakaway (from structured panels) for some time," says Eisner. "I have always known that there is a psychological comprehension of a shape of a panel, and that the page itself is a mega-panel. I am constantly experimenting with the arrangement of panels on the page. Not in the sense of trying to create a "dynamic," as they say in comic books, or an exciting page to shock or excite (the reader). My panels develop as a result of my effort to tell the story. I'm trying to deal in a rhythm. I work in a rhythm. While I'm working, it's almost as if a metronome is ticking away in my head.

"For example, I use space as a time frame. Frequently, I will abandon the outline of a panel at the very end or beginning of a story, and try to create infinite space, letting the reader supply the surrounding background. The panels are generally begotten by me as a result of the nature of that story on that particular page, and the rate of speed and rhythm under which I want it read."

For Eisner, comics are a form of visual reading. In fact, "comics" may no longer even be an accurate word for the medium. As Eisner says, "The word 'comics' is a misnomer. Comics are neither comical nor are they funny anymore. They used to be called the funnies and so forth, but comics as a reading medium has transcended the light entertainment mold that it was designed for. What we're seeing now has been evolving over the past forty years. I think it's a result of the fact that comics in comic-books are complete short stories. They have really taken on a literary task, in a sense. The nature of the subject material requires a more serious approach to the fashioning of the work itself.

"What has happened as this thing has grown, is that the field is attracting people who are devoting themselves to literary merit and serious content. They are more in touch with the potential of the medium. When you get guys like Art Spiegleman (*Maus*, *Raw* magazine), and others who are willing to make a personal statement, then you begin to see material that has literary stature.

"I have always said that this medium is capable of being literature. Not that it is or always was, but that it's capable of it."

Although Eisner has always been an experimenter and innovator, one ideal he has never lost sight of is using the medium for storytelling. Eisner is most concerned with the story, and most of all, the content of that story. As he says, "There are a number of artistic athletes in the field who are incredibly capable of rendering brilliant artwork, but have no story intent or sense. They are unwilling to subjugate their artwork to the story.

"It's a sad thing to say of the field today, but it appears that a great deal of brilliant art is devoted to a vacuous theme. My objection to that is when style and technique becomes the obsession of the artist, when form subordinates substance, that bothers me. I feel concerned about it because the acceptance of this medium depends on the growth of the content. And anything that interferes with the emergence of good content is detrimental to the growth of the medium.

"That's why I'm still awaiting that great discriminating adult audience who will accept the medium as valid literary fare. I can feel it coming, so I'm investing a very precious, totally unreplaceable commodity into this field, time. And I'm beginning to feel that my investment isn't wasted."

A Cartoonist's Cartoonist

ELINOR BURKETT / 1989

From *The Miami Herald*, September 6, 1989, pp. 1D, 3D. Reprinted by permission of the *Miami Herald*. Copyright © The Miami Herald 1989.

If you sneak around back, you can peek into the inner sanctum and catch a glimpse of the legend himself: one of the comic-book medium's founding fathers, creator of *The Spirit*, the first comic book inserted into a Sunday newspaper.

He's the balding one in the polyester pants, the old guy hunched over the desk, scribbling away on the adult comic books he has been penning in the '80s.

He's alone.

The beautiful Miss Cosmek, agent from Planet Mars—who defected to Earth, where laughter, love, and tears are not a crime—is locked away.

Poor Gerhard Shnobble has been laid to rest by a world so distracted by the BIG EVENTS that it never noticed the quiet little man—an ordinary-looking bank guard—who could actually fly.

The Spirit lurks about somewhere, but fifty years after his birth the super-hero is retired from the never-ending battle against evil.

It's hard to imagine how Will Eisner ever hung out with such a crowd. At seventy-two, he looks too much home at Tamarac's Woodmont Country Club, where the company is bland by comparison. He seems entirely too normal to have spent a half century creating superheroes and penning *KA-BOOM!!!* across the pages of cartoons geared to the fantasies of what he calls "ten-year-old cretins from Kansas City."

But the self-effacing guy who slams tennis balls across the net at his wife, Ann, every morning has not only spent a lifetime shaping comic books. To many, he *is* comic books: one of the medium's founding fathers, the guru of the younger generation and the center of an international cult of fans who have remained loyal to his fantasies for two generations. A man who Jules Feiffer, who apprenticed with Eisner for four years, says "had a staggering influence on everybody's work—and still does."

"It's a little embarrassing," Eisner responds, not at all embarrassed, "but someone once said that Will Eisner might not have given birth to comic books, but he was certainly there at the christening."

Honest day's work?

Comic books? What kind of work is that for a grown man? The question has haunted Eisner since he doodled his first cartoon strip as a seventeen-year-old in the Bronx.

First it was his mother, a Jewish refugee from Central Europe.

"'My son, an artist?'" Eisner remembers her moaning.

"'Cartoons? You'll never make any money. It's not a pursuit for a grown man.'"

His mother's lament has pursued Eisner for almost six decades. "Once I went to a teachers' convention to try to convince educators of the value of using comics," he recalls, "I felt like a drug pusher in a schoolyard."

Eisner has never begged for indulgence—from his mother or anyone else who considers comic books the slum of the art world, the back alley of literature.

Not a grown-up profession? Not real art?

P-F-FOOF—H-H-HOOEY!!!

"Comic books were regarded as deleterious reading material because the content was junk. But the medium is capable of being more than funny pictures and entertainment."

Churning out strips

Eisner might have believed it, but for much of his career he had little chance to pen any proof. He was too busy churning out strips about jungle queens and swashbuckling pirates.

By 1940, he was consumed with *The Spirit*, the nation's first comic-book insert in a Sunday newspaper, the adventures of the masked protector of Truth, Justice and Five Million Weekly Readers.

The Spirit was not the first comic superhero. That distinction still belongs to Superman, two years his senior. But he certainly was the least likely: none of the godlike qualities of Superman, none of the panache of Batman. Permanently disheveled, The Spirit was forced to rely on an exceptionally hard head (how could one man get bonked on the noggin so often and not end up with a permanent concussion?) and moral philosophy that liberally quoted both Montaigne and Gilbert and Sullivan.

His creator wouldn't even let the fictionalized vigilante take himself seriously. The Spirit found himself fighting a 1,000-year-old man who looked like Moses walking off the pages of an illustrated Old Testament while battling crooked lawyers with names like "Loophole" and politically connected crooks with names like "Ward Healy."

The Spirit was permanently bemused, a living self-caricature. He had to be: Eisner doesn't even *like* superheroes.

"You can't invest them with subtle characteristics. They take themselves too seriously. You can't put *Mr. Deeds Goes to Town* in a Batman suit."

The "perfect medium"

"This is a perfect medium for adolescent boys trying to work out their manhood. Can you imagine what you would do if you actually met a superhero? If the guy in the chair next to you turned and said, 'I'm going to wipe out evil in the quest for justice?'

"You'd call 911 and have him locked up."

That's precisely what Eisner did with The Spirit. After twelve years of superstardom, Eisner locked his alter ego away in a filing cabinet, shut down his cartoon shop, and turned to more adult pursuits, like making money.

For two decades, he penned comic books as training manuals for General Motors and U.S. Steel, using cartoons, balloons, and too many *!!!*s to teach mechanics to install gaskets in engines.

"Teach with the Speed of Sight," was the company's motto.

By 1974 he had enough money to buy himself the freedom to experiment with his dream that comic books can be more than funny pictures.

The characters emerging from his pen now are the familiar faces of his Bronx youth, the same faces Isaac Bashevis Singer and Chaim Potok have described to us but never shown us. The backdrops are the lampposts and stoops and grates of New York, the city he still loves, even after five years in South Florida. ("A sleep-away camp for adults" is how he describes his West Broward life, which revolves around his work, tennis at the country club and the house he and Ann share in Tamarac.)

Quirky humor

The stories are *Yiddishdik* yarns with the same iconoclastic, quirky sense of humor he could never quite unfetter in *The Spirit*.

Eisner traded in the damsels in distress and the ferocious fiends for the heroes he has always preferred—"the ordinary people whose heroic deeds we never even hear about."

Like Jacob Shtarkah, of *A Life Force*, struggling to find a reason for living, an answer to the fundamental, existential question: "How is a man different from a cockroach?"

Or the nameless character in *New York* who rants and rails before the towering structures of an unhearing city:

BE NOT AFRAID OF THE POWER OF LOVE.

Eisner, the comic-book artist, has emerged as Eisner the poet-philosopher, painting dreams in cartoons and penning his truths in floating bubbles. Where the one-dimensional Spirit existed at a page a day—eight pages a week by contract—the serious writer now struggles like all good writers, laboring more slowly on his creations.

The ideas Eisner conveys are the angst and joy of the adult audience he is finally reaching. "I can no longer address my stories to kids who like Teen-age Ninja Turtles," he said.

Love of old ways

Those kids—many of them fans of The Spirit—bristle at the newest creations of their old hero. They prefer the melodrama of The Black Queen to the despair of the rabbi who tries to make a contract with God for a life without pain. They find more excitement in the crime fighters of Central City than in the tale of the widowed retiree exiled to South Florida by his daughters.

The kids accuse Eisner of being sappy and—God forbid!!—sentimental. "Now I'm dealing with grief, tragedy, even deep romantic feelings that they can't understand yet," he said. "I want to make my readers cry."

Ironically, kids from an earlier era made Eisner an international cult figure. When the flower children of the 1960s turned to comic books as their own medium of expression, Eisner was rediscovered. *The Spirit* rose like a Phoenix, reprinted in dozens of editions for a new generation of fans.

As comic books edge toward respectability, Eisner—the guy who respects Picasso as a serious cartoonist—is being feted in France, Spain, and Italy. A Will Eisner Archives has been established at Ohio State University, which is becoming a national archive for comic books. And in January, an exhibition of his work will be presented at the Royal Academy of Art in Copenhagen.

Re-creating himself

"What's encouraging to me is that when the cultism began, rather than bask in it and endlessly reprint his old stuff," says Jules Feiffer, who included Eisner in his book, *The Great Comic Book Heroes*, "he re-created himself as a cartoonist again."

Eisner is pleased by the attention, the fan mail, the awards, but is still bemused, vaguely reminiscent of The Spirit himself when Miss Dale, girl reporter, smacked a kiss on the superhero's lips after he saved her from the evil Fifth Column.

"I still think of when I was finally invited to join the National Cartoonists Society. I felt like I was the pope in Nirvana sitting there among the greats. Al Capp sat next to me and said, 'I caught your stuff, kid.'

"'Pretty good. But you won't make it in this business. You're too damned normal.'"

Getting the Last Laugh: My Life in Comics

WILL EISNER / 1990

From *New York Times Book Review*, January 14, 1990, pp. 1, 26–27. Copyright © 2011 by Will Eisner Studios, Inc. Reprinted by permission.

It was 1937. The newspaper comic strip was in its heyday. The strips were so popular that some inventive businessmen were starting to repackage them as whole books. The comics field, even in the bleak '30s, seemed to have a bright future. A cartoonist who could draw funny pages had reason to hope, anyway.

I was just such a cartoonist, nineteen years old and out of work. An equally desperate friend, Jerry Iger, and I decided to move into a small office on East 41st Street in New York and start a comics production company, Eisner & Iger (my fifteen-dollar initial investment entitled me to top billing). Like brokers who forecast a sudden demand for pork bellies, we believed that pulp publishers, who were repackaging newspaper comic strips into magazine-size formats, were going to run out of them at any minute. They were going to need original material—whole magazines, written and drawn from scratch. And we, the firm of Eisner & Iger, were there to supply them. There was a little competition from a handful of others, but for all practical purposes we were on our own, working on the rawest sort of frontier, a place with few rules or standards.

Iger, the business partner, kept telling publishers we had this impressive staff capable of cranking out complete books of remarkable quality. But actually the entire staff was just Eisner. I was drawing five different strips in five different styles under five different names, among them Spencer Steele (I always thought anybody named Spencer Steele had to be successful) and W. Morgan Thomas (it sounded so literary). Energetic and hungry, I worked day and night under the lone drawing-board light.

My first effort was *Jumbo Comics* (1938), a collection of stories including a Rafael Sabatini–inspired buccaneer tale, "Hawks of the Seas." In those days, I didn't have much time to think, and little or no social life, but still—and I mean this—I felt something significant was happening. I felt, almost from the beginning, that I was participating in literature, not just exploiting it.

But I was a loner, as cartoonist often are, so, for the most part, I kept my thoughts to myself. That's just as well; it would have sounded pretentious. In the '30s and into the '40s, I was a comic-book cartoonist and nothing more, laboring in what would soon become a kind of artistic ghetto in which people with authentic, if offbeat, talents had to suffer the disdain of the mainstream.

Everything has changed now; comic books are the arena for some of the most inventive expressions of literature. Jules Feiffer's 183-page graphic novel, *Tantrum* (1979), which explores the psychology of a forty-two-year-old man's reversion to a child's state, is perhaps the most remarkable of all the efforts in modern years. Today, graphic novels are included on the list of such major publishing houses as Pantheon, Doubleday, and St. Martin's, and are stocked in establishment bookstores like Waldenbooks, B. Dalton, and Doubleday. It is the promised land for a reading medium with humble origins. After years of denigration by teachers, comics are gaining acceptance in schools, proving themselves as reading tools.

It has been fifty years, and it hasn't been easy; comics have basked in their "golden age" and suffered through their own dark ages. But I feel that my original sense of the potential of comics is about to be realized and that the medium can finally lay claim to legitimacy.

The people originally drawn to the field were raw young talents, mostly men (as is still the case today) with very little training. But they did not lack ambition. They wanted to be illustrators like N. C. Wyeth, Dean Cornwell and J. C. Leyendecker. Comics, they believed, were just a way station. Nobody expected to spend a lifetime at it. Yet many of them remained for the rest of their lives.

It was a true ghetto, the field of comics, trapping these artist-writers in a world of limited outlook. When a cartoonist left the old neighborhood and went "uptown" to show his work to mainstream publishers, the work baffled prospective editors. It wasn't anything like the style and technique required, say, by the *Saturday Evening Post*. To make things worse, when he showed a comic book to an editor it was hard to explain just what his own contribution to the comics was. The sheer volume needed to feed the appetite for magazine-format comic books resulted in production-line creativity in which one fellow worked on ideas and text, another on artwork and a third on lettering and coloring.

The comic book was nurturing great talents who would shape American mythology. In the late 1930s, Superman and Batman arrived. No one among us thought that these heroes were more than successful entertainment; certainly no one thought they would become national institutions. My own efforts, eventually, were largely directed toward a character called the Spirit, a masked crime fighter, meant to be a satirical combination of Zorro and Philip Marlowe. *The Spirit* appeared in 1939 as a comic-book insert, a complete short story, in Sunday newspapers. For the newspapers the move was a reflection of the threat they sensed from the already flourishing comic-book industry. For me, *The Spirit* was a chance to stretch the medium, to reach out to a more adult audience with a complete work of fiction, a true short story.

For the first time I began to receive mail from people other than ten-year-olds in the Midwest: mother and father were reading *The Spirit*, too. And I was able, at last, to deal with story material that wasn't confined to the superhero formula. The Spirit—an ordinary man, officially dead but actually living under a secret identity—was vulnerable; he could be physically hurt, like any other human, and he didn't have even one super power.

For myself and other publishers, recruiting for what was still a "novelty" medium was a matter of seeking out talent that came from other fields, since ours had no history, no labor pool. So before long, I had working alongside me people like Klaus Nordling, a young Finn who had been writing plays for the Finnish theater. He was also an accomplished cartoonist. Perhaps his best-known creation was Lady Luck, a costumed heroine who chased criminals. Also in the studio were Jack Kirby and Lou Fine—both just out of art school—who dreamt of features in illustration. Mr. Kirby, now widely regarded as the king of the superhero creators, left Eisner & Iger in the late '30s; he went on to create Captain America, the Incredible Hulk, and other characters for the Marvel Comics line. Fine was responsible for the Flame. Bob Kane, a high school chum of mine, worked for the studio for a while, then went to D.C., where he created Batman.

The early years of comic books, from the late 1930s to 1955, are called the "golden years' because of the excitement and invention that characterized the new medium, but certainly not because they enhanced anybody's income level. Most cartoonists and writers were paid a flat rate per page of artwork. Moreover, most artists and writers lost all equity in the works they created once they were published. Many of them spent their professional lives and productive juices engaged in perpetuating someone else's creation, sustaining a property for the owner-publisher. It was a poor climate for creative exploration, development, or growth. Only style and the quality of basic draftsmanship burgeoned.

Harvey Kurtzman stands out as an example of a writer-artist who pressed against the conventional with his masterfully written, well-conceived Korean war stories, and of course satire in the form of *Mad* magazine, which he helped to create. But Mr. Kurtzman had no equity in *Mad* and couldn't get any when he tried. Enormously skilled teams like Joe Simon and Jack Kirby (*Boy Commandos, Captain America*) were paid by the piece, owned nothing, and never were able—or perhaps willing—to break free of the confines of the conventional comic. Awesome creative forces were trapped in that stockade.

There was a lot of room for improvement in those days, particularly in content, but before we could improve our work we had to understand what we were doing in the first place. What were the strengths and weaknesses of comics? We had to master the language of the genre: comics have their own grammar, alphabet, and discipline. To get the most out of the technique we had to learn what worked in a frame and what didn't. Which symbols conveyed meaning most efficiently? How could the physical requirements of the cartoon, the frames and dialogue balloons, be used as forceful visual elements? (The jagged-edged balloon that came along to express shock or horror is an example. Lettering that drips with blood is a more flamboyant instance.) In general, the visual imagery is most communicative when simplified.

Because of their simplicity, comics give the impression that they are designed only for the young or people with limited reading capacities. Form is often confused with content and this misperception underestimates the medium's capacity. It would be foolish to deny that there are inherent problems. Comics are dominated by visual content, and an obsession with that often subordinates the literary values. Comics depend on imagery and stereotype. And comics do have difficulty in dealing with abstractions.

But the medium is versatile. It can address an adult theme. It can instruct and amuse, titillate and influence, all with a mental transmission speed greater than words alone. That is one of its major advantages. Its employment of images distilled from our common experience—body postures, for instance, that instantly convey mood—enables it to communicate well both on a cognitive and sensory level.

When I was first approached to do *The Spirit*, I negotiated the right to retain ownership of the character. I had the publishers over a barrel; they needed me. What I needed, although I never actually articulated it at the time, was creative freedom. I felt it would come with ownership. I did not think of myself as a hired hand. And that point of view helped me to feel better about the medium itself and to develop my idea of what it could be.

While many in the field persisted in thinking of comics as schlock, I thought of the medium as writing so full of possibilities that it could even be used as a teaching tool. By the time I was drafted in 1942 I and other like-minded illustrators persuaded the military to permit us to produce training material in comic-book format.

It worked. We used comics to teach servicemen to replace carburetors, repair electrical and fuel systems in automotive equipment, and maintain weapons. All very mundane, but that was the point: comics had to be seen as an effective means of communication. In test after test they outperformed conventional text and photos.

When I emerged from the service in 1946, I returned to *The Spirit*. The staff now consisted of people like Jules Feiffer, whose talent had an intellectual thrust. His skill with words and his social insights influenced our studio; Mr. Feiffer started as a studio assistant but soon became a writer on *The Spirit*. His writing propelled him into a prominent career as a cartoonist, playwright, and author of books, one of the few to make it "uptown."

In 1951, I folded *The Spirit* to concentrate on the broader uses of the medium that I had tested in the military. I spent the next twenty years publishing and producing comic-format educational material for industry, the military, and schools. But the resistance was enormous. A purveyor of comics at teachers' conventions was made to feel like a drug pusher caught red-handed.

In hindsight, I understand the heart of that objection. Teachers, examining the comic books they frequently found in the hands of their students, were put off by the violent imagery, the simplicity of the dialogue (in capital letters) in the balloons, and the stereotyped, seemingly puerile protagonists. Getting past this surface to evaluate the worth of the medium itself was understandably difficult. In 1974, in an article in the *School Library Journal*, I tried, perhaps too soon, to make a case for the inclusion of comics in libraries. Finally, in the late 1980s, when student resistance to reading and a drop in literacy was felt, schools began to permit comics in the classroom.

The field I left behind, the comic book as pure entertainment, did not remain inert, although it was harmed by an atmosphere of fear that persisted from the 1940s into the '50s. Comic books even came under government attack in the early '50s, and in 1954 publishers obligingly imposed upon themselves a "Comics Code" that narrowed the range of the medium. Dr. Fredric

Wertham's eccentric assault in the book *Seduction of the Innocent* (1954) gave voice to the view that the legion of crime and horror comics then on the newsstands abetted juvenile delinquency. The net effect was to feed the negative image and produce formula comic books.

The great breakthrough that enabled comics to emerge as literature came with the "underground comics" of the politically and socially explosive 1960s. In the hands of young dissenters, the comics challenged our intellectual, social, and moral values. The new cartoonist felt no obligation to conform to codes and thus created outrageous work. The subject matter was brutally blunt. With their raunchy, sometimes primitive style, underground comics addressed readers with such impertinence that one had to go back to Honoré Daumier, Thomas Rowlandson, and Thomas Nast to find a comparison. Writers and artists were defying the establishment with a powerful and accessible literary weapon: comics were employed for political protest, personal statements, social defiance, and sexual expression.

In Europe, meanwhile, comic books changed dramatically. American exports of comics like *Mickey Mouse* and traditional adventures like *The Phantom* had long dominated the international marketplace. By the mid-'60s Italy, Spain, and particularly France became the stiles of a special kind of comicbook ferment. Comics from these countries employed art so stunning it was equal to the best of the great traditional illustrators. In an air of experimentation, they produced everything from westerns to the most imaginative science fiction and erotic fantasy stories. These were, moreover, published in hard-cover format, in color, on good paper, and at a higher price than anything in the United States. Superheroes were of no interest. Adults were buying these books with no embarrassment. The medium was invited into the company of the established arts. In the 1960s, the Louvre held an exhibition of comic-book art; the effect on the self-esteem of the comic-book cartoonists the world over was exhilarating. When visiting Paris I recall sharing with fellow cartoonists a happy astonishment at the genuine acceptance we experienced in artistic circles.

The new generation of cartoonists here and in Europe was quite aware of comics' history. They knew the writer Jerry Siegel and the artist Joe Shuster did not share in the profits of *Superman*, and that most other comic-book creators had no proprietary participation in their own works. The underground cartoonists began with a built-in distrust of the big comic-book publishing companies. Like the Europeans, the underground cartoonists in the United States made certain that they owned outright the work they created. They also rejected out of hand the mainstream literature of comics, with its narrow focus and restrictive codes, and they self-published or founded alternative houses. Most prominent in this American group were Robert Crumb (*Zap Comix*), Art Spiegelman (*Maus*), Manuel (Spain) Rodriguez (*Trashman*), Gilbert Shelton (*Wonder Warthog*), and Denis Kitchen (*Mom's Homemade Comics*).

Something else was afoot. The distribution to the marketplace was changing. Traditionally, comic books were sold on magazine racks; cover signs and content were geared to that market. The content was always in danger of causing a negative community reaction because of the books' positions in the children's racks of a candy store or kiosk. The Comics Code with its concomitant cover seal was designed to assure distributors, retailers, and parents that the books on the racks contained "approved" material.

But the underground comics were first distributed in "head shops," places that sold drug-related paraphernalia, T-shirts, and the like. This system flourished until the early 1970s when legal authorities began cracking down on the sales of paraphernalia. Many of these "head shops" went out of business, although a minority became book and comic-book stores. While these shops were beginning to disappear, another distribution system arose. The "direct market" comic-book shop was the brainchild of Phil Seuling, a New York collector. He devised a plan whereby shops would order as many copies of comic-book titles as they wanted from the various publishing houses on a nonreturnable basis. The system was based on retailers ordering exactly what they wanted, in the quantity they needed. Today, more than 3,000 comic-book stores sell the books of about fifty publishers, big and small. Fed by some ten distributors, this direct-market outlet provides a certain safety for very small and experimental publishers, which in turn encourages the flowering of an avant-garde. In this way, the marketplace is helping the medium to bloom, making it easier for unknowns to get published in comics than in any other established print medium.

Around 1972, when I attended my first comic-book convention at the invitation of Seuling, it amazed me. I met the new breed of comic cartoonists for the first time. Long-haired, wild-eyed, and intense, they spoke the language of comics. It was a language that gave voice to their protest and social ideas. I wanted to be part of the excitement again. At first I simply licensed *The Spirit* to the undergrounds. Then, in 1975, I began work on my first graphic novel.

After about eighteen months of labor I sought a publisher for *A Contract with God*, a graphic novel composed of four interlocking stories set in the tenements of the Bronx during the Depression. It was, in format and style, as great a departure from the comic-book conventions as I could master. It was the story of one man's perception of his relationship with God. The book was rejected by the major publishing houses but was ultimately published in 1978 by a small, now defunct publisher, Baronet Books, which got it into establishment bookstores. It got no reviews, neither was it an instant commercial success. The response from adults who chanced on it, however, was warm and encouraging. I had, at last, connected with a serious adult audience. Ultimately it acquired a word-of-mouth following and remains in print to this day.

The following year Jules Feiffer produced his *Tantrum*, a book of substance and psychological insight, in the comic-book language. More recently, Harvey Pekar's *American Splendor* (autobiographical tales of a working stiff in Cleveland, with art by Robert Crumb and others), and Art Spiegelman's *Maus* (a story of Nazi Germany, with cats as the Nazis and mice as the Jews) have attracted serious attention. These graphic novels have been very influential, and I think it would be fair to credit them with having at last established a literary beachhead.

The future for the comic book as worthwhile reading is so much brighter than it was before. These days, I teach a course in comics at the School of Visual Arts in New York, scanning the faces of the students, hoping that enough of the brightest of them will see the possibilities this medium offers. The walls of the comics ghetto have been breached. The comic book is free. Now, the content, rather than the form, has to be the focus. Comics must grow and deal with subjects of value and importance. New, mature artists and writers must see their promise as a genre and become part of the field.

Will Eisner: The Old Man on the Mountain

STANLEY WIATER AND STEPHEN R. BISSETTE / 1993

From Stanley Wiater and Stephen R. Bissette, *Comic Book Rebels: Conservations with the Creators of the New Comics* (New York: Donald I. Fine, 1993), 268–81. Reprinted by permission of Stanley Wiater and Stephen R. Bissette.

Comic Book Rebels: What did you think was possible in the comics medium when you started in the industry, back in 1936?

Will Eisner: I have to give it to you from a personal perspective. I saw comics as a medium wherein I could realize my literary and art ambitions. Most people who came upon comics in 1936 simply saw it as an amorphic entertainment medium. Comics were divided into a few categories; there were daily strips, there were comic pages, and there were single panels. But comic "books" as we call them today were then the result of assembling six weeks of daily strips into magazines that sold for ten cents. Hardly promising as literature.

The thing that struck me, however, was that comics was the answer to what I was personally looking for: a medium which combined the elements which accommodated the talents I believed I had. I mean, I could draw. Also I wanted to be a writer. So I recognized very early that this form employed both elements, so it was possible to do things beyond slapstick in this form and devote a lifetime to it. Most of the other artists working alongside me in the field at the time regarded comics as merely a stepping stone on the way to the real, serious world of being an illustrator. The hope of landing a daily newspaper strip was remote.

So, no one saw comics as a lifelong pursuit. But I saw it as a great opportunity.

CBR: So you then decided to become one of the first packagers of turning comic stores into literal comic books by establishing your own cartoonists' studio?

Eisner: Yes, that was related to seeing the future of the field. In 1936, *Wow* magazine bought my first few pieces. It died after the fourth issue. But by then I recognized that there was a new market. The pulps were dying; the publishers were looking for a new market to replace them, it was easy to see that. It was also easy to see that the source material of comic magazines would soon dry up because they were using only daily newspaper strip material, like *Dick Tracy* and other adventure strips. Pretty soon those had to give out. Besides, there was a finite number of viable strips—clearly, new original material would have to be produced.

I had to argue with my partner Jerry Iger—who joined me when *Wow* collapsed—when I proposed the idea that we would manufacture the content material for these new comic magazines. He said, "I don't see much of a future here." And I argued, "There is a *tremendous* future here because there is no existing source of original material. There are also no complete stories in terms of material." The daily strips had merely continuing stories. So I told him I felt this was a great opportunity.

This may sound like great genius, but it was purely a reaction to being caught in a maze, and saying, "Hey, this is the only way out!" It was pretty obvious to me at the time. Well, Iger agreed after a little while that this *would* be a way to make money. Jerry was important to me because he could sell— he was eighteen years older than me, and "mature." [*Laughs*] I was still only nineteen or twenty years old, and still hesitant about selling. The product needed selling. Events eventually proved my point: complete, original stories came to be the backbone of the industry.

And, indeed, the unique thing about the early comic magazines or "comic books" was the fact that they presented *complete* stories. In fact, in the advertisements on the covers, we would always append the words "Complete Story!" That was a compelling idea for comics at that time. It was a concept that carried pulp magazines for many years.

CBR: So you took the theory that fans of short stories in prose would be fans of short stories in the comics medium?

Eisner: Not quite. There was no precedent. We really did not aim at the basic pulp readers—we just used the idea. There were no schools of comics. There was no theoretical comprehension. Sure, as a writer I borrowed from pulps— I was using my experience in the short story form. It was my early literary nutrition. I was also influenced by the work of O. Henry and Ring Lardner, and Saki, among others. The Thirties, you must understand, was the halcyon days for the short story. It dominated American popular literature at the time. I based story concepts on them.

In fact, one of our big customers at Eisner & Iger was Fiction House, which was a pulp publishing company who were experiencing a downdraft in their sales and were looking for something else to invest in. We suggested they take on comic books, and they did! They distributed the comics the same way as they did their pulps. Part of my selling argument to them was that we were going to take a genre of literature which they knew and understood so well—namely the short story pulp—and simply transfer it to comics. It was a convincing argument.

CBR: You were one of the first—if not the very first—creators to retain ownership over your own comic book character. How did that come about?

Eisner: At that time it was standard practice for the publisher to own all the characters they published.

They felt, as their property, they could properly invest, develop, and exploit it. Besides, to the publisher, artists were really interchangeable—and expendable. They bought the rights to these characters very easily. The rights to *Superman*, for example, were bought by a simple rubber stamp on the back of the paycheck that said, "For all rights and titles . . . " The creator would sign his check every week and ultimately had no claim to anything. But that was an accepted trade practice in the field.

My unique station in owning *The Spirit* came about because I was in the catbird seat, if you will. I was approached by a syndicate a create a comic book supplement to newspapers. This was to enhance the newspapers' competitive position. They needed to compete with what they felt was a tremendously growing magazine force—the comic book—for the younger readers. So I was in a very strong position to retain the ownership of my character. They didn't give it up easily! The way we compromised it was that I permitted them to copyright the strip in the distributor's name because the argument was that daily newspapers would not buy strips that were copyrighted in the artist's name.

It was assumed the artist could get drunk, sick, die—whatever. There would be no guarantee of control or continuity. Whereas if the distributer owned the strip, then the newspaper would be assured of that continuity.

So in order to retain actual ownership, I had a reversion clause placed in my contract that in effect recognized my ownership of *The Spirit*. In effect it was a loan until there was a split-up between us; then the strip would return to me.

The first few issues were copyrighted with the name Everett Arnold, but in effect I was the first comic book creator to own his strip. It was widely rumored that I threatened to set fire to the syndicate if I didn't retain ownership, but it didn't really work that way. [*Laughs*] It was just a good business deal.

CBR: Do you agree this has been the greatest injustice against creators—that it's always been assumed in this particular industry that it's the publisher who should own all rights to a character or comic book title?

Eisner: Injustice or ripoff is not a fair description. There are two sides to it. A publisher—just as the artist—works within the framework of what the market will bear. The publisher essentially felt he needed to have ownership because what he was doing was investing his money in a property, and he was not about to waive proprietorship. The publisher saw it in the long term and was prepared to promote, develop, and sustain the property. The creating artist neither had the resources nor staying power. As a matter of fact—and this *is* a fact—there isn't a major superhero that has survived through today that is still being done by its originator.

Superman and *Batman* for example are the result of *years* of exploitation and creative refinement by many, many brilliant artists and writers. Thousands and thousands of dollars in investing in promotion and exploiting of ancillary product. Which the publisher claims he might *not* have done if he didn't own the property—or if his lease on that property was at the whim of some artist. On the other hand, the artist could not do it all himself. The real unfairness lay in the fact that creators did not share in the form of a royalty. It took many years for that to happen.

CBR: However, you stated the publishers believed writers and artists were interchangeable and expendable. That attitude must have had some effect on the creative community toiling on the publishers' "plantations."

Eisner: Yes, there was a "slavery" syndrome in the fact that the artists were treated by the publishers as replaceable commodities. Saying, "If I own *Superhero*, I can hire anybody I want to do *Superhero*. I can easily find an artist somewhere to imitate the previous artist." Every artist knows that it isn't too hard to find an imitator of his or her style. For years, there was a big joke running around the comics community that if Milton Caniff died, four artists would go out of business; they were all imitating his style.

So, comic artists worked within a then commonly accepted attitude which the publishers had forced upon them by the sheer strength of their position. They could say, "You can be toughminded as you want, but we can replace you." As I recited earlier, the reason my negotiating position was so strong with the syndicate was that I was established, and in the position of owning a fine company, with a good income, and I didn't necessarily need what they were offering me.

Oh, yes, I needed what they were offering me in terms of a new arena, *that* I wanted badly. But I knew that unless I had the creative control—which came with owning the property—I couldn't achieve that new audience for *myself*. My strength with them lay in the fact that I was a proven producer and they could not take the risk of going with an unknown quantity. Not in the newspaper field.

CBR: What motivated you in "pushing the envelope" with the then radical approach you brought to *The Spirit*, right from the very start?

Eisner: From the outset I began to experiment. As far as I was concerned, I was taking on *The Spirit* because it would provide me with the opportunity to employ the medium as I felt it *could* be—innovatively! By 1940, '41, I believed earnestly that this medium was a true literary/art form, and that I was going to spend the rest of my life doing it. I *knew it*. As a matter of fact, somebody recently unearthed an old 1940 interview in the Baltimore *Sun* in which I said just that. I remember being embarrassed afterwards, because when I got back to New York, a number of the cartoonists accused me of being "uppity!" [*Laughs*]

But as I said, a "slave mentality" does inhibit creativity and innovation. If you tell a slave, "Look, this is as far as you can go," a slave begins to accept this. He just says, "Yes, master," and does not make waves. The people who are constant experimenters by nature are the ones who resist creative enslavement, no matter what the cost.

I am one of these.

Even when I undertook *The Spirit*, I couldn't abide the rules and standards the syndicate wanted. Most were very simple but confining things; like they wanted me to draw the exact same logo every week! They'd plead, "We're just asking for a very simple request. We're not trying to interfere with your creative freedom—just please give us the same logo every week like they do for *Superman* so we can advertise *The Spirit* on our trucks! Is that too much to ask?" [*Laughs*] It *was* too much to ask! The logo was part of the story, you see! Integral to the ambience of the whole strip.

CBR: Was that your way of insuring your creativity wasn't running the risk of being "enslaved" by the practices of the industry at that time?

Eisner: Yes and no. I wasn't doing it because I felt enslaved. I did it because I felt *free*. I felt that here was my chance to exploit my career dream: I wanted to establish this medium as a literary/art form. That meant pushing on the perimeters (and parameters) of the medium as much as I could. What drove me then—and still drives me today—is the desire to always climb over the hill because I could see something new that could be done on the other side.

I'm an experimenter. Well, that's what *The Spirit* gave me: total freedom to experiment. It was far more free than working in any other comic book house—even my own publishing house! In newspapers I had found a place where *I* could be the master of my product rather than the newsstand marketplace! Because the newspapers at that time really had no accurate way of measuring the success or failure of a comic strip character. Not like a comic book publisher, who makes creative judgments by simply adding up the number of copies sold. So for me, it was total freedom. Not to run wild, but to try anything I felt needed to be tried. The precedent for me was *Krazy Kat, Polly and Her Pals*, and so forth.

CBR: In what other ways did you rebel against the status quo of your contemporaries of the Forties?

Eisner: Well, my tendency isn't toward sexual exploitation or mindless violence for the sake of violence. My discipline was my own creative integrity. I wanted what I was doing to be accepted, ultimately, as something serious. The fan mail that I was getting mostly dealt with *what* I was saying, rather than *how* I said it. I enjoyed that. My memories of that period of *The Spirit* was that I was a "Young Turk," if you will. I felt more revolutionary then; more *avant-garde* than I ever felt in my entire career. Except, perhaps, years later when I finished publishing and began *A Contract with God*.

I've always felt somewhat akin to the *avant-garde* comics. I don't know if I've ever been regarded as part of it, but I always felt a part of that movement.

CBR: You took a long career turn in the Fifties and Sixties by working outside of the mainstream comic book industry. Was that a conscious choice, or did you possibly feel that by then you were something of an "outcast" in terms of where you fit into the comic book scene?

Eisner: No, I wasn't an outcast—I never wanted to get into the comic book industry! Instructional comics was yet another adventure for me. It was more attractive to me.

Remember, a number of things happened to me along the way. During World War II, while I was in the Army, I made a pitch to the Department of

Defense to sell them on the use of comics as training material. I had fallen into the training department somehow, and had sent up a memo saying that there is another medium which was not being used that could train soldiers faster than anything they presently had. When you're twenty or twenty-one you are cocky like that! I convinced the Ordinance Department to use comics as a training tool. I created a character called "Joe Dope" and I was then the first one to get a two-page comic in an official Army training manual.

This created quite a shock. It was an impertinence at the time. The military publishing commanders felt that what I was doing was a threat to them. My comics implied that their regular training material was not readable. Which was indeed true!

So during the war, I discovered a totally new application of comics which I carried in my mind when I got out of the military. When I got back to *The Spirit*, I occasionally received calls from former military types who were now involved in the publication departments of major corporations like General Motors and U.S. Steel. They asked if I could do any of their training material in comic form. Of course, being a New York City boy, I said, "Sure!"

So I started a new company because I saw this as an exciting opportunity. As far as I was concerned, the comic book world held no real interest for me anymore. I had no desire to be part of it. I suppose it sounds a little pretentious, but even though money was always important to me, it was not *that* important if it stood in the way of my doing something very, very valuable in itself. So I saw it as an opportunity to make money, as well as a way to open up a whole new field for the medium. Later, around 1952, I began to contract with the Defense Department to repeat the success of comics in World War II. I produced *PS Magazine* monthly.

CBR: The Fifties was also a time when the comic book industry was regularly under attack from parents groups and society in general as a negative influence in America, not a positive one.

Eisner: That never fazed me. The only way that attitude hurt me was when I tried to sell teaching material in comic form to schools. The teachers would have nothing to do with it! But from a career point of view, since I never saw the need to pursue doing pages for any of the major publishers of comics, it did not affect me. I also never really saw the need to publish my own comics, though I did do a couple on my own that were failures. But essentially I was interested in the industrial use and instructional application of comics as a very interesting educational tool.

CBR: Just what is it about comics that made you feel it could be such a potent educational tool? All of us were brought up with the general understanding from our educators that comics had virtually no intrinsic educational value.

Eisner: That concept confuses form and concept. Comics is a literary form that employs images. Imagery communicates ideas in milliseconds, whereas words have to be decoded. Images transcend language barriers. Comics is an arrangement of images in a sequence, if you will. This lies at the core of the idea that a comic, if well done and properly executed, can convey a complex thought. Those of us working in this medium had never realized, until others started writing about it, that the subject or the content tends to shape the way we *communicate* with this medium. That being said, let's carry it to what's happening today.

We're now living in an age where information is moving at such a startling rate that we must create communication that rapidly transmits ideas. What is needed is some kind of "visual machinery." So we invented electronic machines that can transmit pictures and ideas quickly, simply, wildly, and inexpensively.

Comics is a way of transmitting ideas through words and images via print. One does not eliminate the other; they are interactive. The culmination of the words and images that we string together is what makes it so easily understandable. There are limits to it, of course. Words also still convey a great deal of internal thought and abstract characterization. But the essential reason that comics work so well is because of the visual imagery. And imagery is the fastest means of written communication in existence.

CBR: When you came back to the comic book form in the Seventies, it was really as part of the underground comix scene rather than within the mainstream industry. What led you there?

Eisner: Several things happened. In 1972, I had the opportunity to sell my company. I had also reached a point in life where I wanted to continue to touch all the bases, do all the things I had wanted to do. The other thing that happened was that Phil Seuling had a convention, and invited me down there.

I was astonished to discover a lot of young men walking around carrying old copies of *The Spirit* that they were trading back and forth. There was also a young fellow there with long hair named Denis Kitchen, and he was publishing underground comix. And he asked me if I would let him reprint some of *The Spirit* stories. I looked at all the underground comix and I suddenly realized what was happening: this was the new revolution in comics!

I attribute to that point in time as being the renaissance of comics as a literary/art form. With the artists like R. Crumb and Gilbert Shelton being the hard-core revolutionaries. They were using comics to attack the Establishment. They were not using comics purely as pandering entertainment. They were using it almost like graffiti. Sure they were writing for other "heads" who were dropping acid and such, but in the process they were still saying *something*. They had no other place to go to express themselves. It was *their* medium. They were being as "impertinent" as I was in the newspapers and the Army and the schools. Only more so!

"*My God*," I said to myself, "*they are using this medium as a true literary/art form.*" So I got caught up in that. This was a chance for me to do all the other things I always wanted to do. Again, I've always responded to opportunities in creativity, just as I've always responded to opportunities in business.

CBR: And that next opportunity for you was to basically create the first graphic novel, *A Contract with God* (1978). Creating an entire new market as well as a new format for the medium.

Eisner: I don't think in terms of market . . . I think in terms of audience. At the time there was no channel to the audience I sought except through the establishment bookstores. I hoped that I could break into the established mainstream market; I was in pursuit of the older reader. The format was intended to serve the content. I created the term "graphic novel" on the spur of the moment. I had written the book and rendered it in complete pencil form and started to look around for a publisher. I called Bantam Books because an editor there had known *The Spirit* and had known of me. When I go the editor on the phone, I said, "I have something new for you here. Something very different." And he said, "Yeah, what's that?" I looked down and I suddenly realized: *I could not tell him this was a comic book!* I wanted desperately to get a meeting, so I said, "Well, I have a graphic novel here." And he said, "Oh, that's interesting—I never heard of that. Bring that up."

So I came up to his office a few days later and he looked at *A Contract with God*, and then he looked up at me and said, "You know, it's still a comic book." [*Laughs*] I was advised to find a smaller publisher. But that's how the form got started.

CBR: Do you think the general public in this country is at last changing their attitude towards the medium; that they're now seeing comics as a completely legitimate "literary/art form"?

Eisner: Yes, there *is* a substantial change. The fact that a comic book was recently given a Pulitzer Prize can't help but have a tremendous effect on the reading attitudes of the American public. All my professional life I've been fighting that stigma. I remember well that when I told a teacher, "I make comic books for a living," their eyes would go wide in horror, and you can see in the pupils of their eyes two superheroes battling one another. And I had to explain, "Wait a minute, wait a minute, this is something different. This is an entire *medium*."

Old reading habits die hard, but they are changing. The fact that *A Contract with God* is still in print after fifteen years is an enormous victory for me, because as a comic book by any other name, it has survived. The average shelf life of a "comic book" as you and I know it is quite brief. So people are paying attention to this form now, as they have been in Europe for years.

CBR: Of the graphic novels you've done since, which has been the most satisfying, overall?

Eisner: From a creative point of view, the book that gave me the most satisfaction when I finally completed it was *A Life Force.* The reason I say that is that I followed the conventions and the structure of a classic novel. *To the Heart of the Storm* was a kind of autobiography which took effort and angst and two years of my life.

But I haven't attempted yet to do something like Jack Jackson's historical comics. I regard what he's done as very important, and deserving of more attention than it's gotten.

CBR: Will, looking back on your career as a whole, what do you think has been your greatest influence on the medium?

Eisner: It would be hard for me to say; I think it should come from somebody who has a good overview of the field. Any answer now would be a carefully wrought guess! The influence I hope I will have left, above all, is that comics are a valid literary/art form, and that it will continue to enable us to ultimately achieve a serious, adult reading audience. Hopefully, the body of work I've produced proves it.

Self-portrait in *The Spirit*, May 3, 1942. Reprinted by permission.

The Spirit, October 6, 1946. Reprinted by permission.

The Spirit, November 30, 1947. Reprinted by permission.

The Spirit, June 26, 1949. Reprinted by permission.

The Spirit, August 14, 1949. Reprinted by permission.

Poster drawn while Eisner served in the U.S. Army during World War II. Reprinted by permission.

P*S: The Preventative Maintenance Monthly, vol. 1, no. 1 (June 1951), cover by Will Eisner. From 1951 to 1971, Eisner was artistic director for this digest intended for U.S. Army personnel.

From *The Spirit* No. 1 (Kitchen Sink Press, January 1973). Reprinted by permission.

From *The Spirit* No. 1 (Kitchen Sink Press, January 1973). Reprinted by permission.

Preliminary pencil sketch for a color
print in *The Spirit Portfolio* (Collectors'
Press, 1977). Reprinted by permission.

Preliminary pencil sketch for a color
print in *The Spirit Portfolio* (Collectors'
Press, 1977). Reprinted by permission.

A Contract with God, originally published in 1978, widely popularized the term "graphic novel." Set in the same neighborhood as Eisner's later graphic novels *Dropsie Avenue* and *A Life Force*, *A Contract with God*'s four novellas in comics form dealt with Jewish immigrant life in New York City.

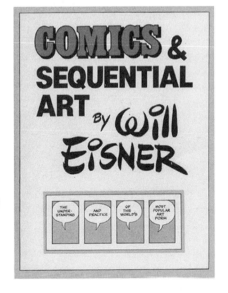

Comics & Sequential Art, published in book form in 1985, was one of the first analytic overviews of the comics form, examining both its formal principles and methods for creation. It began as a series of essays and lectures Eisner wrote for courses he taught on comics.

Self-portrait by Eisner
drawn for his interview
in *Heavy Metal* in 1983.
Reprinted by permission.

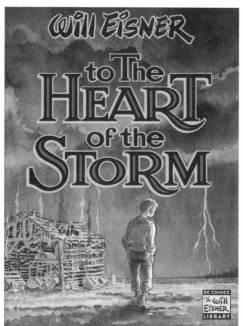

To the Heart of the Storm (1991), one
of Eisner's autobiographical graphic
novels, is set during World War II.

Design for a bookplate in 1993.
Reprinted by permission.

Life on Another Planet
(1993), originally serialized
in the *Will Eisner Quarterly*
as *Signal from Space*.

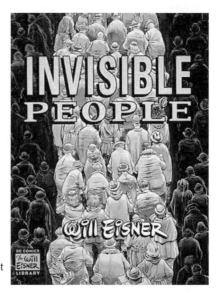

Invisible People (1993) collects three linked graphic novellas about anonymous life in a big city.

From *The Yellow Press*, a comics anthology published in Dublin, Ireland, in 1994. Reprinted by permission.

From *The Will Eisner Sketchbook* (Milwaukee, OR: Dark Horse Comics, 2003). Reprinted by permission.

WILL EISNER

THE SPIRIT OF COMICS

1917-2005

Self-portrait of Eisner as graphic novelist waiting for his readers and fellow comic artists to catch up. Reprinted by permission.

Night of the Paper Noir

PETER DePREE / 1996

From Comic Book Marketplace, No. 38 (August 1996), 30–63 and No. 39 (September 1996), 45–57. Reprinted by permission of Gemstone Publishing, Inc. All rights reserved.

Program Notes: In a discussion about art and cinema once, actor Rod Steiger winced when I called his cab scene with Marlon Brando in *On the Waterfront* "larger than life."

"Kid," he said with a cocktail of sadness and bemusement, "there IS nothing larger than life."

And so it goes with the collective memories of Eisner and a handful of his Tudor City artists. There IS no projector to replay that innocent, tragic, creative, noir past.

Not really.

But here's a buffalo nickel anyway, it will get you on the el that crosses neon-lit prewar Manhattan, clattering towards a cramped brownstone apartment-studio where (Holy Crow!) Blackhawk and Sheena, The Ray and the Spirit, Mr. Mystic, Joe Hercules, The Strange Twins, and "the idle heiress" Brenda Banks—Lady Luck—await.

Against a backdrop of tinny improvisational jazz, the cinematographer orchestrates a helicopter pan through the computer-generated '40s neon . . . The entire roof of the skyscraper is given over to filming the documentary, crammed with a variety of sound-stages: Wildwood Cemetery, an exotic medina, a sludge barge, the Tudor City studio . . .

Author Voice-Over: "How much Will culled from the flicks and how much from the mood-choked alley and byways of night-lit NYC is open. He adored them both equally. That he found much of it grist for the atmosphere of Central City in 1940s Manhattan is certain."

SCENE I/RAINY FOOSTEPS

The camera rolls back as Eisner, domino-masked, strolls toward it. His face is up-lit. A technician holds a boom-mike to the puddle-splashing footsteps.

"In the fall of '39 I was approached by the Des Moines Register Tribune Syndicate and Quality Comics Group publisher E. M. 'Busy' Arnold to produce a comic book insert for syndication to Sunday newspapers across the country. The creation of the necessary characters in this sixteen-page free-standing supplement was left to me. For this I created *The Spirit*.

"I was a 50 percent partner in Eisner & Iger then and prior to signing the agreement with Register Tribune Syndicate, I approached Iger and discussed it. Since our stockholder agreement stipulated that if either partner wished to leave the company, he must give the other first refusal, I sold him my portion."

Will walks out of a swirl of soup fog and leans somewhat theatrically on a prop wharf piling. "One of the deals in the agreement between Iger and me was that I was not to raid his shop. We agreed to have a vote and I could take a few artists out of the shop who would want to join me. Bob Powell, Lou Fine, and Chuck Mazoujian said they would prefer to come with me—behind remained people like George Tuska and Reed Crandall."

One who didn't make the leap, but deserves mention, was a kid named Kurtzberg alias Kirby: "Jack Kirby was at Eisner & Iger for a relatively short time (circa 1938). Jack was a hard worker, very attentive to what he was doing. He was quite fast, quite strong in his draftsmanship and everybody in the shop admired him. Kirby was the guy who always took on stories with a gritty look. Powell loved to do what he called 'classy stuff' where the artwork was kind of decorative. Each guy had his own style. As I remember him, Kirby had very little patience with intellectualism (laughter) . . . He was not interested in it. He loved adventure. High action was present in whatever he was doing. In my book *The Dreamer*, I refer to him as 'Jack King,' and relate a little incident about him that demonstrates that. His dynamism always reminded me of John Garfield—that kind of hard drive, a seething internal—not anger, exactly—but certainly competitiveness. I still maintain that deep inside he was The Hulk! (laughter)

"In the Eisner & Iger shop he kept pretty much to himself. Rather shy, he didn't socialize too easily. His name was Jack Koenigsberg back then."

As the film crew takes a break to rearrange the lightning, I hurry over to the studio bar. A P'Gell extra pours me a Bacardi, and I move to the skyscraper's parapet to enjoy the cool breeze off the nocturnal continent of 1990's Manhattan spread out below in all its twinkling majesty. Then a familiar face is at my side. Joe Simon is excited by the Eisner footage: "Yeah!" he agrees with Will's take on Kirby's personality, "Absolutely, absolutely!" But then he chuckles—"*Koenigsberg*? It was Kurtzberg. Ask Will if *he's* losing his mind too!"

I down my drink and tell Simon I need to get back to do the next Eisner interview segment, but he grabs my arm to share an irresistible anecdote: "I signed on as a chief editor at Fox Comics at a time when Eisner & Iger had split with Fox. (Fox was in the same building with DC Comics, the Grand Central Palace at 480 Lexington Avenue in NY.) Eisner pulled out with all his staff because he sensed legal difficulties because *Wonderman* was being sued by *Superman*. So, when I became editor at Fox, Fox had decided that all the editors would be named Mr. Roberts—didn't even have a first name, just Mr. Roberts. And so if we left him we wouldn't have a past, so to speak. Fox had this idea: we ran an ad in the *NY Times* for the artists who did The Flame, the artist who did Wonderman, 'Call Mr. Roberts at Fox Publications.' The idea was to deplete the Eisner-Iger studio and hire everybody away from him. But the funny part is that Eisner himself had used these names, he was the artist who did several of these characters! Eisner, naturally, didn't call to answer the ad, and very few if any of the artists did. Because so many of them were Eisner himself! I had a fake name, and Eisner had all these fake names! Like a comedy."

Author VO: "The choicer strips are overwhelmingly powerful—Eisner never feared exploring deep emotion—and one or two gems play out across the page like perfectly balanced, self-contained paper movies. 'My trademark is stagecraft,' Will has said before, a directorial track exemplified in *Hurricane*.

"This short, 1949 paper noir is a classic example of Eisner's rich use of sable shadows, powerful emotion disguised beneath sardonic, witty dialogue, and hi-caliber panel direction. Snappy repartee from crime melodramas is introduced at just the right moments. What we might mistake today for a nostalgic or camp tinge was actually a special magic, one that never wasn't there."

The author waves his arms over Denny Colt's fifty-foot long face.

"These crisp blacks, tightly plotted were complexly stylized without seeming at all so."

The author pauses in the title-black and gazes up directly into the camera:

"No comic cinematographer had tighter control of his camera, or was as daring and eager to travel the really extreme regions of the graphic terrain. Although other comic artists explored the black/white synergy (including

Toth, Caniff, Wood, maybe a half dozen more . . .) few were able to exploit it as lushly—and often surprisingly—as comics' foremost noir director, Eisner."

Tight shot on Will's hands filling his pipe: "In the course of my agreement with Busy Arnold and the Register Tribune, we set up a partnership, under which I would produce The Spirit, the ancillary characters (Lady Luck and Mr. Mystic), plus three other magazines—*Uncle Sam Comics, Police Comics,* and *HIT.*"

It was a daring move for the twenty-two-year-old entrepreneur: "I ventured into this, leaving a perfectly acceptable situation with Eisner & Iger—I was dissatisfied writing to a comic book audience consisting largely of thirteen- and fourteen-year-old kids—not the older audience we have today. The adult newspaper audience gave me the platform to exercise something I had been dreaming about since I came into the field—an opportunity to write comic *literature*! Free to write anything I wanted, I focused on detective stories, creating a free-moving private-eye who could roam throughout the city. I wanted my stories to center around the city, because my entire literary nutrition consisted of tales by the '30s short-story writers of city life like O. Henry and Ring Lardner. Since this freestanding, free-moving detective would be outside the law, I could have him do anything, giving me the fulcrum for adventure, or whatever kind of stories I wanted to do." Thus was born Denny Colt, a lean and fast tenderhearted outlaw hero.

"Keep in mind, I planned storylines far beyond the 'crime-does-not-pay' syndrome pandemic in those days. I discussed the ideas with Busy, proposing at first a simple detective or freelance investigator, but he objected, feeling the Syndicate would find a 'costumed character' (a euphemism for today's 'superhero') easier to sell. We battled that back and forth and finally I conceded, but under no circumstances did I want to do a straight superhero. Superman was very hot at that point, Batman was beginning to boom, and the Syndicate was determined to break into this comic book market, which to them read costumed characters. I compromised—'Alright, I'll give you a costume.' I put a blue suit on him, gave him a domino mask, gloves. But that was as far as I would go. They accepted that. It was a 'costume' as far as they were concerned!

"In a 1940 *Baltimore Sun* interview, just when I began *The Spirit*, I said I believed strongly that this was a true literary form. History has proved me right. As far as I was concerned, this was a medium I was going to spend my life in. And I believed implicitly that comics had capabilities of being *literature*, treating subject matter far beyond the simplistic 'trash 'em, beat 'em up' kind of story."

We take another break before shooting the next scene, and again I run into Joe Simon at the bar: "Simon & Kirby was next door to Will Eisner in Tudor City! 1942–43. But I never saw his setup there and I don't think he came over. We were usually competitors. No, we were *always* competitors. But we admired him and his work, and he admired our work, I think.

"I was up at his studio a couple times with some friends when Will was at Busy Arnold's place on Madison Ave., and I saw Lou Fine working there, and the guy who did Plastic Man, Jack Cole. All these working artists were so nice. The writers? I don't know, they're usually too drunk to talk. We used to call him Bill, and I had to train myself to start calling him Will, because everybody else did. In those days it was Bill Eisner. And he had a sixteen-year-old secretary, Libby, who was in love with him. There was this engraving salesman, Arthur Weiss, who was in love with Libby. Ask Will if he remembers Libby, she was a very pretty girl."

"By and large I worked on *The Spirit* alone," says Eisner, "with the exception of a letterer. When I left Eisner & Iger to start *The Spirit*, I rented a two-room Tudor City apartment as my studio. (I never liked to work at home.) One of the rooms was my studio, the second occupied by other artists who came with me to produce this magazine section. Beginning with Dave Berg (who did Blackhawk, a character I created) the group included Lou Fine, Bob Powell, Tex Blaisdell, and Chuck Mazoujian. Later on we had a young kid come by in the afternoons to sweep floors and be of help—a kid named Joe Kubert. We all know what became of him!"

(A newspaper spins out of the screen with The Spirit section) Author VO: "Eventually reaching a whopping five million copies per week, the *Spirit* insert made the entire Tudor City bullpen syndicate cartoonists with millions of readers!"

"Unlike the more formal Eisner & Iger shop," Will continues, "it was a very casual working studio, just guys sitting around in an apartment, really. The room was stripped of the usual furniture, just drawing boards and chairs, tabourets and stuff like that, with material pasted on the walls."

The grips dolly-in to a mockup foamcore model of the studio with a light burning, presumably late into the night.

The author stands over the model as a lean 6'-6" man with sagacious eye gestures and points: "Tudor City," Tex Blaisdell explains, "was a posh uptown development of expensive apartments on the water, with uniformed attendants, strict parking regulations, the whole bit. We were up on the high ground in the Woodstock Tower—this building here—over the East River with a long downhill cliff to the water area. Out the back window you could see the river. Down below, though, near this handball court here, was this slaughterhouse! That sort of put a crimp in the neighborhood.

"When you came in the door of the two-room apartment, that's where we sat, what was probably supposed to be a living room, and then there was a door in the middle of the room turning right into the inside which was probably the bedroom where Bill had his setup. And the bathroom was off there too. It was smallish, it wasn't a huge place at all. It was cramped because we had so many guys in there—eight or ten drawing boards jammed into the living room. And more people moved in as time went by, and we had some writers sitting over in the corner. Dick French was there, he contributed to Blackhawk writing scripts . . . but Will mostly did it himself. Chris Hansen did artwork of some sort. Then we moved in Chuck Cuidera to do Blackhawk. Part of my duties was to help him finish up when Chuck couldn't make deadline. I did backgrounds and touchups . . . and I did the same thing with Lou Fine because he was so slow with his gorgeous pencils. If Fine couldn't make his thirty pages in thirty days, I'd help him sometimes. And once in a while Bob Powell would feel like having help so I would work on Mr. Mystic. Chuck Mazoujian was such a good artist he managed to snare himself a position in an executive capacity over at Pratt and left. Pratt was sort of a big university-type art school. You graduate with a diploma from Pratt and what you are is accomplished! When he stopped doing Lady Luck they moved in with Nick Viscardi. But after the war he shortened his name to Cardi . . . we teased him about getting his Vis shot off during the war. Nick's still around . . . but I've lost track of him. With luck he's retired."

"Generally," Eisner remembers as he joins Tex and the author at the model, "in those days (the beginning of 1940) I worked from 9 A.M. till well past midnight, many times. I had this little couch in my room (you can see it here if you look closely) and would sleep there overnight occasionally. *The Spirit* was a very demanding project—the entire sixteen-page section had to be produced weekly, with no margin for error or lateness. Whereas in comic books or graphic novels you've got a lot of 'slippage,' in the newspaper business— like radio or TV—you have no fail-safe time! It has to be delivered on a certain day.

"The coloring was done at the engraving shop, not internally, by making a silverprint, or black-&-white proof, of the line art. The color was suggested with Dr. Martin's Dyes, and then a code applied to each hue, which gave the engraver the combination of Ben Day screens to create that color.

"Late 1940," Tex relates, "I was looking for work, and somebody suggested I go see Bill Eisner. (Nobody called him Will—to friends, associates, and family . . . he was Bill.) Bill thought my pitiful samples showed something, so he said, 'I'll give you a trial week and pay you fifteen bucks. Be here at nine o'clock every morning and I'll give you something to do.' I was living in Whitestone, Queens, an hour's trip on the subway. He started me out on Spirit backgrounds, giving me a pile of his printed material as reference. So I started filling in blacks and crosshatch textures, and this, that, and the other thing.

"Wednesday, he came around and looked at what I was doing, and I was replicating a texture he used previously. 'Who told you to do that?!' 'Well you gave me these things to look at and I saw that in this circumstance that's what you did, so I'm mimicking it.' 'Okay, you're hired,' he said, 'I'll pay you twenty-five bucks for the week and you just come in every morning.'

"They roughed the artwork in and if necessary I would touch them up, but I mostly rendered them, tightening the pencils and inking. I would do some of the textures on covers, like if he had a stone wall, I might get to do some of the rendering on the stones or something like that. I remember doing scripting just on Blackhawk . . . Bob Powell was there doing Mr. Mystic, Chuck Mazoujian was doing Lady Luck, Lou Fine was sitting over in the corner doing The Ray. Bob Powell was in the other corner. Chuck Mazoujian was in the middle of the room. Davey Berg was over there."

Davey Berg.

"I don't know what everybody else called him, 'you lousy sonuvabitch' or something," Tex chuckles, "No, he's very nice. As a matter of fact he's one of the coupla guys that came to my wedding."

"Tex was sort of right-hand man to Will," Al Jaffee recalls. "He did backgrounds and may have done lettering and did a lot of consultation with Will. He was in Will's office almost all the time, problem-solving and helping out."

Cut to night scene, author VO: "A scrawny kid with sleepless circles under his eyes clenches his fists in anticipation and gazes out over a night-lit 1941 Manhattan as the el goes clattering on through the chill night . . . That buffalo-nickel ride on the el brought him to a bedroom apartment too small for ten artists but roomy enough to hold a Milky Way of superhero adventures. Joe Kubert remembers the Tudor City studio like it was yesterday:"

"Will was so involved and so much a turning point and an opening up for me coming into the business, I couldn't begin to tell you. I was about eleven or twelve years old, just starting out at the High School of Music and Art. That's as long as I've known Will. And this has been an ongoing relationship. Until he moved down to Tamarac, Florida, we were able to see each other quite often.

"Somehow I was directed up to Tudor City, just trying to break into the business. I don't know if Will himself hired me or Tex Blaisdell—who is actually teaching at my school now! Tex was one of the first guys I met working up at Will's office. In all probability," Kulbert continues, "it was Will who hired me because he gave me the last word on everything. It was through that full-time summer job with Will, that I also met Jerry Iger. Jerry and Will were collaborating on several publishing deals."

Here's how Tex recalls the whiz kid destined to do big things with Hawkman: "Kubert was six or seven years younger than I, a snot-nosed little punk when I first met him. But a swell handball player. We would go out at lunch time and play handball down by the slaughterhouse below Tudor City. Oh, did it stink . . . wow!"

"I lived in Brooklyn," Kubert goes on, "east New York, and attended the High School of Music and Art up on Convent Avenue and 135th Street. It took me about an hour and a half by subway—at a nickel a ride! That was a little while ago (laughs.) After school at two thirty or three o'clock, I'd ride all the way up to 135th and Will's place was off 42nd Street on the East Side, Tudor City, where the U.N. now have their offices in Manhattan.

"My initial duties were sweeping up the place. Chuck Cuidera was doing Blackhawk up there at the time, and I had the privilege of erasing, cleaning up, and whiting out his stuff. Bob Powell was doing Mr. Mystic. I was really lucky to be able to see that original work going on under my hand, it was a wonderful learning experience."

"I worked right through the summer. They were turning out *Spirit* pages and magazines at the time at his Tudor City studio setup. He also allowed me to do half-pages at the end of the seven-page supplement they supplied the newspapers. Looking back now, and remembering how terrible the stuff I did was . . . it's amazing that he gave me those kinds of opportunities—I was just a kid! His permitting me to learn on the job like that was just a marvelous, marvelous opportunity. Most of the other guys I knew were sixteen and seventeen and already out of high school by that time. I was lucky enough to be able to do it while going to school and during the summer . . . which gave me a real head start."

"I'll never forget that place as long as I live. I remember that as clearly as if it happened yesterday. It was a regular two-bedroom apartment with Will separated from the rest of us in one of the bedrooms where he worked by himself. The rest of the bullpen—the letterer and other artists—took the other room. I didn't really get to see Will too often because he was ensconced in the master suite working like crazy. In addition to Cuidera, Powell, and

Tex, Dave Berg who works for *MAD Magazine* was just starting to work there and there was Nick Viscardi who did Lady Luck after Powell left. Absolutely outstanding artists, an inspiration to anyone who wanted to break into the business. And I might add, the kindest and most patient people in the world! Here's this young kid flittin' around and aching to do this kind of work, and I guess they recognized it. They spent all kinds of inordinate time with me teaching me the way to do things. It was just a wonderful experience."

Camera dollies back as Dave Berg speaks. The caller was asking him to remember six months spent in a dim, cigar-box studio tucked way back in the early '40s—all the way across the country and more than a half century ago. (Oy vey! But how was it that he recalled it with such crystal clarity?)

Camera follows as he moves back to the glass and furrows his brow. "I've had a long career now, but that period when I was in Eisner's Tudor City studio was the most interesting I've ever had in all these years. All the memories! They're all kinds of memories!"

Back on the stage set: Later that night we find Eisner sneaking out from his cot after another eighteen-hour day, prowling NYC subways at night in search of choice characters like some noir vampire bat. Story settings, villains and heroes, snatches of dialogue crystallized in wharf spume and thick manhole steam. Much of that Central City chutzpah energizing the Spirit strip was absorbed during these nocturnal forays.

Story conference: In response to your query re: "How much of the Spirit's personality is in Will Eisner?" Well, how much isn't?

The façade is lit with fake drizzle and, after being fitted with a pair of lapel microphones, the author and Eisner stroll slowly through a cosmetic recreation of 1940s Manhattan: "The city—New York—has always fascinated me, so my work has centered around an environment—like Faulkner's South, John O'Hara with his lower aristocratic class environment in Pennsylvania, and so forth." In spite of the drizzle, it's a hot summer night in the stage-like setting and many are asleep on the fire-escapes. A Panaflex on a giraffe-crane tracks us along the crowded alleys and avenues with down-angle shots. We pass a kosher slaughterhouse then down an alley of sweatshops to a cramped honkytonk tucked under a clattering el line. The streets are packed with ethnic extras—Irish, Italian, German, Eastern European Jew, Chinese . . .

Eisner drinks it in: "The big city has always intrigued me as a place of great theater with a huge amount of story material constantly available, an environment I know and understand. All the lighting and shadow work on my characters is derivative of city lighting which comes from above, whereas in a rural environment, light comes from all sides. The streetlights and alley-shafts and so forth that I lived with influence my art. To this day, I draw these things sans reference because I have a keen visual memory of them."

When Dave Berg told me he had always viewed Will as an older brother figure, he didn't really have to. You hear it in his voice: "Will taught me something important . . . He said—'You're not a cartoonist, you're the director, the actor, the set designer . . . the whole motion-picture, is you!' I have never forgotten it, and I still work on that.

"It was the first job I ever had. Now Tudor City itself, especially in those days, was quite a prestigious neighborhood. Technically, Tudor City is not a city, it's a group of houses called Tudor City. Will cobbled together a studio out of an apartment. Unfortunately he chose too small and compact an apartment, we were even in the kitchen! I still remember exactly where everyone sat.

"I discovered Eisner in 1941 when I was twenty years old. Somebody at Cooper-Union showed me some *Spirit* work and said he was related to Will somehow. He showed my Cooper-Union classroom work to Eisner and Eisner said—'Yeah, tell him to come Monday.'

"Will called him back later—'Hey! I have no room to put him in! Tell him not to come.' Well, he didn't make that call so I showed up Monday, and Eisner exclaimed—'Oy! I told him to tell you not to come, I have no room for you!' And I'm standing there and he says—'Well, as long as you're here I can use you. We'll make room.' He starts pushing things around, creating a little corner, but he didn't even have a desk or a chair for me! Within an hour one of the supply houses delivered a drawing table, chair, and tabouret. If I had gotten that message it would've been a whole different beginning, because he was the best to start with, so brilliant, so talented."

Kubert agrees. "I tell ya, I can almost smell the place! I can smell the India ink, I can smell the aroma of the comic books themselves, the pulp paper they were printed on. It's as vivid to me today as it was when I first walked in there to work. I remember where the guys had their tables stacked up against the walls in that comparatively small room. In retrospect of course, I was just a kid, so that the place probably looked a heckuva lot bigger to me than it actually was! But I remember that there were four, five guys in what might be called a studio—in actuality a living room and bedroom. We were stacked against the perimeters of the walls. My job was sweeping up the place, keeping things tidy, but really the preponderance of my work involved cleaning up the other artists' work when they were finished inking, erasing the pencil from underneath the ink, whiting out, stuff like that. It is part of the procedure instead of wasting the artist's good time in erasing—if you have seven, ten, fifteen pages it may take you quite some time to clean up the whole job, and would waste their time and their talent. In two or three hours these guys could bang out another page instead of erasing their material, and that's why they hired me.

"Okay, it really is a menial job, but to me it was just great. I loved it, loved it. That was to me one of the greatest experiences I could have had at that time, simply because it permitted me to see the work, to really examine it and find out how the heck they actually put it together. I got really enthusiastic about what I was doing! I recall working on some Blackhawk illustration and artist Chuck Cuidera was working right there in the room. The cover design had Blackhawk climbing a hemp rope, silhouetted against the moon. I even recall which cover it was! (Laughing.) As I was whiting it out, I got so involved with the little hairs sticking out of the hemp rope that, instead of just cleaning it up, I started putting hairs into the rope! I was so enthusiastic about what I was doing that I didn't realize what the heck was happening. I was so proud of what I had done . . . till I gave the stuff back to Chuck. 'Chops' looked at it and kind of shook his head with a tsk-tsk—'Look Joe, just clean this stuff up. Don't draw!'"

Story department: Such a trivial detail to remember this many decades later—but pivotal, drawing the hairs on a hemp rope! Where's that brat who plays the young Kubert? Let's get an over-the-shoulder shot of him drawing here.

If Kubert experienced those historic days as a slumber party atmosphere where he could eavesdrop on the older boys' wisecracks and pickpocket artistic shortcuts, Eisner deemed Tudor City a more formalized creative hotbed: "In a shop like that there's a *tremendous* amount of influence between members, like a schoolroom or art class where you have an opportunity to see what the other guy's doing, which can't help but influence you! 'Oh yeah! That's a good idea, I think I'll try that kind of stuff in what I'm doing.' That plus a healthy dose of competition certainly had an effect. Cross-influences pervaded the shop's atmosphere."

Al Jaffee agrees: "The Tudor City experience was very short but very interesting and vivid. Great talent. And it was so invigorating and interesting because we were creating *together*.

"You know, I've spent my life freelancing and you just sit in a studio by yourself all day, but being in a bullpen with the likes of those guys there was a lot of excitement and you're picking up all kinds of tips. I'd stand there and watch Powell and Nick doing their thing, watching how they ink and all that kind of stuff and it was just fascinating."

Dave Berg recalls assisting Cudeira: "Blackhawk was done by Chuck, he started it and I would assist him doing backgrounds. Around '41, before WWII started. Chuck was a very good artist. (He was half-Italian, half-Jewish. The other Chuck—Mazoujian—was all Italian.) I remember he had a very interesting airplane and when there was a smaller version of the plane to draw, I would do that. That kind of thing. But Chuck handled the scripts himself."

"It wasn't as fractured doing the work back then," Kubert remembers, "Today you have pencilers, inkers, background people, and people who do just breakdowns for somebody to refine the pencils. At that time every artist that I know of did the whole job: penciling, inking, and very often the writing and lettering as well."

Tex sees the same distinction: "The main difference back then was that most of the guys did the whole thing themselves. They've become increasingly specialized since. In those days we did the whole damn thing ourselves, in the case of Bob Powell, he wrote and drew it, and so did Chuck Mazoujian, and Nick. Lou, though, could hardly be depended upon to ink because he took so long to pencil. But Chuck Cuidera contributed to the story ideas and drew it all himself."

"I'd brown-bag it just like I did when I was going to school," Kubert continues. "It took me about an hour each way to commute back and forth from New York, and I was paid for that the munificent sum of $12.50 a week. Now that was a lot of dough, dough that I sincerely appreciated! It was not long after the Depression, and 25¢ was still a helluva lot of dough. I have no arguments with that. It's probably more than I was worth at the time! (Laughs.)

"My only stint on *The Spirit* involved inking Lou Fine's pencils. I tell you, I was so young and naïve Lou Fine's pencils *didn't even frighten me!* I learned so much from just watching Lou work. Just to give you an idea, his pencils were of such a nature that it became dependent on the inker to select the right lines. Lou didn't just do an outline of the figure; you could see the *construction* or the *building* of what he was doing. And then it was up to the inker to select the right places to put the ink lines down. *That* was a real learning experience. Although detailed, his pencils were not completely cleaned up, so he allowed a certain margin of flexibility to the inker, and I was just lucky. *Really* lucky!"

Al Kotzky, the next youngest to Kubert, worked over the Secret Master's breakdowns too, noting the profound impact it had on his own style: "As a matter of fact," he groans, "Lou's penciling was so good I often ruined them. It was amazing just sitting behind the guy and seeing him go through his stuff—and then working on it yourself! It's had a lasting effect. He knew how good he was yet he never bragged about it, and he treated me completely as his equal, instead of just a young kid starting in the business. He was about twenty-five and I was just eighteen at the time."

Others qualified their admiration for Lou's interpretation of Eisner's character: "Lou preceded my being there," Feiffer recalls. "He was there during the war years, and started out imitating Eisner's style which didn't seem to me right for the Spirit *at all* and I didn't care for it. I ignored those years."

"Lou was a very quiet, sweet person who just sat there and did his great stuff," Tex recalls. "But he didn't contribute to the songs and snappy patter that went on in the workroom. He was sort of a short guy with tremendous shoulders and arms from dragging his paralyzed legs around. He'd come in on his crutches, barely able to maneuver by himself, and sit over in the corner, standing his crutches behind him. He didn't have any personality. He just sat there and did his gorgeous material . . . and made everybody gulp and swallow when they looked at this stuff he could do. Even though he fussed with it so much he couldn't maintain a fast schedule, it was so great anybody would buy it."

Oddly, Al Kotzky, the man who would end up knowing Lou best, remembers it differently: "As far as I know, he never used a crutch, he may have worn a brace but I couldn't see it because of his trousers. But I was never aware that he had something to help him, he just had a limp."

"I admired Will Eisner," Joe Simon says, "He was probably my favorite creative person in the whole business. My favorite *artist* was Lou Fine. He was also Jack Kirby's favorite artist. I know that Jack was a fan of and greatly influenced by Fine's artwork."

Lou Fine died early, but Berg recalls late night gab sessions with the lame wizard: "Lou was two floors above us and I often visited with him. There was no room for him in our studio because we were all jammed up, so Will got him another small apartment. He could afford it, Eisner was doing financially very well. By the time he went into the Army he had $300,000 and was about twenty-five years old—*during the end of the Depression!* That was such a huge amount of money in those days, like having a million dollars. Remember, he was a publisher/editor and he was making big money."

The time was ripe for it. Kubert recalls a thriving four-color industry back in those early '40s: "There were about twenty-five different publishers. The two largest at the time were DC and the place that put out Captain Marvel, along with more than twenty other smaller places. I used to make the rounds regularly with my buddy Norman Maurer, we attended the High School of Music and Art together. And because we had the same affinity for this kind of artwork, we grouped together and would go out almost every day after school, or play hooky, and hit every publisher and every editor we could scare up with work. This is during and after the time I was working with Will Eisner. Norm and I were constantly on the go. Norm had worked with Charlie Biro doing Crimebuster and Daredevil—at about the same age as I. As far as I'm concerned, Will Eisner is one of *the* certifiable geniuses in our business. Everybody and anybody who has seen his work and has read it, has to appreciate it for what it is."

Feiffer, in turn, characterizes Kubert as one of the few remaining grandmasters: "Joe's drawing over the years developed into some of the best art one sees in comics. I admire him enormously. And there's a lot of good graphics out there, but I don't know the names of these people. I don't read comics anymore."

"I was with Eisner up to about '43," Alex Kotzky remembers, "when I went in the service. A friend of mine from high school, Al Jaffee, (right, the *MAD* fold-in artist) decided he wanted to go up and show his work to Will 'cause he'd been up there before, and he figured as a good excuse to take my work along. Because apparently if he went up on his own, Eisner might have just given him another quick shrift! So he took my work up and I got the job, penciling and inking *Spirit* backgrounds. Al got a page, Inferior Man. I was penciling for Chad Grothkoph who worked for DC Comics and then when Al took my stuff up to Will, a few months before Pearl Harbor, I left Grothkoph."

Al Jaffee offered more background on the story: "After graduating from the High School of Music and Art, I was living at home in the Bronx and going to work by subway. I was nineteen and created a feature called Inferior Man—a silly Superman take-off (but considering Superman couldn't have been very old back then, I guess I was a bit ahead of my time!) When somebody mentioned that Eisner might be interested in something like that as a filler, I went up to see him in Tudor City and was really surprised when he offered me a job at $10 a week. And that's how the whole schmeer started. He gave me a desk behind Dave Berg, and Dave and I became close friends, going out to lunch together and so on. I can't remember anything other than Dave Berg eating mints all the time! He constantly had a bag full of mints that he consumed.

"I did Inferior Man as a one or two-page filler for Quality and it appeared in *Military Comics* ('Stories of the Army and Navy'). I was doing the whole thing including the lettering. I got to know Frenchie (Dick French) a writer who worked on *The Spirit*, and Tex Blaisdell, and Nick Viscardi. I envied Nick because he was such a terrific comic book artist and looked up to him as "the older guy" because he had more experience at that point than I did. They were the big guys, Bob Powell was doing Lady Luck; Dave Berg was doing Death Patrol; Uncle Sam was being done by Lou Fine with Eisner's assist; Chuck Cuidera was doing the lead feature in *Military Comics*, really beautifully done. But the Spirit was really the powerhouse. Outside of the studio I didn't have access to it because it didn't appear in any New York City papers! (I think it appeared in Philadelphia and a few other places.) But from what I did see—a lot of originals up in Tudor City—the stories were just great. But to me the design aspect, especially his splash pages, were brilliant. I felt that Will was a fantastic designer whose designs carried the stories forward brilliantly. I think he was a twenty-three-year-old genius and I was twenty, or something like that. I was in awe of Will Eisner, even though he wasn't that much older than me. Sheesh—I don't even know if he's older than I am *at all*! My memory of Will was that he was just an awesome *wunderkind*! He was so young and so smart and so quick and so bright and just a very talented guy, and the Spirit was kind of like . . . magic!

"But then Will had to let me go, for whatever reason. He said he liked my stuff and all that but he let me go and he arranged for me to go over and do the same thing with Ed Cronin and his group, very nice man, one of the early people in the comic book business. He had a little studio and I did a couple of Inferior Man's for him, the same character. They all had some tie-ins. I was just a kid interested in drawing for whoever would buy it. And then that kinda broke up and I was on my own. So, I said to Alex Kotzky 'Why don't we form a partnership? I tell you what, I'll take a sample of my work and a sample of your work, I'll cover the Bigfoot comedy angle and yours will be the great straight stuff.' Alex was really excellent and he did just beautiful drawing of various kinds of superheroes for Timely. I made a portfolio, a couple of pieces of mine and a couple of pieces of Alex's, and I went out to Eisner and Eisner *immediately* wanted Alex! So that was the end of our partnership, because he hired Alex."

Kotzky picked up the story: "That first week that I started working there Eisner sat down with me to point out some of the things I was doing wrong—'You either gotta produce the stuff, or we can't use you.' Which gave me pause to think. But after a coupla weeks I got the hang of it and from then on it was smooth sailing. I was there with Chuck Cuidera, Tex Blaisdell, Sam Rosen was the letterer, Bob Powell did Mr. Mystic, and Nick Viscardi did Lady Luck."

Did Kotzky feel the hectic deadlines hampered the artists? "No, I don't think so. They worked at a fairly leisurely pace. Four pages per week really didn't seem to be any strain on Nick Viscardi and Bob Powell. Then again, *everything* was good as far as I was concerned in those days, and when I think back on it now there wasn't anybody other than Will or Lou Fine that I really thought was great stuff."

"Al Jaffee," Berg recalls, "was at the studio for a very brief period doing Inferior Man, a single-page continuing feature in one of the books. But, as he confessed, we hardly paid him $10 a week or something like that! That's the only thing about Eisner, he's not a big payer, especially compared with Gaines who was very generous."

But Will had a soft spot too. "In mid '41," Tex recalls, "I went and asked him for a raise because I wanted to get married. He blanched—'How much did you imagine?' Well, I said, we figured out that we could do it on $35. So he regained his color and said 'That'll be fine.' He gave me the extra ten bucks and we got married on it. And on that $35 we had a little rattletrap car my grandmother had given me, a '31 Plymouth with a rumble seat, and a three-room apartment, *with* garage. And every week on the way home I put $5 in the bank and bought a book from a bookstore down the block. On $35, with groceries, gas, and everything, you could do that in those days!"

"Powell's name was really Polaski." Dave Berg chuckles. "He came home from a rich, noble family in Poland. His Majesty really let the rest of us know it. He also did something that I thought was very peculiar. He was engaged to a girl and had her picture plastered all over the studio. He goes away one weekend and comes back married to *another* girl! It was the weirdest thing I have ever seen. He met her that weekend while engaged to another girl and they ran off and got married . . . in one weekend."

"Powell did an airplane feature," Jaffee recalls, "not Blackhawk, Loops 'n' Banks or something like that, a Flying Aces kind of deal. His style was not as realistic as the superhero style, more of a kind of crossing over from traditional cartooning of an earlier era into the modern super drawing stuff of the Milton Caniff school of that time."

"Bob Powell," Joe Simon supplies, "was fifty-three when he died. Bob was from Buffalo. Powell wasn't his real name, he had some kind of Polish name, one of those ten syllable gizmos."

"Originally," Berg continues, "I was hired to be Eisner's assistant doing Spirit backgrounds and helping out whenever I could, and when he wasn't using me the others would. But very quickly I was out of that because I had my own success and was busy with my own features.

"It was an unbelievable time, so interesting—a very positive and very pleasant situation being with him. Will changed my life with three words. The first time he gave me anything to illustrate, I read the script and said—'Will, this isn't a very good story.' 'Can you rewrite it?' he shot back. I said, 'I'll try.' Well I did. For which he said the words that changed my life: 'You're a writer.' I had no intention of being a writer, but from then on . . .

"He then assigned me the job of writing the first issue of *Uncle Sam*, the whole book! What a jump—here I'd never even thought of being a writer! But I did it with such enthusiasm, I was so excited, a whole new field had opened up. The book was extremely successful. I only did the first book though. Tex Blaisdell and I would talk over the plot and then I would write it. Tex was a good assistant, he could do backgrounds.

"We were late turning out *Uncle Sam* and Will had me come in on Saturday, he and I did final touch-up. That was a new thing to me, to work on a Saturday! It was a five-day week and that's the first time I ever heard of it. Well, that's the kind of office Will ran. Will inked my pencils, and said he was thrilled with the job I did. I also penciled most of the comic before it was handed out to inkers. Some of the books that have come out since have gotten the information wrong, giving the art credit to the inkers instead of to me and Tex."

Freelancers popped in occasionally. Kotzky recalls Klaus Nordling, "a short, Finnish guy with a moustache who came in after Nick Viscardi but he didn't work in the studio. He wrote his own stuff (like Lady Luck) at home and delivered the work to Tudor City.

Berg shrugs: "It was unfortunate that I had to leave the office but they were overcrowded, with all of us jammed into that living room and kitchen. I didn't get fired, Will moved me to another studio he had part-ownership of, but I didn't like it and didn't stay there long. It was such a changeover from having the best talents of all. He shipped me down to his other office, and I didn't like those people whatsoever. They were terrible and amateurish . . . and I stayed there only a very short time."

"Occasionally," Eisner reflects, "I'd have someone like Powell help me on backgrounds, but I was working pretty steadily and quite heavily. I had people come in and do lettering for me. In those years it was people like the late Ben Oda, a classic letterer in-shop until later on when I had Abe Kanegson—the one whose lettering I always admired and who worked best with me and had a philosophical affinity for my work. He appeared in my shop after WWII, in 1947. I don't know whatever happened to him. As a matter of fact, Jules Feiffer and I tried to locate him years later, but he seems to have disappeared."

Tex recalls the lettering genius this way: "Abe Kanegson and Bill had a terrible fight at some point, they yelled and screamed and jumped up and down and Abe quit. I ran across him later after the war, when I had pages to do. He did my breakdowns and I discovered he was pretty good, I didn't have to fix anything . . . All I had to do was put faces on it and ink it."

"I always required imaginative lettering," Will continues, "because I regarded it as a vital part of the art, integral to the story, not as a necessary evil. I sought to achieve sound-effects by having some letters done heavily in boldface, some lightly, some in differing styles, to accommodate the story thrust."

INTERMEZZO

As the cameraman take a break, Eisner strolls across the studio stage set to get two period bottles of National Bohemian pale beer chilling on the fire-escape. A skinny kid tosses a push broom into the closet and dashes offstage, presumably to catch the el back home. A muscular, redheaded man with a cork-stemmed Japanese brush over his ear and Coke-bottle glasses lurches by on the crutches, a pile of oversized Red Bee original art tucked under his arm. When I reach out to tap his shoulder my hand passes through him. As he trudges upstairs to another apartment, you can almost make out the rose wallpaper through his ghostly holographic form (courtesy of ILM—industrial Light & Magic.)

Author Voice-Over: "It is only then that I realize it was Lou Fine."

SCENE II

The camera begins to roll for the next interview scene: "So you made the letterers an integral part of your storytelling package?" "A major comic book house with a bloated bullpen tends to be an assembly line," Eisner nods, "But I made big demands on my letterers. I worked with them, made them part of the storytelling itself. They liked the idea. Nothing really good is done without enthusiasm. All I needed to know was whether they cared. The letterers were people I would not hire unless I knew they were philosophically connected to what I was doing. So there was no question about it. To begin with, these are guys who came into the shop because they wanted to be part of the creative process and wouldn't be there unless they did."

There was no question who had final cut at Tudor City: "In my case, it was a Will Eisner studio, and everything coming out of my shop was material I had to take responsibility for and be identified with. Consequently, the artists who worked for me had to be people I would be willing to be identified with, who identified themselves with me.

"In the earliest Spirit days I did all the writing, penciling, and inking—everything but the lettering. Later on, as I got busier and more involved with other things, I would do the penciling and have the bodies inked. But the heads were always done by me and the writing essentially was done by me. I also handled the creation of characters outside of *The Spirit*. Take Blackhawk, for example, now owned by DC Comics . . . I created it in-shop, usually a rough drawing or blue-pencil, and then would turn it over to somebody in the shop. After Dave Berg took over Blackhawk we hired another freelancer Dick French to script it. After Berg left, Chuck Cuidera took over drawing it. In that particular book, the writing was always freelanced."

I interrupt to ask Eisner about one of the greatest Blackhawk artists ever.

"I didn't have much to do with Reed Crandall. He came in the shop toward the end of my Eisner & Iger tenure and worked there for a while, then I went on, so we didn't have much interaction."

Dave Berg recalls the Crandall tragedy: "Reed had money coming in to him. Bill Gaines was very good about that, he paid royalties. Now to locate him. Well he had to hire detectives to find him so he could pay him. And he said when they found him he was in very bad condition. But he gave him the money. Crandall was so talented."

"Pretty soon," Tex recalls, "Will hired Charley Cuidera to do Blackhawk. We didn't call him Charley, we called him Chuck. But he preferred 'Chops.' Don't ask me why. So when we created Blackhawk as a committee in the office in 1941, with everybody contributing something, there was a Chinese character swiped dead from *Terry and the Pirates*, and Chop-Chop was his name. And Charley . . . Chuck . . . Chops . . . wanted him in there as one of the characters. And Bob Powell created one of the other characters, and so on."

Segue sequence: The lights dim down. Rain thunders through the studio. The background morphs into a starry sky with the Blackhawk plane high overhead.

"Way back in the Eisner & Iger days," Will goes on, "I created Sheena, Queen of the Jungle by making the first drawing. I actually drew and executed the first cover, but the story was turned over to Mort Meskin. That's generally the way I created characters at Tudor City too. In the case of Lou Fine who preferred not to do any writing, I worked up a thumbnail of a character then orchestrated the scripting before Lou took over. You have to keep in mind that the character of the studio in those days was much akin to a woodworking shop system, with the master designer omnipresent. If a problem arose on a page they were working on, we would talk it over or I would come by and say—'Gee, this doesn't read right, why don't you do it another way.' There was a lot of control on my part because, again, I felt responsible for, and would be *identified with* whatever came out of the shop. But there was plenty of industrial training involved. Lou Fine might be doing something and I'd come over and say—'Well maybe you oughtta draw older-looking shoes.' The advantage I had in a shop like that was that my entire staff were salaried. I was not buying freelance—a device I instituted when I started Eisner & Iger on the theory that it would give me total product control. Because then I could say to the artist—'Well, look, I don't like this, do it over, do it another way.' He would be willing to do it because his salary was fixed, unlike a freelancer who loses money if he has to change a page." The artists had the opportunity to work overtime for bonuses as well. "It was practical, but risky, because it made production iffy. If you were looking to get four pages from an artist out in a given week and you asked him to change two or three, he might not make deadline! But we had robust morale, the shop was tightly structured, everybody had a great deal of respect for each other, no animosity. As a matter of fact there was a lot of collegial family warmth there."

Berg concurs: "We often did things together on Saturdays. I remember one time we all drove up to Yale to watch a football game."

I asked Berg if he had any representative photos: "In those days who was messing with photography? I wasn't, or anybody else."

Eisner continues: "The guys would go out to dinner together, they socialized. A good, warm shop."

But the staple interaction were the marathon cross-studio conversations, with the war always in the background like the sucking rumble of a giant wave building. "All very interesting," Berg remembers. "Very intelligent, very talented, with conversation going on all day on a very high level, very *intelligent* conversation. We would go on talking at our drawing tables. Of course the war would be the biggest subject, which was developing in Europe. We still weren't in it, but then it did happen while we were at Tudor City, and then of course suddenly we were in it and the whole bit. The writing was usually done at night (I did my writing the night before) so the conversation could continue uninterrupted. Those long discussions are why I say I've never been with another group like it."

Kubert recalls a shop-wide work ethic: "The impression I have today is that there was a professional attitude, not a lot of kidding around. We got our work done, first and primary. But I remember vividly being able to play handball with Tex downstairs during lunch break, so it wasn't all that rigid. But when we were up there working, we were working."

Tex recalls it as more lighthearted: "We just babbled and made silly jokes and sang the good old songs—typical cartoonist studio, nothing sensible gets done."

"The thing that hung over like a dark cloud," Jaffee feels, "was the looming draft and the war. That was kind of affecting most of us. I think we were all very eager to get our careers going, knowing that we're going to get caught up in the war fever."

"I got there in October," Kotzky recalls, "and then Pearl Harbor came along, so most of the conversation was devoted to how we would beat the Japanese in six months! It didn't quite happen that way but there was a lot of kidding around and joking with one another."

"One of the things that made it work," Eisner feels—"was that I was a player-manager, like in baseball, out there on the field working with them, fellow worker as well as shop owner. It wasn't as though I were a boss sitting in the front office way at the end of the hall, remote. If a problem came up I could sit down at the guy's board and demonstrate exactly what I was talking about with my own drawing. We respected each other. I enjoyed their regard professionally and they enjoyed my regard.

"There was a kind of EC spirit, except my guys were working in-shop. In the case of EC or *MAD*, the artists were all freelancers by then, coming into the shop only to drop off their work, whereas in my shop the work was created while the artists were there, between nine and five every day. Working in the shop, they didn't have the kind of separation as individual freelancers had—an atmosphere distinct from our team feeling. Everybody I ever knew working in the comic business was in it because it became something he'd rather do than anything else. When they started in my shop in the early Eisner & Iger days, the artists regarded the comic field as only a stopover. I was the only one around who regarded it as a lifetime occupation. (Berg will protest: "I had the same idea. Although I did a lot of the adventure stuff, I wanted to be in comics to do 'life stuff' too.") Most of them aspired to the world of illustration, their primary aim. Lou Fine was always dreaming of being an illustrator, and later became one. Chuck Mazoujian went into advertising, illustration—he's a member of The Society of Illustrators now, a portrait painter and a very good one."

"We were all just kids when we started this thing," Joe Simon explains, "It was one of the very few places we could go. Sure, we'd rather have been illustrators, or advertising artists, but when you're twenty years old you're not going to step into a magazine. But you could probably do it in comics. Will was nineteen when he started and had Eisner-Iger by the time he turned twenty!"

"The business was so lively and exciting," Al Jaffee enthuses, "you know, *that was the Golden Age*. And so many top-notch people who could have been illustrators for the *Saturday Evening Post* couldn't get work and went into the comics just to pay the rent. If Norman Rockwell was a young guy at that time he'd be doing comic books! You got fantastic people, I mean Lou Fine was an illustrator of top magnitude—and there he was doing comic books!"

Eisner reflects on the stable's interaction: "Even though I couldn't socialize fully with my artists (I was their age, sure, but I was the shop owner) there was, nevertheless, a good friendly relationship. They would bring their dames up. I remember Chuck Mazoujian brought his wife-to-be up and we had dinner together one evening. The Tudor City studio was used for what we called 'illicit purposes!' Remember, we were all bachelors then—the key was available! I don't remember any difficult times, any anger or professional distance between us. There was always a good deal of respect we enjoyed between us."

Episode wrap: When I found Will for the next shoot he was standing in the Tokyo Rose bar location shot, arms outstretched, being measured for a zoot. P'Gell sat across from Eisner reading her portion of the script, in a froth over not having enough lines. I caught a hint of Coco Chanel and Nile-green eyes. I pulled my eyes away from her creamy ivory décolletage to the bartender working a silverplate Graf Zeppelin cocktail shaker, and back again.

(Camera: Give me a gritty, contrasty B&W film here. Let's get Will to walk slowly through these venetian blind shadows.)

Peter DePree: You saw the panel as analogous to a film frame?

Will Eisner: Not quite the same way. Major influences on me were not only film but live theater. As I grew up through the '30s, I was very interested in theater and stage design. So I saw it as theater, but incorporated film nuance heavily during the early Spirit days and the early comics that I did, largely because I realized that reading was being influenced by film. We tend to be influenced in our comprehension by other media to which we're exposed. MTV today has tremendous impact on the current reading rhythm and acquisition. Lacking the patience for longer, involved works, we want shorter, crisper stories packed with sound-bites. These are the influences. Visual literacy comes from film in modern society."

(Will and Peter walk across a bluescreen backdrop which will later be retouched with a computer-graphic of the old modern and deco picture palaces.)

"I did turn to film a great deal to employ 'camera techniques.' I was very, very impressed with Fritz Lang in those days, a real fan of his films—*Metropolis* and *The Cabinet of Dr. Caligari* were favorites—and I paid a lot of attention to the new photography and imagery films were producing. I wasn't trying to emulate film, I was *employing* the visual language influenced by film. For example, film was using the camera as the reader's eye. Perhaps you'd be looking through a keyhole watching something happening. I frequently used a scene where the reader was looking through his *own* eyes—a story seen entirely through the eyes of the reader. Experimentation is very much a part of the fun, enjoyment, and satisfaction I have in this medium. I'm constantly pushing the envelope.

"I used to pay a lot of attention to the Man Ray surreal, experimental films. And of course I grew up on the Saturday afternoon serials in theaters. These were the years when filmmaking was really growing into maturity. The '30s and early '40s were the grey years of our society, all films and most magazine illustrations were in black-&-white. Everything was black-&-white."

Camera on DePree: It was a time of noirs like *Dark Passage, Nobody Lives Forever, The Big Sleep, Maltese Falcon, Double Indemnity, Hangover Square, The Big Clock, Criss Cross, Fallen Angel* . . . Coinciding with this '40s dark cinema, Will's books acquired a campy angst that arched into high art at times. That gritty German Expressionist lighting, those destabilizing camera angles and moody backdrops were techniques the resourceful Will saw ways to incorporate. And something subtler.

Eisner: "What the film noir provided me with was evidence of the kind of rhythm to them that color obfuscates.

"In communication you always take into account the external influences on your reader and you link with them by these references. Some of the Spirit stories like *Hurricane* reflect a film influence in the staging, but the experimental movement of panels and frames is something totally removed from film. Remember that in film you're unaware of panels; each frame is the same size and same shape and is flashing by you. In comics, each frame/panel has technically a different size and shape which plays a crucial part and meaning in storytelling. A comic book frame impacts on the story's emotional content—a very sophisticated technique that I examined in depth in *Comics & Sequential Art*. The frame does more than simply separate and contain the flow of action. The shape of a frame has an effect on the emotion, rigid frames quite another. A long narrow or oblong frame contributes to a feeling of crowdedness, of being imprisoned, or implies great depth. A vertical frame has a different meaning than the frame that's wide and flat."

DePree: "Steranko once told me that to him a wide, flat frame evokes a sense of calmness and steadiness.'

Eisner: "Yes, because it relates to the natural function of your own vision. For example, the reason that you—a human animal—widen your eyes when you're in terror, is because you want to see as much as possible—by which you can better negotiate your escape routes. A wide frame removes you from direct involvement with the characters, and gives you a bird's-eye view. So the reader becomes an observer from a distance. I agree with Steranko, there's a calming quality there."

DePree: "Like this panel in *Hurricane* of Satin and the Spirit looking out over the ocean sunset—the only panel on the page that is long and flat."

Eisner: "That's right. There's a reason for it. In the '40s I was still experimenting with these ideas. The wonderful thing about working in comics is that on-the-job training process. So I'm constantly probing. I hadn't fully refined these devices, but I knew why I was doing what I was doing.

"I did use a lot of motion-picture references in *Hurricane*.

"In this medium, you have neither sound nor motion. You have to imply motion, availing yourself of whatever visual experience your readers have had relating to motion. This leads one to resort to the visual clichés used in film. Without sound and motion, it becomes a totally different medium.

"I wondered about possible influences from Orson Welles's flavor of baroque noir . . . I was extremely flattered a couple of months ago at a meeting of the California Cartoonists' Professional Society when one of the men there told me that he knew Orson Welles very well, and said Welles had been reading *The Spirit* with fond avidity. And I just ballooned into the ceiling because I admired Orson Welles tremendously, thought he was one of the most experimental filmmakers.

"I was very much aware of Welles in 1940. Whether *Citizen Kane*—a very strong film visually—came out before or after I began *The Spirit*, I can't remember, but I certainly recall being tremendously impressed. Welles used a visual language very, very effectively. Which is what we do in this medium, the visuals being here a form of language. You can safely say that if I wasn't influenced by him, I'd be much surprised! (laughs) The term 'influences' is frequently misused in our business. There's a fine line between imitation and influence—but a big distinction in my mind. Influence is the absorption of concept whereas imitation is mindless copying. We all work on our predecessors' shoulders. It's impossible not to, because the visual impressions and selections you make, what you think is good, are invariably predicted on what you've seen before."

DePree: "Your short stories worked as self-contained units that could have stood on their own, without the focalizing lens of Denny Colt in many cases."

Eisner: "Exactly. That's a very good point, which harks back to how at the inception I was more interested in doing stories than a serial cartoon character. The difference between writing about somebody like The Spirit or about a superhero, is that once you create a superhero his powers are so all-encompassing you're trapped into limited narrative material. Stories built around his remarkable powers tend to be repetitive as you wind up constantly reapplying the same themes to different situations.

DePree: "Steranko notes in his *History of Comics 2* that if the Spirit was injured he would wear a bandage or exhibit a bruise—sometimes for several weeks of strips! When he got socked, it hurt, and he suffered accordingly. It made The Spirit more believable than many of the other characters."

Eisner: "I'm glad you chose that word because I've always begun my stories with the implied plea: 'Believe me.' I'm a storyteller and in telling stories you start with asking for that. I'm constantly reaching for the reader's recognition of reality.

"The Spirit tale that has always been my favorite was *The Story of Gerhard Shnobble* since it represents the first time I allowed myself to go flat out for a 'literary' theme. It epitomized the philosophical statement which I regard as the true distinction between the entertainment story and the story that makes comics literature. The comics form historically was identified with pure entertainment. I believe that the turning point in the history of comics as a literary form occurred in the late '60s in San Francisco in the underground comics. Because there, for the first time, comics were employed as a protest medium in which the authors were making social statements.

"I worked generally on two-ply Bristol board using a Japanese brush, which takes a great deal of skill and finesse because it lacks resilience and won't snap back the way a sable-hair does. There were two reasons why I found them preferable to work with; the main reason was they were *cheap!* The second reason was that very early on I was interested in Oriental art and woodcuts, recognizing in them the forerunner of comics. Look at the early Japanese woodcuts—the Hiroshige prints are a good example—and you'll be struck by the tremendous similarity between them in the line art and so forth. Although the Japanese brush gives you a truly beautiful line, it takes tremendous control. The only other guy in our shop who could master them—outdo me in fact—was Lou Fine."

Kubert recalls this temperamental tool all too well: "I worked with the

Japanese brush and used it for quite some time. That again was one of the things I was able to pick up and learn about while working up there next to those guys, but I could never get the hang of working that brush the way Will did. He was just a whiz with it. The Japanese brush, which the Japanese and Chinese use to write the language, has a very fine point, but the hairs are dead. The brushes we use today have the ability to snap back to a point. If I'd lean on it during a stroke it would stay in that position. It was difficult to get accustomed to, but it was a beautiful tool when the other guys used it."

I asked Will if he used the brushes solely for large black wash areas.

"No, you used them all the way. I used the pen only for backgrounds—chairs, tables, doorways, picture frames, and stuff of that sort. As a matter of fact, the fluidity of that brush . . . the open mouths with the saliva lines so popular in modern comics comes from Lou Fine who employed the Japanese brush that way. It was stumbled upon because the Japanese brush didn't hold ink quite the way sable brushes do. You made the black areas by stroking it in but not all the way, so the ink spread a little differently. Just like the odd-shaped panel; each of these techniques resulted from experimentation."

Kotzky, who today employs a civilized Winsor-Newton #3 on *Apartment 3G*, remembers: "As a matter of fact I used the Japanese brush some of the time too, as did Lou Fine. Today I have some old ones laying around and can't imagine how we used it because there isn't any resiliency in the body of the brush!"

(The following interview scene is shot on a fake beach set. Feiffer, Eisner, and DePree sweat under the halogens. In the background among a cluster of plastic department-store palms, stand silhouettes of the famous Spirit fatales.)

DePree: "Will, you share with Chester Gould the technique of using flamboyant character names."

Eisner: "Gould preceded me. Again, it has to do with influences. I always believed that names somehow take on the characteristics of the personality themselves. And I always felt the way Gould did, that to relate the names to the nature of a character was very important to the creation of the character themselves, like Skinny Bones, or Silk Satin. P'Gell was taken from Place Pigalle, a WWII Paris street packed with prostitutes! The GI's always knew about Place Pigalle and I thought—'Oh great—let's call her P'Gell!' I was especially interested in her because she was so amoral. (Laughter.) Skinny Bones was based on a girl I knew. Silk Satin I liked too, the highly romantic gal. I was always intrigued—not only professionally but personally!—by women who had a competence and identity all their own. I never really thought much of

Ellen—the girl next door. In romance adventures the winning of the "good" girl is dull. But to seduce someone like Silk Satin, or P'Gell is an accomplishment! That's something. That's worth the game."

These Eisner femme fatales were spellbinding to Feiffer: "The Spirit's relationship with women I found fascinating. Will wrote some very strong women characters. Even Ellen Dolan, the girlfriend, was powerful in her own right, very opinionated and strong, which always intrigued me.

"I thought Satin—who became Sand Saref later on—was the most interesting, because she was kind of a cross between Caniff's Burma and the Dragon Lady. She was my favorite. P'Gell I never cared for. But I think Will liked her the best."

Kotzky makes a good point: "Although the police inspector, Commissioner Dolan, was my favorite, they were *all* good. They all harmonized together, which made it a great feature."

Eisner continues: "All my characters are generally based on people I've known or a combination of them. Even the characters I do today are drawn from a combination of several people I've known.

"I start my story with a thumbnail. In the Spirit days, instead of a thumbnail rough, I would work right on the board itself. Generally I would plot by making a laundry list of the script (something I still do to this day), usually starting with the *end* of the story. Knowing what the story's going to end with, the rest of it becomes a problem-solving exercise in which I lead up to that conclusion. So, unlike a lot of writing that I've seen in the years I've been in the business, I don't start off with a doorknob and build a whole house around it—I start off the concept of the house and begin tightening the details. I would rough out the Spirit story on the page, and I always had seven pages so I knew precisely how much space I had to tell the story—and then I would write it down on a sheet of paper and make a numbered list so on each page I knew what I wanted to cover. It works for me. I know a lot of writers who start off with a catchy opening line and then just keep writing until the end. When I work on my graphic novels now, I start with the end in mind but can develop the story until I finish, which may take a hundred pages or more. Lacking that luxury on the weekly seven-page Spirit, I had to preplan each page meticulously beforehand—like taking a bologna and slicing it!"

DePree: "Might that have inadvertently improved these stories by forcing you to approach them as an organic whole and work within a limited space?"

Eisner: "Any discipline or pressure tends to improve what you're doing. I'm a firm believer in deadlines—deadlines tend to force the best out of you. If you have too much time, you tend to get sloppy and do shoddy work. I rarely had patience with the complaint—'Well, I didn't have time to do this.' The best solutions to problems come to you quickly. And in the reasoning process of creating that solution is when you develop wonderful things.

"I never wrote with a standard script, never used a typewriter in all the years I've been working. I write the balloons and do the images almost simultaneously. I believe that the image comes first and the text comes afterwards.

"I would dramatize the action and then hear the text. Text in my stories always—even on *The Spirit*—is a result of the action. The classic procedure is to first write a script. The artist will then take that script and append to it the images that it calls for. I do the reverse: my images evoke the script, I discuss that idea in the new book I'm writing, *Graphic Storytelling*, a textbook follow-up to *Comics & Sequential Art*.

"Even to this day, although some of my graphic novels have been done in wash or color, most of my work centers around black-&-white line, which I prefer. Originally the book *Signal from Space* (since retitled *Life on Another Planet*) was color, but now is being reprinted by Kitchen Sink in black-&-white. It looks a heck of a lot better, is far more readable, and will be even more successful without color."

Kotzky recalls Eisner's devotion to the work: "Will was certainly a hard worker. He would come in on Sunday mornings and work till the night and then he'd have the stuff ready for us to start working on Monday morning. His penciling was semi-rough. He laid in the backgrounds, how he wanted them, and then Tex and I started repenciling the backgrounds and inking. And there usually was quite a bit of background. You would think there wasn't enough to keep us both busy, but there was."

Certainly, what the artists recall as a series of compassionate scenes were punctuated now and again with misunderstanding. Tex recalls how his job in the Eisner/Quality stable mysteriously ended: "Alex Kotzky came in towards the end of my Tudor City tenure, at the end of '41. An unfortunate happenstance occurred which I was unaware of at the time. I noticed that I was sitting there idly, and the work that I had been doing, mostly on *The Spirit*, I noticed that Al was taking over at his drawing board in the kitchen. So I sat there for almost a month not hardly doing anything! Finally, I confronted Bill—'Listen, I don't feel right about taking my pay because I'm not doing anything!' He instantly brightened up and said 'Well, I certainly appreciate your attitude and well . . . alright.' And so we terminated the association at that point."

What had happened emerged much later: "Bob Powell, it turned out, had approached Bill saying he wanted more money. Bill tried to explain to him that he couldn't give him more money because the product wasn't selling appropriately, and of course cost of living went up but his income didn't. Bob had a short fuse (which of course Bill was aware of) but they laid off that subject. Bob was moved to tell him that Bill's fair-haired boy (me) had referred to Bill with an anti-Semetic slur. Which, of course, I had not. That was why his attitude towards me had cooled and why he hired Al Kotzky to replace me without even saying anything to me. Bill was a gentle soul and he invited me to lunch along the way there, and now I realize that what he wanted to do was discuss the situation, but couldn't bring himself to do it. So we just parted with that dark cloud hanging between us and—I didn't even know what it was!

"So I went out freelancing and made a helluva lot more money. Bill was affiliated with Busy Arnold, and Busy didn't think it was a smart idea for Bill to let me escape after spending a year there learning their secrets of production and storytelling. He said 'Send him over here and we'll keep him in the stable.' Busy gave me work at $15 a page, the top rate in the field at the time! But those pages were twelve panels and one was required to write them and draw them and ink them and letter them for that fifteen bucks, which worked out to a little over a dollar per panel. Oh boy! But it was more money than I had ever been paid before. Meanwhile I was doing work for Lloyd Jacquet, a lovely man, at nine dollars per page, writing and drawing comedy material which is my normal bent. He packaged comics for publishing companies like Curtis, *Saturday Evening Post*, and they had this line of comics they were financing, but of course the minute they were able to not bother with it they dropped it, same as Sidney Hillman did when he got *Pageant* magazine selling. Although these guys were ashamed to be affiliated with comics, comics paid their rent! As soon as they could afford to get it somewhere else, they quit. Lloyd had several publishers he produced finished books for, and I was doing an imitation *Li'l Abner* type of thing for him. But it didn't have twelve panels, on a page, only five or six. And it was fun stuff to do so I kept on doing it for nine dollars a page. Combine that with the Busy Arnold work and by the time they came and drafted me, I was making $175 a week! $175 a week in 1942 was a fortune! I never made that much money again until I did *Little Orphan Annie* in '68. Of course once I was succeeding they came and drafted me in 1942 and dragged me off kicking and screaming."

Dave Berg too was just hitting his stride when WWII tripped him up: "The other job Will gave me was *The Death Patrol* after the guy who did that feature went on to other things. I did *Death Patrol* for almost a year. That was completely mine, took over completely—art, scripts, you name it. That too was an instant success and I immediately started getting fanmail. (Which, incidentally, I never actually received because the main office was in Connecticut and we were in Tudor City!) *Death Patrol* was very popular and kept going for years because after I went off to the Army other people took it over. *Death Patrol* made me famous. The man who was doing it ahead of me has since passed away. Of course he then became famous with *Playboy*.

"It started with a group of prisoners who were released so they could fight the Nazis. In each story one of them would get killed and another would replace him. Then Busy Arnold whined—'You get these swell characters and you kill em off! I don't *like* that!' So he insisted I had to bring them back. And I had to write a special story how they all came back!

"But then it was off to the war. I spent a few months with *Captain Marvel* and then went into the Air Force."

SCENE III: PEARL HARBOR

"Then we all go off to war, okay? Then we come back."
—Dave Berg

The first hint of the disintegration of the Tudor City studio came through the mesh of Will's tortoiseshell and red-mahogany radio: "The music I listened to was mostly classical, I've always been a classic fan," Eisner recalls. "As a matter of fact, on the Sunday Pearl Harbor was surprise-attacked, I was in the studio.

The New York Philharmonic Carnegie Hall concert was on and I remember it being interrupted with the announcement that Pearl Harbor was bombed. And I knew that my number would be up very shortly because I was draftable."

Tex recalls the Japanese sneak-attack this way: "I was home in my married apartment six months after my wedding, reading the Sunday comics when we heard it over the radio that morning. I didn't know where the hell Pearl Harbor was anymore than anybody else did. My father, the ex-marine did, and explained to me what that was all about, that the news reports were crap, that what they had done was sink the entire Pacific fleet—which they did not tell the public."

"I was in my father's apartment in the Bronx," Al Jaffee recalls, "when I heard the newsboy shouting over and over downstairs—'Pearl Harbor bombed!' I was twenty."

"My draft board gave me an extra six months," Eisner says, "because I needed to get someone to replace me, giving me a chance to organize the *Spirit*'s continuation. After the six-month deferment, I went into the Army in '42. So I had a year and a half working on the prewar *Spirit*." The war was everywhere, Irving Berlin's *This Is the Army* was just opening on Broadway when Will was inducted.

En masse, there was a mad rush to get all the comic characters covered. Dave Berg remembers the chaos: "Lou Fine was upstairs. The war started and we were all leaving to go into the Army. So Fine, who was lame, was going to take over and I was assigned to write the first *Spirit* for him. And I did, but that particular one didn't get published because he didn't get the characters right. He was an excellent artist but it was a new character he was unfamiliar with. It wasn't until the second script that he got it. So the first one was junked, unfortunately. So Lou continued the *Spirit* while Eisner was in Ordnance."

(Editing: Left behind, lame Lou Fine's light burning late into the night— the Secret Master tucked away in the garret apartment Will rented exclusively to him, would ghost *The Spirit* through the War Years.)

"I was with Eisner at the most six months because then the war started and the whole thing broke up." But for so short a time, in this artificial world of mass-production, Berg was missing Eisner already: "I got my notice and they said I would be going in a certain amount of months, so I took an easy job at Fawcett doing *Captain Marvel* for a few months."

Things seemed good. Well, not horrible anyway. The personal aspects were gone: "They had a mass-production idea because they knew they were going to lose everybody, so they crammed in as much work as possible. The whole three years I was gone, my work kept coming out! I told the GIs in the barracks or tents—'I did that,' and they wouldn't believe me! 'But you're in the Army for three years—how could you have done it?' It looked as if my career was uninterrupted.

"Eisner did posters and pamphlets for Ordnance and I did them for chemical warfare. Only I went overseas. Iwo Jima. I was in that mess."

SCENE IV: "BEST FRIENDS"

Too young to go slug it out with the Japanazis, Kubert got another big break: "I worked with Lou Fine during one of my high school summer stints—just about the time war broke out, '41, '42. Will had gone into the Army and Lou had taken over the strip. And by that time I was kinda improving my work a little bit, enough anyhow to be able to do inking on *The Spirit*, and one of the jobs involved my commuting up to the Stamford, Connecticut satellite office Busy Arnold ran, where Lou and Alex Kotzky were working. *The Spirit* was being done there, and Lou was the guy who did all the penciling. Alex was one of the inkers, and I was the other one. Here I was inking on *The Spirit* (laughs) only a few years after I started out sweeping up the joint!"

His astonishment is reasonable—if the erasing had been monkey work, Kubert was not handling the true finesse stage of the process, usually allocated only to the established pros.

I hit a nerve when I ask Kotzky if he remembers Lou Fine: "How could I forget *Lou Fine*?! Around January of '42, Will hired Lou to do *The Spirit* because Eisner got called for the Army. And they moved the place up to Stamford, Connecticut, Busy Arnold's offices.

"My family lived in NYC but I would go up there and work Monday through Friday and then come home by train, returning Monday morning. I stayed in a family home which rented rooms. I inked *The Spirit* while Lou penciled. We worked together in the same room for a little over a year until I was called into the service. I admired Lou very much. Then Joe Kubert came up to Connecticut with his father around Spring of '42. Although the artists didn't last long enough to form deep friendships in Tudor City (they were constantly being drafted) when we got to Stamford we had a tight group up there: Gill Fox, Jack Cole, Lou Fine, myself, and Aldon McWilliams. Aldon was very good on destroyers, battleships, and nautical things. He went into the service and became a master sergeant."

Kotzky hands me a B&W photo with crinkle-cut edges someone snapped back in the '40s with a Kodak Baby Brownie. It shows him working next to Lou in Stamford.

"I didn't do anything except backgrounds at Tudor studio, but once I went up to Connecticut I freelanced evenings on other comic books like *Manhunter*—on top of the eight-hour days with Lou on *The Spirit*. (I get photostats from readers who remind me of what I had done back then, some of which I don't remember at all!)

"Quality editor Gill Fox was up there and we became good friends and still keep in touch. He was in the same office but then he felt the hot breath of the draft and went to work on a farm hoping to get deferred. But it didn't work out, he went in a month before I did.

"Another guy who sometimes came in and worked in the Stamford office and who lived in Stamford was Jack Cole, *Plastic Man*. Swell cartoonist."

Jaffee agrees: "Cole, who committed suicide, was gifted, one of the top imaginative cartoonists. I admired his work enormously. *Plastic Man* was brilliant, the concept was so exciting, the imagination just fabulous—almost like animation is today where a figure squeezes through a keyhole."

"In Spring of '43, six months before I went into the service, Kotzky continues, they moved Lou Fine and I back to the Lexington Avenue Quality office. They started me doing covers for all the books, because they just didn't have any other artists available, they were all in the service at that time. So for the six months before I went into the service, all I did was covers, five a week! *Plastic Man* and *Blackhawk* and all those features, doing the whole thing myself. I eventually went overseas with the Fourth Infantry Division. I was in England for about a day, then Belgium, Luxembourg, France, and Germany.

"Lou was very warm and friendly and a great friend to me," Kotzky grins sadly. "We would get together often and go bowling up there. Even though Lou had a bum leg and his wife had a very serious heart condition, they would come out with us and even if they didn't bowl they would sit around just to be with us. But since I was so young in comparison to the others, (Cole, Lou, and Fox were all twenty-five, twenty-six—seven years older than me) when they did socialize and ask the wives over, I was too young to be invited! But Lou would have me over for dinner by myself and he was a great friend.

"Stamford was a wonderful city. Just like a small town. In fact we worked across the street from the town hall. There was a little triangle outside, sort of a lush lawn with red picnic tables shaded by ancient oaks. I vividly recall many lunchtime picnics there with Gill Fox, Lou and his wife, Aldon, Jack Cole, and the whole bunch . . . So, quite a group.

"And I remember at Christmas time that was the first year that *I'm Dreaming of a White Christmas* came out, and they played that constantly, all day long on the bells. '42. What an idyllic year for me."

SCENE V: TAILORS' SONS

Meanwhile, with Eisner and Jaffee at the Pentagon, Tex scrunched up in a B-29, and Kubert, Kotzky, and Fine holding down the four-color fort, Davey Berg found himself in a different world entirely: "They sent me to a very special school at Edgewood Arsenal for chem.-warfare. As a sergeant, I was thoroughly trained with the officers. And then after having learned everything, I came back and could write pamphlets and so on. And then, towards the end of '45 my Colonel said—'Well, training's over. Let's fight the war.' And I shipped overseas.

"We were Air Force, a P-47 outfit, and ran the airfields. I was the sergeant in charge of things. Our pilots would take off every day and protect the B-29s which was our main job. Although when the war ended our commanding officer let on that we were only marking time because our real job was the invasion of Japan . . . You would not be talking to me, I would be very dead, cause they were fanatics. The Marines had to kill just about every one of the 21,000 Japanese packed onto the tiny island of Iwo Jima. The only POWs we had were captured wounded. Nobody surrendered. We lost 6000 killed and a lot wounded. I wasn't a Marine so wasn't in such danger as they were, but there was still plenty of sniper fire and aerial bombing. But I felt I did my job. We took the island for the airstrip.

"Towards the end of the war I did have another very interesting assignment. After Iwo Jima was taken, it was pretty safe and becoming civilized and they formed a volunteer newspaper. They began to use me as a war correspondent and I was sent to different places."

I push through the heavy scarlet drapery and find Tex Blaisdell on the studio balcony. I offer him one of the cigars Joe Simon keeps handing out and light it. Through the pungent smoke he drifts back: "Dick French I socialized with because he happened to be my brother-in-law, I married his sister Elaine. While I was out gallivanting, winning the war singlehandedly, she was a chorus girl, a showgirl in a succession of shows, primarily USO. She worked at the Roxy theater as one of the Roxyettes, imitation Rockettes. And at Radio City. She was also in Clifford Fisher's *Folie Bergeres* for a while until it folded."

Since his May '42 induction, Eisner had been doing a variety of features, including *Joe Dope*, at the Pentagon. Jaffee recalls running into him there: "Our war careers crossed. I was brought up to the Pentagon and bumped into Will in one of the coffeeshops and we got to reminiscing together. He was a warrant officer and I was a Sergeant. I had washed out of pilot training and had to be reassigned and the only Air Force MOS they could come up with was that I was sort of a draftsman/artist. They shipped me around in various places doing that kind of thing and then a Dr. Howard Rusk started a convalescent rehab program and needed people to prepare pamphlets and make illustrations of returning problems of soldiers and equipment and therapy so I got the call and was shipped up to the Pentagon. I was there for a couple of years working in the Air Surgeons office assigned to Colonel Rusk who later went on to become very famous creating the Rusk Institute for disabled people and I made posters and did all kind of things there for a couple years."

"While I was doing comic strips at Coast Guard Headquarters in Washington D.C. during the war," Joe Simon fills in, "Will was in the Army doing his comic type of illustration thing. *P*S* (*Preventive Maintenance Monthly*) which he did for years.

"I lived in the former Egyptian Embassy in D.C., which they had converted into a rooming house. I was doing *True Comics*, a weekly Sunday strip syndicated throughout the country, and the deal was that the Coast Guard would allow me to do the strip so long as every third episode was a Coast Guard episode. (The whole thing is a comedy, isn't it!) I was also doing things for DC Comics while in the Coast Guard, and did a whole full-size comic book put out by Street & Smith—*Adventure's My Career*—to draw recruits into the Coast Guard Academy. Street & Smith liked it so much they sold the thing on the newsstands, so we had a million circulation there.

"Will, myself, and Alfred Harvey were all in the public information division. Alfred was a lieutenant in the Pentagon, publishing comic books for the Army. The three of us would go out for drinks occasionally, and Busy Arnold used to come in and take us around the Washington D.C. pubs. But we couldn't keep up bar-hopping with Busy . . . nevertheless, we did the best we could.

"Will was a very nice looking young warrant officer, personable, well built, looked sharp in a uniform." Then Simon recalls something which makes him laugh furiously: "Of the three of us, our fathers were all tailors! And so was Jack Kirby's father!"

"In 1946 I returned," Eisner recalls, "opened a Wall Street studio, then moved uptown to larger offices where I conducted a publishing company."

One of the first orders of business for American Visuals' young CEO was to patch over a festering misunderstanding. "So comes now after the war," Tex recalls with a deep sigh, "there was a telephone message left by Will, my wife told me." It was with a mix of curiosity and trepidation that Tex scooped up the Bakelite butterdish phone: "So I called him, and he explained to me that he had finally discovered that I had never said any such thing so that Bill wanted me to come in with him again at his new studio down on Wall Street. Right after the war, late 1946. He got home two weeks before I did, and it was around Christmas time, and he wanted me to come in there and he was gonna give me a piece of the action and we would set up shop and go. And I said four years I've been taking orders. I wanna stand on my own two 'feets' and be a freelancer. Which is exactly what I did. I didn't take Bill's offer. Which in retrospect I should have. Hindsight is 20/20. And I did all right anyway, but I should have. I would've been better off had I gone back with Bill. But he did say that he had discovered that Bob Powell was the troublemaker and he apologized for . . . whatever, and all that stuff."

The pages Tex eventually freelanced for American Visuals in '46 took Will by surprise. "Bill and I did *Baseball Comics*," Tex recalls, "I drew it and he put faces on the main characters. When I showed him the first page or two of pencils he gushed: 'Jesus Christ, I didn't know you could do this stuff!' The whole time I was working there he didn't realize I could do that kind of work!" (To get a rough measure of Tex's artistic range, one should bear in mind that later in the syndicates he would work on, for example, *Popeye* and *Prince Valiant*—simultaneously.)

I find Davey Berg at the rooftop studio bar working on a bone-dry martini: "I get back from the war," he recalls, "and there's a message for me from Will. Will was dropping *The Spirit* and venturing into another business. And I mean *business*. He was a businessman! And so he brought Jules Feiffer and me over and I would write the stories and then rough-in pencil layouts for him, and Will would finish it. He didn't need much penciling. At *MAD* now I do very tight penciling because they have to check it over, but with Eisner you just gave him stick figures, very rough. And he drew with his brush. Yet another remarkable thing about him."

But Eisner reflects on the brutal tempo of the new schedule: "When I got out of the Army in '46, John Spranger worked for me doing pencils from my roughs. He would do tight pencils and I would ink over them. It worked back and forth—I did whatever I could to deliver under a production schedule that was very tough, and which just got tougher and tougher as I began doing other things. But occasionally I would get all excited and do the whole thing."

Berg marvels as he recalls that energy: "Will opened up the new business doing creations in a variety of fields, for a slew of different accounts. He would buy up businesses and run them, but also handled PR for other companies. And I did some freelance work for him on that. I did a lot of safety things which the government was buying and distributing. He got a lot of good accounts. If you want to know the one big thing about him, here is this fantastic talent as an artist and a writer but he's also a fantastic businessman! I never heard of anything like that! And he was brilliant at it!"

SCENE VI: WALL ST. WHIZ KID?

"I was a groupie"
—Jules Feiffer

One of Will's more valuable postwar acquisitions was a young kid, nobody's idea of a star draftsman or another Lou Fine, but smart: "I was about seventeen years old in '46," Jules Feiffer recalls, "and was looking for work. Although I hadn't worked in comics I was a big Spirit fan. I had some samples, a comic book feature I was working on—*Adam's Atom*—with another fellow who wrote it while I drew it. It was done in a kind of serial comic style—rather badly—and that's what I showed Eisner. I looked him up in the phone book, and he was then on Wall Street in Lower Manhattan (I still remember it—37 Wall Street) and went quite nervously in, and he's sitting in the outer office." Eisner had duplicated the insulating floor plan of Tudor City: "The odd arrangement was that Will sat where the receptionist ordinarily would, in the outer office where he had his drawing table, a rather dark, windowless room, and inside, a larger room than where Will lived, were his staff: letterer Sam Rosen; John Spranger who did some penciling and some inking (he had a wonderful pencil technique, drawing large, clunky, blocky characters. He was terrific at drawing fights. I don't know whatever happened to him.) Dave Berg, and I forget who else was around at the time. Later on he hired Jerry Grandenetti.

"Will thought my samples were terrible, thought I had no talent at all. But I was such an enthusiastic *Spirit* fan and knew so much about Eisner's career he couldn't help but hire me. So I mainly got hired because I was a groupie. The salary was non-existent, absolutely no pay at all for the first few months, then he laid off everybody for the summer. I forget what the circumstance was. After the summer he hired me back for $25 a week—my first cartoonist's salary—to erase pages and black in areas and do a few backgrounds (which I was miserable at) and stuff like that."

With his vast accounts, Will was always on the lookout for promising talent: "Jerry Grandenetti was working as a renderer in an architectural firm in 1947 and came to my shop when I was looking for an assistant to do backgrounds on *The Spirit*. I decided that a guy who could do architectural rendering would make a superb background man. After working in my shop for a while, he began experimenting with figure drawing, gradually developing proficiency at it. His very strong, controlled brush style impressed me. I don't think he had any comic book ambitions until he worked in my shop for a while—there he established himself as a cartoonist. Up until then I don't know whether he had done figure rendering at all, but he began to learn his craft by inking my work. I would pencil and he would ink the bodies."

Feiffer recalls the renderer-turned-comic-artist fondly: "Jerry Grandenetti and I became good friends when he came to work for Eisner. He couldn't draw at all in the beginning. He had studied architecture and draftsmanship and couldn't draw the human figure very well. But through sheer perseverance and will, he taught himself and succeeded brilliantly, doing some beautiful work, and his backgrounds were quite wonderful too."

Eisner: "Some could ink in the style I wanted and some couldn't. I don't remember who my favorite inkers were but Grandenetti was especially proficient, I always trusted him."

"The only thing done out of that shop was Will's material," Feiffer continues, "the other Spirit Section features were done by artists in their own studios. And then later on, '47 or '48, Eisner started putting out magazines like *The Kewpies* and *Baseball Comics* that I was involved with."

I ask Will if he wrote *Hurricane*, one of my favorite *Spirit* episodes, which leads him to consider the merging of his storytelling with Feiffer's: "Jules was beginning to write *Spirit* stories for me. He first came to my shop as a studio assistant, then began to write balloons, progressing later to scripting full stories. But (laughing) one of the interesting things is that we've lost track of which stories each of us wrote. So we don't always agree. But he remains a very good friend and we stay in close touch. This is understandable because we were very closely involved, and frequently I would tell him the basic story idea, and he would go ahead and script it. We reached a point where we were so attuned we could integrate our writing. So, in the case of *Hurricane*, I'm pretty sure I wrote that story . . . but only 'pretty sure.'"

Feiffer remembers: "We both would come up with stories. Some would be my idea, some his. This came about because after working at this job for a while I used to complain to him that I didn't think *The Spirit* stories were nearly as good as during prewar years. I thought he was a better writer and the stories from '39 and '40 were better told and more interesting. (Amazing the stuff I was able to say to him and not get fired—apparently I had a lot of nerve!)

"One time he got so angry he said—'If you think you can write a better story go ahead and write one.' So I did. And to his credit he thought it was very good, and from that point on I was the house writer (for no increase in pay at all) and just thrilled to get the job. I would lay the stories and dialogue out on scraps of paper and show them to Eisner and we'd go through them and then I'd lay them out on the page and he would change them and rewrite.

"I learned structure from radio dramas of the time, which don't exist anymore, shows like *Suspense*, a half-hour weekly drama that was a strong influence on my writing.

"I didn't do any of the drawing. You have to understand that my technique for doing this sort of work was seriously inadequate. However hard I tried I never developed the kind of brush line necessary to be in the comic book profession. Whatever my ambitions were, I just wasn't able to do that kind of work. I didn't have the line for it, didn't have the mind for it. The writing came much more easily and I could have fun with it, which set me off and running.

"Whether I lived up to my own pretentions, I have no idea. I know Will was impressed, and that I loved doing it, and it also taught me a lot about my craft that I was able to apply in later years to my own work."

Dave Berg, for one, recognized the unusually incisive brilliance of his acerbic coworker: "I remember telling my wife—'Feiffer's a genius if he ever gets a break.' Well, of course it turned out to be true. I somehow thought he would never get that break, but he got it. And he hit some great heights."

Like the pre-WWII Tudor City bullpen, Feiffer's stint was interrupted by a war: "I got drafted out of the job in 1951. But actually through my first months during basic training I was writing *The Spirit in Outer Space* ('Mission . . . The Moon'/'Heat on the Moon'/'Rescue', 1952) for Wally Wood."

Although the Eisner/Feiffer/Wood outer space *Spirit* teamup ranks as a fan favorite, Feiffer felt it interrupted the strip's characteristic line: "I've never understood Wood's work, never was a fan of it. It always seemed to me heavy-handed and wooden. He swiped techniques from Alex Raymond and others and heavied them up. I just never thought he was a very good artist. I didn't like that style, preferring Eisner's looseness, fluidity of line and movement."

Eisner's artwork, indeed, was as billowy as a zoot-suit, with snap-seamed holding lines. I asked Feiffer if he thought the Japanese brush contributed to that fluidity. "No, I think it's just his state of mind. He has it to this day if you see his work."

Berg sheds light on Wally Wood's subsequent tragedy: "Woody was a sad story. He had a lot of troubles he suffered from, severe headaches. He started to fall behind in his work, and for one year I ghosted his comics at *MAD*. I've kept that secret for a long time. But then while we were on a *MAD* trip to the Virgin Islands he told everybody off. I said—'Well I'm not gonna help you anymore.' And without my helping him he couldn't do it and so eventually they had to fire him. And people were saying I got him fired. Yes I did, but not for the reasons they think! It's because I refused to help him anymore. They think I went up to Bill Gaines and said—'Fire the man!' I didn't do that.

"But still you could never forget the Nazi things he said they were so terrible.

"Nobody at *MAD* knew it until he died. Then I said—'Okay, now I can tell you. I ghosted his work.' Though I penciled it, he did the finishing, and that's why they couldn't tell. It was still his style. Everybody used to tease his wife for coming up to the *MAD* office with him . . . But she was coming up there to keep him from drinking! And then little by little I began to find out the whole story. She's still active last I heard, a colorist in the comic book business. Tatjana."

Feiffer continues: "I was the only writer. Marilyn Mercer, Will's secretary, actually did some script work in the early years, but no one else did any writing after I began working on *The Spirit*.

"I socialized to some extent. Mercer and I became good friends, and used to see each other and have lunch. She was the first person who introduced me to the writers at the *New York Times*, and she brought me into the world of journalism, media, and reportage that I didn't know anything about.

"Jerry Grandenetti and I saw a little of each other and hung out a bit, and he too was from the Bronx. But mostly I saw Abe Kanegson, who became my closest friend in the office and my mentor. Abe did lettering and backgrounds. He lived a few blocks from me in the Bronx and we used to see a lot of each other. He was four or five years older and it was always an older brother/younger brother relationship, never co-equals.

"I wrote *Rube Rooky of the Major Leagues*, and had the back page which Eisner gave me as a reward for my labors. It was my first experiment with my own strip, a single-page gag about a kid which tried to deal with kids' life, more or less realistically, as I knew it in the Bronx. It built up some small following, coming out a year or two before *Peanuts*, and in a somewhat similar mode."

I asked Feiffer if he thought Charles Schulz may have taken something from that as the basis for *Peanuts*.

"It's hard to tell. But whether he did or didn't, what he did was carried so much further than I was capable of that it hardly matters."

Feiffer remains in awe of Will's work: "First of all, the high intensity, the belief and credibility of the characters—with each other and within themselves—was unparalleled in comic strips except for *Terry and the Pirates*. Caniff and Will were the two best storytellers in comic history. No one told stories better than those two. It was that storytelling which interested me, and what we later learned to call the film noir style of *The Spirit*: the realistic settings, the use of sounds like dripping faucets, the flying newspapers in the street, which seemed to me such a realistic view of the city that I grew up in: the grittiness of it, the lowclassness of it, the lower depth feeling about it. Look, there's nothing middleclass about *The Spirit*! But it had for me a rather glamorous feel.

"One script I wrote which was very personal to me concerned sound. 'It will take you seven minutes to read this story, and in that seven minutes somebody will die.' I wrote the script in real time. As you read the story from beginning to end it takes that exact amount of time in the life of the characters. It was fun, a challenge. And then there was a story about a man going blind which I wrote and Eisner contributed to (or maybe he wrote and I contributed to—I forget the exact genesis) but that was a lot of fun. The Fables that he wrote at Christmas or at Halloween and the satires, when he opted for humor, were of great interest to me."

I ask Feiffer about the same favorite *Spirit* episode I asked Will about: "My memory is that I wrote *Hurricane*. But Will's right, it's hard to say because we worked so closely together. And whether I wrote a story or not, I was writing—or trying to write—quite deliberately in his style rather than mine. Even when I came up with a story, I was coming up with what I thought was an Eisner script. When I finally began my work, it wasn't *at all* like *The Spirit*.

"From that day to this, I never knew what's going to happen. When I'm writing *now* I don't know what's going to happen until five or fifteen minutes ahead of time. I make notes in my work of what I would *like* to happen, but it often veers away. I relish the spontaneity."

Around the time Feiffer was drafted to Korea, Davey Berg recalls a moment that may or may not have signaled, to paraphrase Hemingway, The End of Something. "I didn't like my position as a Marvel editor because I wasn't creative but judging other people's work. I was very unhappy in that job and didn't want it, didn't ask for it, Stan Lee decided I should be an editor.

"The last thing I did with Stan was *Combat Kelly*, about the Korean war. I was able to switch from serious to lighthearted to the real cartoony. Stan and I got to be very close friends and he took me aside one day and said—'We've over-produced, we're going to have to close down for a while. Look to jump elsewhere.' And I immediately went to *MAD* and that was it. But the fact that he only gave *me* the tip. And they did close down for some months.

"I'm the only one from Tudor City who stayed in, who continued, and the rest went off into other fields. Chuck Cuidera became a high-ranking officer. I saw him for the last time when the Korean war started, ran into him at Grand Central by accident." The half-Italian, half Jewish *Blackhawk* artist looked sallow in the faint subway light. Their voices rose through the cavernous immensity of Grand Central's Concourse. "Chuck says—'Well, uhm, they called me back and I might as well make it my career.'"

"He was very high up, I think he was a colonel. He gave it all up and became a professional soldier. It's amazing that with all the really top talent they had I think I'm the only one that stayed with it."

"Actually," I tell Berg, accepting another round of martinis from the drifting studio waitress (a Sand Saref lookalike stand-in) "just the reverse may be true. Kubert runs a thriving school for comic artists in Dover. Tex teaches there. Feiffer, of course, is still an incredibly productive (not to mention successful) cartoonist. Kotzky reaches millions with *Apartment 3G*. Your buddy Jaffee *still* draws for *MAD*. Joe Simon is collaborating on a Captain America poster with the Hildebrandt Brothers."

Joe Simon overhears and laughs over the film crew hubbub: "Why quit? It doesn't require a lot of heavy lifting!"

And Will?

Animation Sequence: Let's do this epilogue in Eisner's impressionistic style. Tenement background. CLOSE ANGLE ON WILL: "I work alone now pretty much, writing and drawing myself. I do my own lettering now, which I never did in my *Spirit* days. And I still have this abiding belief that this medium is capable of far more than just adventure and entertainment. In fact, it's happening now. I feel very, very vindicated in my early judgment."

After Tudor City, long after, Will still experiments, creates, stage manages: "Lately I've been working on graphic novels. This last year I completed *Dropsie Avenue: The Neighborhood* and am wrapping up on *Graphic Storytelling* and then I'll probably start on another graphic novel. Meanwhile *Graphic Storytelling*, which hopefully comes out Spring of '96, is all ready to go now. It will probably be published by my company Poorhouse Press, which publishes *Comics & Sequential Art*, and distributed to comic stores by Kitchen Sink Press."

"I haven't seen Will in a number of years," Berg laments. "The last time was at a dinner. He got up and spoke and singled me out to the audience, saying it was people like Davey Berg who set the pattern for what all the comic books are doing today, giving me credit for being an innovator and setting patterns which haven't changed since."

And much of that credit, Berg feels, goes to Will, who had an unerring instinct for where the rich veins of potential lay in his artists: "'Your real talent is in writing,' Will goes, and I didn't pay attention to it. I had no desire. It was a nice hobby, but I wanted to be an artist. Will says I was a writer, and it certainly turned out that they used me more as a writer. And here I am studying all those years to be an artist! There was a shortage of good writers. There still is, the whole thing is in the writing, and it's hard to get. Even with *MAD* it's very hard to get good writers. Of course the switch to *MAD* is a whole different thinking, it isn't comic books anymore. I really found myself at *MAD*. Everything I had done prior to that seems to go into it, a training ground. And now I was a commentator, and still am today. Although it's done with humor, there's a lot of thought that goes in behind it. I start off with a big idea, whittling it down to the bare essentials. In the '60s, there was a lot more writing in my thing. Now they've decided they want big pictures, so instead of four panels they say—'Do two panels.' So I can't write as heavy anymore. Everybody says they liked them more when there was more writing. Unfortunately we have people over us who say—'Now we want a big picture.' So, I enjoy the *drawing* of it, but feel hampered in the writing. I can't say everything I want to say. They are now selling my original artwork. The '60s and '70s *MAD* material, that twenty-year period—now that's valuable. They're going for pretty good money.

"My wife played this part: she researched. I would tell her a month ahead what subject it's gonna be, and she would go to textbooks and so on and get me all the information, which I had honed into story form with a punch line. Everybody says—'How do you know so much?' *I don't!* My wife looks it up! So that was a very good method. She loved doing it too, she misses it."

Kotzky and I discuss Lou Fine. "I talked to Lou a few times in the '60s by phone. I would sometimes run into him coming out of his New York office, but we never really got together after that. He was doing a lot of advertising, in fact he would do as many as three of those third-page ads you see in the Sunday comics per week—a very good percentage. But later when television really took over, not only did he suffer but Johnstone & Cushing, a big outfit with many different artists working for them, just about went out of business. Television really messed everybody up."

Tex and I are admiring a piece of Lou Fine twice-up original artwork, a *Black Condor* cover. Tex traces the delicate feathering with a fingertip: "Twenty, thirty years later I saw a photograph of him, you know? standing on his own without crutches. And I don't know whether they figured out a way to put braces on him so he could function without the crutches, or what. But he seemed to be maneuvering around . . .

"If I hear one of the songs," he says more quietly, "that's a time machine. You hear one of the old songs, it jerks you back to that time, to Tudor City."

Joe Simon reflects back on Eisner's opus: "Will's artwork, much as my own artwork, has changed with the years according to who's working with him. Bob Powell was the same way. Will Eisner by himself—I loved his artwork, extremely creative." Simon feels nobody could set up a shot like comics' noir director: "I still remember his three dimensional logos which were masterpieces in themselves. I loved his work! Jack liked Will Eisner too."

"Will did just one style," Kotzky notes, "but what he did was very good. And his creative imagination in the writing field was marvelous. Somebody who established his own style and then led the way for all the others . . . Will Eisner."

Feiffer considers how Eisner's current work has seasoned into impressionism: "We've both gone our separate ways, but I think the sort of thing he's doing with *A Contract with God* and *Dropsie Avenue*—how he has evolved that storytelling aspect—is just wonderful. By the time I had left, the Spirit was mainly a walk-on character who would come in and tidy up the drama, which was almost always about other people in other situations. Now Will has taken those ancillary characters and subplots and socked them squarely in the foreground, and does it beautifully. The autobiographical aspects of the work especially intrigue me.

"Eisner belongs to a generation of rather witty cartoonists, something that seems to have vanished entirely. We now have comics on steroids: essentially humorless, very ostentatious, and they take themselves on so seriously. Frank Miller's stuff—as skillful an artist as he is—is wildly pretentious, and, because of that, funnier than he realizes.

"Often when you're a kid and go to work for somebody, admire someone, the years will put that person into a different perspective, you'll see them differently or think that the work really wasn't that great in the first place. Eisner is just the reverse of that.

"When I think back upon the creative work he did, I find it still way in advance of much that's going on today. Remarkable." Feiffer thinks back on the Jewish artist who delighted in creating Xmas fables, the protean creator who dreamed of P'Gell and Sand Saref, Skinny Bones and Sheena, Ebony White and the Blackhawks . . . "And simply in terms of our relationship and personal contact, it's been one of the great pleasures of my working life." His last three words are hushed: "I cherish it."

So does Kubert: "The main focus of what we do in this business is storytelling, and Will is the storyteller supreme!

"When he was teaching regularly at the art school at one of the better colleges in New York, Will often asked me to come and lecture his class, which I was more than happy to do, and he has come here to my school to address the students as well. It's been that kind of friendship. This is a relationship that started when I was eleven years old, and I'm a couple of years older than that now and it still maintains itself. I feel pretty much the same way about the guy. He's been terrific."

Dave Berg was the last to leave, he grabbed my arm: "When you speak to Eisner again, write this down, say to him, 'may your name be inscribed in the Book of Life.'"

Berg grinned at my curious look: "Will's not a religious man, but he'll understand it." Then as the elevator doors were closing he added, almost as an
afterthought: "I always looked at him as a big brother."

Notes to Story Department: With the crews gone, the giant crane cameras
and elaborate sets broken down, the roof of the skyscraper is bare now—
only a few loops of clipped celluloid, some sawdust, the foil wrapper from a
bacon cheeseburger. I pull out my small spiral notepad and begin laboriously
to write: Dramatist, businessman, filmist, by twenty-two a crusty, wise old
studio director, copiously wealthy at the tail-end of the Depression, wandering the predawn alleys and docks of Manhattan, Will was the man we found
behind the domino mask.

That's the one version.

A more acceptable approximation of the truth comes from an understanding that half the life was lived creating the characters, the other—some say
better—half spent sharing that character's adventures with his team of
artists.

That may be melodramatic or it may not. What matters here is that Will orchestrated as many real life characters as fictive ones (he gave Kubert, Feiffer,
and Berg their first art jobs, after all, and most of the rest of the bullpen their
first art jobs that really mattered.)

Enduring his enlightenment and awestruck by the speed of his successive
creative ideas, the Tudor City crew found themselves as artists through a man
who could see beyond a primitive portfolio into the gut of the artist instead:
All I really needed to know, Will said, was whether they cared.

Will Eisner's Vision and the Future of Comics

R. C. HARVEY / 1998

From *Cartoonist Profiles* No. 132 (December 2001), 48–54. Reprinted by permission of R. C. Harvey.

In 1978, Will Eisner published a hardback book of short stories told in the comics medium. The stories were set in the 1930s tenements of the Bronx where Eisner grew up, and Eisner had been mulling over this material for at least twenty years. Entitled *A Contract with God*, the book was Eisner's first work in fiction since leaving the world of newspaper comics in 1952 in order to concentrate on producing instructional comics. Since 1978, he has created thirteen similar works, the most recent entitled *Family Matter*.

The stories in *Contract* are about ordinary people confronting certain events in their lives—sometimes everyday events, sometimes unusual (even shattering) events. "In telling these stories," Eisner wrote, "I set aside two basic working constrictions that so often inhibit this medium—space and format." In other words, he imposed no length limitation upon his storytelling; and he permitted the needs of the story to dictate the page layout (number and size and arrangement of the panels).

Eisner called *Contract* a "graphic novel," a term that subsequently caught on. Comics in this format—long narratives in a single publication—ushered in a new era for cartoonists, and with that, a host of prospects and problems.

Eisner had believed in the literary merit of the comics medium since entering the field in 1936, but comic books have traditionally been aimed at a juvenile audience, and that history constitutes one of the chief obstacles to the development of the medium. We talked about this and other matters one day in February 1998 in Eisner's office in Tamarac, Florida. The conversation went like this:

Eisner: It's hard to get into an accepted status. I'm struggling with that right now with this new book, *Family Matter*, which is really aimed at an adult audience. All my books are always aimed at an adult audience. Big joke in the industry is that Will Eisner draws comics for people who don't read comics. [Chuckles] I'm coming to the reluctant conclusion that there is a stout wall of prejudice out there among adult readers against anything with dialogue that's encapsulated within a speech balloon. It makes the book suspect and translates it into a totally different category. If there's a balloon, it's comics; and if it's comics, it's for kids or idiots—or it's supposed to make you laugh. And therefore I can't take this book seriously. I don't know what we can do about it. Jules Feiffer solved the problem by having no balloons—just words alongside heads; and that seems to make it more acceptable to an adult audience. I have a feeling that if he put balloons around that dialogue, he might have some resistance. It wouldn't diminish the quality of what he's saying, but he would lose some of the acceptance by the audience.

Harvey: You mentioned that once before. And I remembered later the first time I saw Feiffer's cartoon—I was in college at the time—in the *Village Voice*. And I remembered thinking, This is different. There's something—it looks like a cartoon, but it's not quite a cartoon. So I think you might very well be right.

Eisner: I've got another thing on the boards that I'm working on. A collection of memories of real incidents that happened to me on one of my field trips to Vietnam when I was doing *P*S* magazine. And I did this with no balloons. Just words floating next to speaker's heads. It's a story in which the principal character is talking to the reader, the reader being a participant—a sort of eye witness—in the action. I don't know whether that'll help or not. And it's a limited solution. It only works on material where all the dialogue comes from one person; I don't know how you could eliminate the use of the balloons in other situations. I'm a purist about the medium itself, and I just can't see breaking away from the balloon. The balloon itself—the shape of the balloon, and the outlines of the balloon—has a storytelling capacity to it. So I'm afraid what's going to happen is that the audience is going to have to turn itself around and accommodate itself to me! [Chuckles.]

Harvey: You have alluded a couple of times to the need for better content in comics. Could you elaborate on what you mean by content?

Eisner: The comic book medium is no longer a novel medium. Comic books have been around as comic books for sixty years, and it's no longer enough for the medium to simply demonstrate high action, terrific artwork, and characters flashing all over the place. There has to be content, or story. Comic books have to tell something. I equate it with typeset. If you get a book, and you set it in Old English type—or some very unusual type style—it's not enough to sell the book. You have to say something with it. To me, comics is somewhat like typeset: it's a language, and it's always been a language. The art within that language is an art form. It's sequential art, which consists of pictures arranged in a sequence to tell a story. That's the core of the medium. But it is nevertheless a storytelling or message or communication device, and consequently the survival of this medium will be based upon the content—the message.

Harvey: And the content has to be something more than superheroes can't achieve the illusion of reality except in the comics medium. You can see them in movies, but you know there's a trick. Special effects. But when you see them in comics, it's not a trick. This is the way they are on the page—they fly, and they do all these feats of strength. It's endemic to the form almost.

Eisner: The reason for it is that comics is a participatory medium. The reader is participating. In film, he's a spectator. You're just watching it. In comics, you invest the action with your imagination. If you have five people sitting in a room reading the same comic book, I'll guarantee you that each of these five readers are hearing a different soul, if you will—and we believe what the character is doing because they are imagining it as they are doing it. If you're showing Superman leaping off a tall building jumping across a huge chasm or his eyes blazing a hole through a brick wall, you see that in your mind—you close your eyes and you see it, and you feel it. And film has to devise special effects. One of the reasons films have turned to comics as a source of material is because the technology of film has become sophisticated enough now that they're able to do in real form the kinds of things that comics have always done. So that's a big difference.

Another reason for the success of movies about Superman and Batman is that the characters are pure circus. All the movie had to do was do a circus character—the thing that Barnum and Bailey used to do. As a matter of fact, here's some trivia for you: Superman's costume comes from the circus. The strong man in the early circuses had that costume. They came on with a skintight suit and shorts and a cape.

Harvey: Ahhh—and the strong man had the cape, too! And of course they wore the skin tight thing because—

Eisner: Showed their muscles.

Harvey: Getting back to content, one of the ways that content might be different is to have different subject matter. When I was a kid, you could get comic books that were detective stories, westerns, romance—there was a range of genre. Is that part of what you mean by content?

Eisner: Only part of it. Because we're talking about genre, which is kind of easy to do. You take a superhero and put a cowboy costume on him, you've changed the genre, and all the bad guys are in different costumes, too. *Star Wars* is nothing more than a western with aliens as the bad guys. What I mean is something deeper than that. I mean that the story has to have intellectual content; it has to touch on something that the reader wants to hear and understand. I guess the best example I can give you is the short story of the thirties—stories by Ring Lardner and O. Henry. I grew up on them, and they influenced me. They were telling stories with human interaction. That's the difference.

Harvey: I've seen a number of comic books in the last ten–fifteen years where obviously the person producing this book felt that if he told a story in which sex figured importantly, that this was a mature theme. And I've always objected to that—really, a trivialization of the idea of what maturity is. There's a whole lot more to maturity than that.

Eisner: Absolutely.

Harvey: And the stories that you do are stories that have content and have a mature theme because they're dealing with the human condition in some way.

Eisner: That's exactly what I'm talking about.

Harvey: So many of the people who are producing this stuff haven't lived outside comics very much.

Eisner: You bring up a very important point. What we're dealing with is life experience. Now, the reason I don't attract the fourteen-, fifteen-, sixteen-, seventeen-year old reader is because in my stories, I'm talking about heartbreak. And heartbreak to a seventeen-year-old is a lot different than heartbreak is to a forty- or fifty-year old. Teenagers haven't had the life experience; they haven't been able to feel the things that I expect a reader to feel.

Harvey: And when a mature person has a heartbreaking experience, it's his life that's affected, not just his romance with the prom queen. Those are dilemmas for the adolescent mind, and they're real enough, but they don't run deep.

Eisner: Oh, they feel pain. But you don't learn much from an adolescent predicament. I talk about the Hernandez brothers [who produce comics about life in the barrios of Los Angeles]: they're giving you a slice of life inside another culture, which I can learn something from. That's very important. But the superhero stories—the cowboy stories—these are not real things. I don't learn anything from them. As a reader, I want to see something that can give me some life experience.

Now, my *A Contract with God* has held on over the years. My readers are mostly adults. Since 1974, I've reasoned that all the people who started reading comics twenty years earlier are now thirty-five or forty years old, and I asked myself, Would they continue reading Superman and Batman? Would there be enough for them? Would the stories be satisfactory? I've been gambling that these readers, raised on comics, would probably still enjoy reading comics, still enjoy the medium, if they told a different kind of story, a story about the kinds of things a forty- or fifty-year-old person would be interested in. I was partly right because *A Contract with God* is still selling. The thing that keeps me going is the fact that people say, I got your book and I love it, and I read it two or three times over the last few years. And that's great. That book's doing what I want.

Harvey: There's been a lot of handwringing recently about the terrible condition of the industry. But it's the market situation everyone's concerned about—not the quality of the product so much. And I don't think that comic book publishers—particularly the smaller houses—devote enough imagination and energy to how their books are marketed. They produce material that's going to be sold in bookstores in "graphic novel" sections that are really like little ghettos of comic art. Instead, they ought to aim at sections of the bookstore with books of similar content. If you had a science fiction graphic novel, it would go into the science fiction section—not the graphic novel section, not the "humor" section either, where so much comic art winds up.

Eisner: You've got a good idea, but let me tell you a story about that, a true story. *A Contract with God* was first published back in 1978 by a small publishing company, and the publisher called me up, and said, I've got great news for you—Brentano's in New York, big establishment bookstore on Fifth Avenue, is taking copies of your book, and they're carrying it in the bookstore. It's like someone calling and saying the Vatican is publishing your book! So I contained myself for a week, and a week later, I ran up to Brentano's on Fifth Avenue, and I found the store manager, and I said to him, I am the author of *A Contract with God*, and he said, Oh, yeah—I had that two weeks ago; did very well. I said, Where is it?

And he said, I had it on the table in front of the store, and it sold very well, and then James Michener wrote a book, and so I had to take yours off the table and put James Michener's book there.

And I said, What did you do with mine? Well, he said, I brought it inside, and I put it in with religious books since it's about God, and, he says, this little lady came up to me and said, What's that book doing there? That's a cartoon book; it shouldn't be in with religious books. So I took it out and I put it into a humor section where they have people like Stan Lee and so forth. And someone came to me and said, Hey, this isn't a funny book; there's nothing funny in this book—why do you have it here? I took it out of there, and I didn't know where to put it.

And I said, Where do you have it now? And he said, In a cardboard box in the cellar; I don't know where to put the damn thing.

Harvey: Oh, no.

Eisner: And that's the story. As a matter of fact, I understand that even *Maus* had similar kinds of problems. They displayed it on the counter in the front of the bookstore when it first came out, but I don't know where they keep it now. They have it in the bookstore; it was a bestseller so they have it well displayed. The problem is that the major bookstores have no categories for comics. They picked up this word I invented, graphic novel, which everybody uses, and they have a section—they put a spinner in, Walden did, and they load it with graphic novels.

Part of the problem is that a lot of the so-called graphic novels that are turned out now are counterproductive. Physically, they don't look like serious stuff. When we get one of the major houses doing a collection of old Superman stories and calling it a graphic novel, it doesn't look like the other graphic novels. It looks like a big, fat comic book. And then you get some of this violent superhero stuff that some of the young people are turning out today—these metallic ladies and so on [laughs]—

Harvey: You think if you touch them, they'd click.

Eisner: Oh, sure, sure! And they're always drawn in pseudo-seductive poses. I call them "pseudo-seductive" because I can't imagine being aroused by a girl like that just because she's got a skimpy costume and iron breasts. [They both laugh.] Anyhow, the bookstores just don't know what to do with them. Not right now. But they will figure something out. What's going to happen is that they're going to begin to discriminate among the media, among this media, in terms of the various comic books that are worth keeping in a section called "graphic novels," and then it'll come about. It'll take some time, but it'll come about. It has to come about. There's no other way for it to go. Comic books do sell. They produce income.

And Walden and Dalton and Barnes and Noble and Borders and the rest of them can't ignore this for long. They've got to capture that market.

The problem is not comics. Comics are doing fine. It's the market that's doing badly. Lots of good stuff around. Good artists working in the field. There's nothing wrong with the medium.

Harvey: No. And I've said as much myself. This could be the beginning of a new golden age for the medium. But the market is the problem. And marketing, which ought to be the solution, isn't homing in on the special audiences that might be interested in the books if they knew about them. My contention is that every book deserves specific market research in order to find its audience. I realize that small publishers don't have the resources for this kind of thing.

Eisner: I'm a publisher and I can respond to that and tell you that it's very hard for publishers to market a book that way. They have to put out anywhere from $10,000 to $20,000 to $50,000 to get a promotional program going. Is a publisher going to do that when he doubts in his mind that he'll sell 50,000 copies of the book? Now Random House might do a better job. They have a lot of machinery that's calculated to do this sort of thing.

Harvey: But as you say, capitalism creates a powerful will.

Eisner: Right. If there's profit in it, somebody's going to figure out how to do it. And I think there will be a profit in it. As I said, I'm betting on the fact that everybody under the age of fifty grew up on comics as a sort of literary nutrition and still would enjoy reading comics if they could find something of real interest for mature readers in comics.

Harvey: Most of them still do read comics—the funny pages of the daily newspaper! So we know the interest is there. I've thought too about the nurturing of a future audience, and I think that as a rule, the comic book industry is not doing that with sufficient enthusiasm. In the early seventies, there was a great demand on the part of a fairly vital fan readership for more mature comics, comics that were not just pablum for eight-year-olds, and I think the current "grim and gritty" superhero trend emerged in response to that demand. But what about young kids? The tie between Saturday morning television and the comic book stand is not as strong as I think it ought to be. Some company ought to invest in their future by investing in that audience so that those kids get in the habit of looking for comic books.

Eisner: They're trying to do that now. They're becoming aware of it, turning out *Looney Tunes* and comic books of that kind. The problem is that the marketplace for comics has changed over the years. The corner newsstand is no longer there. We get our daily newspaper delivered. And so we don't go to a newsstand where we might find other things of interest—comics, for example. That's one thing.

The second thing is that even in supermarkets, where a lot of comic books are on racks today—kids don't go there. And there isn't the selection there even if they did. A third factor is that the price is too high. You're dealing with three dollars for a thirty-two-page newsprint color magazine that has a lot of advertising in it. DC runs four or five pages of advertising. So every story is interrupted with a commercial every few pages. The little kid that used to get a copy of *Mickey Mouse Comics*, a kids' book, no longer gets that. First of all, he hasn't got the money; secondly, he'd rather watch games on his computer at night.

Another thing that's happening is that parents are buying these books and giving them to the kids. Consequently, you have to get the approval of the parent for a comic book. The parent reads it and says, Yes, I like this book, and my kid's going to like this. It's a decision made by a parent. So these things are changing, and I don't know whether we'll ever get back to the ten-cent comic book, but that was the engine that drove the early comics—the Golden Age and the Silver Age. You could buy a comic book for ten, twelve, twenty-five cents. But today, it's a costly venture to buy a comic.

And here's another factor. The method of distribution. Comic book stores take in their stock on a non-return basis. Whatever they order from a publisher, they have to keep. They keep it as back issues, and there's a market for back issues now, so it works. Newsstands have 100 percent return privilege. Makes a totally different market situation. Even Barnes and Noble gets its books on a fully returnable basis. This means that the publisher publishing in a returnable market is faced with a much greater gamble, greater risk, than the guy publishing in the comic book market. What does that do? The publisher publishing to a high risk market tends to select properties that have as little risk to them as possible. So if you come along with your book with a collection of great cartoons from the 1920s, the publisher that's publishing for the Borders market says, Well, this is going to be of interest to a very limited audience; maybe I'll take this book on, and I'll print 5,000 or 10,000 copies.

And he's very nervous about it. The publisher in the comic book market does a preliminary promotion on the book, sends out a leaflet to all the comic book stores, and Diamond, the distributor, takes orders. And before the publisher goes to press, he knows how many orders he has, and consequently he can do a relatively low print run because he needs to have only enough copies to fill the orders. So he can take on new and different properties because they aren't as risky for him. Big difference.

Harvey: The direct sale (non-returnable) comic book store was a big plus for the whole industry.
Eisner: Exactly. It still is. It's my contention that if the return privilege gets back and dominates this market, you'll have a drop in creativity the likes of which you've never seen. Right now, it's fairly easy—a better than fifty-fifty chance that some publisher, whether Fantagraphics or Acclaim or whoever, will take a book because the risk is relatively low, so you can afford it. And thus, new material gets into the field—new artists, new writers. Unfortunately, there's no simple answer.

Harvey: I don't think there will ever be a simple answer.
Eisner: But it's the comic book market that's in trouble. The comic book product is not in trouble. Some of the best talent in America is producing comic books. Alex Ross and Frank Miller—guys of that caliber. You didn't have guys like that working in comic book business in the fifties and sixties, the so-called Golden Age. These guys were uptown doing illustrations for *Collier's* and *Saturday Evening Post*. So these are good times now. We've got good authors and artists, good production, we just haven't solved the marketing problems.

Interview: Will Eisner

TASHA ROBINSON / 2000

From *The Onion: A.V. Club*, September 27, 2000. Reprinted with permission of THE AV CLUB. Copyright © 2010 by ONION, INC. www.avclubs.com.

When Will Eisner co-founded the first "comic art shop" in the late 1930s, he took one of the first steps in an epic career that would significantly change the face of comics in America. Eisner's studio—which employed Bob Kane, Lou Fine, and Jack Kirby, among others—was one of the first to produce original comic books in an era when "comics" meant newspaper funny strips. But the company was only a few years old when Eisner left to launch the groundbreaking weekly series *The Spirit*, a standalone newspaper insert that gave Eisner freedom to experiment with his visual style and begin the creation of a new form of communication. After ending the series in 1952, Eisner spent twenty years pioneering the use of comics in education, from military instruction magazines to elementary-school visual aids. In the early 1970s, he returned to fiction with *A Contract with God*, the first in a series of ambitious, influential graphic novels that told real-world stories in expressive, innovative ways. Today, at eighty-three, Eisner is far from retired. This year alone, Dark Horse Comics published his new anthology *Last Day in Vietnam*, NBM Publishing released *The Last Knight* (based on *Don Quixote*), and DC Comics began republishing his classic works, including the first installment in a projected twenty-five-book library of *Spirit* treasuries. Eisner recently spoke to *The Onion A.V. Club* about his new projects, his old projects, and the future of his chosen medium.

The Onion: How's life in Florida for you, compared to life in New York City?
Will Eisner: Very comfortable. This is a very solitary business, and you're always working in a small room. Whether this room is in New York City or in Florida really doesn't matter in the long run, except that life in Florida is very

comfortable and very good and very healthful and very enjoyable. At first, I
didn't want to come down here. It was my wife's idea to come down here, and
I didn't want to leave New York. New York to me is the center of the Earth.
I used to enjoy flying up to teach at [New York's School Of Visual Arts], and
to walk around the city and get a carbon-monoxide fix. But life down here is
quite good. It's healthy and stress-free. I believe very strongly that people are
responsive to their environment, and if you're in an environment where there
is a great deal of movement and action, you kind of respond to it physically
yourself. Kind of abstract thinking, but I believe it.

Onion: Given how closely your work is tied to big-city life, are you worried
about the impact on your writing?
Eisner: Oh, no. When you're talking about the human struggle for survival,
it's endless. New York City is a fountainhead of stories. It's a big theater, and
there's always something going on. I'm never really out of stories. There's always a new challenge, and my style is to constantly explore or experiment, so
I'm constantly probing beyond what I've done before. I'm never happy with
what I did yesterday—not because I think I did a bad job, but because there's
more to do. This is a medium that has not fully reached its potential.

Onion: You've been responsible for a lot of innovations in the medium over
the course of your career.
Eisner: Most of the things I've been given credit for are the result of either
desperation or an attempt to solve a problem. *The Spirit* itself was an attempt
to solve a problem. At that time, newspapers were getting very worried about
the fact that they were going to lose a lot of their younger audience to comic
books, so they were looking for someone who could create a comic book for a
newspaper. That gave me the opportunity to do something I had wanted to do
all along. That led to innovation, just as the so-called "splash page," which I'm
credited with innovating, was a result of the fact that this was a free-standing
supplement in the newspaper, very much like TV guides in newspapers today.
I knew that if I didn't get the reader's attention as he flipped through the
Sunday newspaper, I might lose him. So I began to innovate on the covers.
Also, I had only eight pages—seven pages, later on—to tell the story, so I had
to bring the reader in very quickly, set the scene very quickly. Then, another
thing I did that was called innovative at the time was I never repeated the logo
the same way in each successive story. The syndicate was furious with me over
it, because they felt they couldn't market this thing. *Superman* had the same
logo all the time, and every comic strip had its same logo, but I felt I would be

losing my readers. I was after an adult reader, and the comic-book world was really a ghetto as far as I was concerned. So innovation is constantly the result of an attempt to solve a problem, to reach out beyond where you are.

Onion: You were also the first person to use the term "graphic novel." Is it true that you made that up to avoid pitching *A Contract with God* as a comic book?

Eisner: Yes, that's a true story. I was sitting there on the telephone talking to this guy, and I said, "I have this new thing for you, something very new." And he said, "What is it?" And I looked at it and realized that if I said, "A comic book," he would hang up. He was a very busy guy, and this was a top-level publishing house. So I called it a graphic novel, and he said, "Oh, that's interesting. Bring it up!" I brought it to him. He looked at it, looked at me over his granny glasses, and said, "You know, it's still a comic. We can't publish that kind of stuff."

Onion: What about your use of silent panels, furthering a story without dialogue? You were the first there, too. What problem were you trying to solve?

Eisner: There, too, I was dealing with a reader that I felt was more sophisticated than a comic-book reader. By creating a series of pantomime panels without dialogue, without balloons, I'd get the reader to supply the dialogue. This is a medium that requires intelligence on the part of the reader. It requires a contribution, a participation. This does not occur in movies, for example. This is the prime difference between comics and film: Film is a spectator medium, while comics is a participatory medium. You participate, your reader contributes to it, and you have a sort of dialogue with the reader. And the reader is expected to draw out of his or her life experience the things you're suggesting or alluding to. As I go on in this medium, I've become more impressionistic in the work I'm doing. I've experimented with that. Currently, in a new book I just got out called *Last Day in Vietnam*, I experimented further in having the reader become part of the story itself.

Onion: *Last Day* has a theatrical feel to it. Reading it is like looking into a stage.

Eisner: That's exactly the way I think. I don't think in terms of film; I think in terms of live theater. The reason for that is that in live theater, the audience is part of the scene. The audience is privy to the scene. In film, the reader is a camera. They move you around; you see things from bird's-eye views and worm's-eye views, though knotholes, in extreme close-up, and so forth. I use close-ups, but not that often. Mostly, in the last few years, I've kept my reader on the same level as the action, as though he's looking at a stage. It's very important for me to maintain contact with the reader, because I'm writing to someone, and I'm desperately eager to achieve believability. Not so much realism as believability.

Onion: The stories in *Last Day in Vietnam* are all true stories from your own experience, aren't they?
Eisner: Yeah.

Onion: I understand the Army actually sent you to Vietnam and Korea during wartime so your military instructional comics would be more realistic.
Eisner: One of the requirements of the contract was that I would go out into the field at least once or twice a year. That way, what I was doing would be far more authentic than working from photographs.

Onion: Did you actively want these trips for the experience, or did you have to be talked into going into combat?
Eisner: I wasn't eager to do it. I mean, I didn't volunteer for it, but it was part of the thing. After a while, I rather enjoyed doing it, because I came away from it more knowledgeable than when I went there. When I got back to the drawing board, I was reporting more than anything else.

Onion: Why a book about Vietnam now?
Eisner: Over the years, you carry with you little snippets of scenes or things that do not deserve a whole book, but they're part of a lot of little things you want to divest yourself of. I'd just completed a rather heavy book called *A Family Matter*, and it was a serious piece of work. I was thinking about doing something a little lighter. I was flipping through these *Spirit* books one day, and I saw a story I'd done many years ago in which this man, I think he was a sea captain, was talking to the reader. And I said, "You know, I never followed up on that." It was a great idea, because I was turning out stories every week on a heavy schedule, and I could never really follow up on good ideas or carry them out. So I said, "I'd like to try this." Anyway, these ideas have been in my head for some time.

Onion: The artwork is very different from your usual work, with the heavy canvas texture and the light brown ink.

Eisner: It's very gritty. The reason for that was that I wanted it to look like a sketchbook that comes right from the field. I wanted a feeling of grit.

Onion: When you were planning, did you think about identifying your market?

Eisner: I don't write to a market, but I'm talking to somebody when I write. I guess you might say I'm like the Ancient Mariner: I've got a story and I want to tell it to somebody. I don't sit down and say, "There's a big market right now for mutants trashing each other, so I'm gonna do two mutants trashing each other." None of my books are done for a market. I have a very small market when you come right down to it, compared to, say, *X-Men* or *Spawn*. I don't write for these people at all. It's very hard to talk to them about heartbreak.

Onion: Do you think all of your works address heartbreak on some level?

Eisner: Probably. I'm dealing with the human condition, and I'm dealing with life. For me, the enemy is life, and people's struggle to prevail is essentially the theme that runs through all my books.

Onion: You often say that you don't write for people who read comics; you write for adults. Where do *The Princess and the Frog* and *The Last Knight* fit in?

Eisner: [Laughs.] Those were a little vacation I took from the business of writing this kind of stuff. They were the result of another attempt at innovation. About five or six years ago, public television here in Florida asked me to work with them on developing something that would get them into the literacy field. I developed what I called a reading experience on television. I took the classics and reduced them to a little half-hour show in which there was no animation in the art, but the balloons were animated, so the language would pop in as the characters spoke it, and that would force the reader to read it. Well, it never went anywhere: They couldn't get enough funding to pursue it, and I was left with a bunch of stories I had roughed out. I showed the stories to my agent in Europe, and he said he had five publishers in five different countries who wanted stories. So I did the *Moby Dick* adaptation as *The White Whale*, which hasn't been published here but appeared in Europe. After that, I did *The Princess and the Frog* because I was leafing through a Grimm's fairy-tale book one day and discovered, to my astonishment, that the princess was not really the nice girl I always thought she was. So I did that, and I then did the Don Quixote book *The Last Knight*.

Onion: The mixture of fictional adaptation and biography was kind of unusual there. Why suddenly introduce Miguel Cervantes as a character at the end?

Eisner: I couldn't resist making the statement. I felt very sympathetic to Don Quixote. I think many of us in this business are Don Quixotes. Anybody in the business of innovation is in pursuit of something that nobody else believes exists. These were adaptations, so I took that liberty. I had a lot of fun with them.

Onion: Do you have any plans for more in the series?

Eisner: Yes, but . . . [Laughs.] I have to have time for it. I just finished a book that DC is going to publish in the fall, called *Minor Miracles*. It's this series of stories that take place on Dropsie Avenue, making the case that there are little miracles that go on all the time. So . . . I probably will one of these days. I have roughs for about four or five more, including *Oliver Twist* and a couple of others I should be able to get to. It's just a question of which comes first.

Onion: DC Comics is reissuing a lot of your books this year.

Eisner: Oh, yeah, that was the sweetener that made the deal as far as I was concerned. I had about thirteen books that would have been remaindered if DC hadn't come along. I'm still in pursuit of the serious readers, the establishment readers, and DC represents an opportunity to ultimately reach them. They have the legs and they have the access, so maybe my books will find a place in Borders and Barnes & Noble and all the other bookstores where I want to be.

Onion: About a year ago, you said in an interview that you wouldn't want Marvel or DC handling your reprints because you'd lose your personal connection with your work. Has that been a problem at all?

Eisner: Did I say that? I should have written a denial immediately after that. At the time, I was still thinking in terms of my past practice, which was to stay with small companies. I've always been successful working with small publishers, and I had never really thought that DC would reach the point where I could regard them as a comfortable house to be with. When they came along and made the offer, I thought about it very carefully and realized that by this time, with their Vertigo line and so forth, they had moved well beyond the standard comic-book house that they were back in the '70s and '80s. So it was easy for me to make that decision, and it's worked out very nicely.

Onion: What is it like seeing the early-1940s *Spirit* stories back in print again?

Eisner: Well, I love the package. I think the package is marvelous. I try to avoid looking at the artwork because it makes my toes curl. [Laughs.] I want to grab a pencil and redo it. "Oh, my God, did I get away with this junk?"

Onion: Where is the art coming from? Do you still have the originals of those strips?

Eisner: They've done a remarkable job, and the modern technology is absolutely stunning. The original artwork for that era does not exist anymore. I have the original artwork from 1945 on, but for that period, there's no original artwork. What they've done is picked up, from collectors, actual copies of the issues from that time, then somehow bleached out the colors, kept the line art, and restored the colors. They've done a stunning job, and the coloring is absolutely accurate. I said I would like to have the paper simulate the newsprint, with the color being the flat color we used at that time. They agreed to do it, and the results have been absolutely splendid.

Onion: How do you think modern readers will react to them?

Eisner: I don't know. I suspect that they'll look at them as quaint collections of some kind. I must say I was amazed that the character has survived. It's still got young readers. Apparently, the basic stories have survived largely because they're fundamentally sound stories. You must remember that these stories were written for an adult audience, for a newspaper audience. Consequently, there's more depth to the stories than you would have if they were written for young comic-book readers. As a matter of fact, the proof of that is that *The Spirit* was never successful on the newsstand in competition with *Batman* and *Superman* or any other superheroes. But the last report I got from DC said that the first archival edition has sold well beyond what they expected, so it's doing very well.

Onion: Over the last twenty-five years, one of the things you've consistently said in interviews is that we're right on the brink of an industry change, that comics are about to become more intellectual and more respected. It just hasn't happened yet. Do you still think it's about to happen?

Eisner: [Laughs.] About twenty years ago, I think, I was giving a talk to a bunch of distributors. When I did *A Contract with God*, I said I had opened up a toll booth in an empty field, waiting for the highway to come through.

[Laughs.] I can hear the trucks out there. I don't agree with you: If you look around and see what's being published, you'll see that the level of at least 5 percent of the comics production of this country has risen well beyond what it was twenty years ago. You've got *Maus*, you've got Jules Feiffer, you've got Harvey Pekar, Neil Gaiman, and Alan Moore, people of that caliber who are in the field turning out high-quality stuff. There's a lot of good stuff, but it just hasn't reached a critical mass where it will establish itself in the marketplace. We're not very different from jazz. It took a long time for jazz to achieve a position in the musical world where it was considered legitimate music. Slowly but surely, we're getting there. I'm still carrying the flag on that, and I still believe it.

Onion: But the mainstream still considers Moore and Gaiman to be anomalies, to the extent that the mainstream is aware of them at all. Do you think America is ultimately capable of accepting comics as a literary medium?

Eisner: Ultimately, yes. Ultimately, they will, especially because of the dynamic that's occurring in society right now. We're in a visual era. We have to communicate today with imagery, because there's a need for speed of communication. Comics—the comic medium, the idea of sequentially arranged images with some text to convey an idea and tell a story—have found the place between text and film. We deliver information at a very rapid rate of speed. Very often, our information is not as deep as a body of text, but a lot of people haven't got time to read a large body of text any longer. So I would say the growth of our society, the conduct of our civilization, is on our side.

Onion: What about the growth of the readers? Do you think people have changed in any essential way since you started your career?

Eisner: I think people are essentially the same. Everybody is in a continuing struggle to survive, or to prevail over life. The environment we live in is changing. In modern society, the rhythm of life is so accelerated that our attention span is shorter, and our patience is a little shorter. We're looking for faster gratification, quicker solutions to things. I have to address it with the writing I'm doing now. It's influencing students I've talked to. The Internet and MTV are changing the rhythm of reading. We want solutions more quickly, more rapidly. If you look at MTV, you find that there's no attempt to provide intervening action between a beginning and an end. So the readers I'm writing to now are less patient with a great deal of involved detail than they were back in the '40s and '50s.

Onion: What about the growth of new technologies? How do you think that will affect the comics industry?

Eisner: That's another thing that's challenging us. The way I see it right now, the Internet is a vehicle of transmission. And the vehicle of transmission does not alter the fact that comics is a language that combines image and text. Whether it's transmitted or broadcast over a computer screen or done digitally, it's still going to involve the same kind of intellectual process that anybody working in comics today has to employ. I don't believe that print will disappear. It may no longer dominate our communication world, but it will not disappear. The whole process of arranging images in a sequence to convey an idea—whether it's transmitted electronically or by paper and print—remains. The only difference is in the technological skills that are employed.

Onion: Are there still skills of comics creation that you're trying to master?

Eisner: Oh, yeah. In the last few books I've done, I've spent a lot of time trying to master the ability to transmit internal emotions. It's very hard to do with single images, very challenging. What I'm continually working on now is not so much my pen-and-ink skills or my brush skills; I've long ago mastered those. I'm spending a lot of time now in minimalization of the technical drawing, the draftsmanship of detail. I prefer to spend my time trying to arrange and posture the human character in such a way that it conveys an internal emotion, what's going on inside him. Passion, the transmission of passion, is very important.

Onion: Your background settings are becoming minimalist, but your characters are still detailed, which is exactly the opposite of the style of many modern independent comics.

Eisner: I'm very conscious of that. The works you refer to are really obsessed with movies and animation, and they're trying to emulate motion pictures and animation. Japanese manga have their basis in animated cartoons, and they're very skilled at portraying action and fast movement, but there's no internalization, no depth, and that's the big difference. Yes, I believe that cartoons are a form of impressionism in the world of art, and I try to be as impressionistic as possible. It's for that reason that I began, with *A Contract with God*, abandoning the rigid panel arrangement that dominated comics for so long. I felt it enabled me to invite, or involve, the reader much more. You give a reader a blank background, and the tendency of the reader is to supply the background out of his own imagination or his own experience. I learned that from one of the comics that influenced me tremendously early on, *Krazy Kat*. If you examine [George] Herriman's early work, you'll see that he had a visceral instinct for this kind of thing. After studying that as a kid, I thought, "Gee, this guy's got something here."

Onion: Why not extend that to the characters, then? Why not use more iconic characters that readers can identify with?

Eisner: The reason for that is that the human being has to be fairly precise. When you look at a person, you look for small details that reveal the character to you. Heavy eyebrows may mean something to you, and a sharp nose or thin lips mean something to you. Those are details that have to be expressed, because you can't create abstract people. Creating abstract people loses the relationship that you want to develop between the person and your reader. The reader has to look at a character and say, "Oh, I've seen him before. I know who he is and I know what he's like." The background can be impressionistic, because we remember backgrounds impressionistically. You don't come away remembering the number of rivets in the bridge; you just remember the feeling of the bridge.

Onion: Is it true that you prefer to work in black and white?

Eisner: Yes. Black and white gives me the closest contact with the reader. It reaches the reader without interference. Color has a tendency to interfere with the dialogue. Color is almost like a large orchestra playing behind the art, you know? You can't hear a thing. I don't think color is bad—I've used color in the fairy-tale stories and I'll use it on covers—but I don't feel I need it inside the book. In the last book, *Family Matter*, I used the brown coloration: not full color, but monochromatic color, largely because I wanted to create a mood. Color does help create moods. I like a lot of my books to run in brown ink rather than black ink.

Onion: Why brown?

Eisner: It has a dreamy quality. Psychiatrists have told me that people dream in brown. I don't know how true that is. I think I dream in black and white. But it creates a warmth, and it's not as strident as harsh black and white. A lot of my books have been in black and white. For instance, *The Heart of the Storm* was all in black ink. That seemed to work there.

Onion: Speaking from a purely idealistic plane, where would you like to see the industry go from here?

Eisner: I would like to see more sophisticated material. I would like to see the comics industry reach a point where good comics material is reviewed in the *New York Times* and treated at a level equivalent to oil paintings and good literature. I'm hoping we'll see more of that. I believe it will happen, and I'm hoping to be around when it does.

Eisner Wide Open

TOM HEINTJES / 2000

From *Hogan's Alley* http://cagle.msnbc.com/hogan/interviews/eisner/home.asp. Reprinted by permission of Tom Heintjes.

Tom Heintjes: What challenges do you see cartoonists facing that they traditionally haven't had?

Will Eisner: Before we can discuss any challenge facing a cartoonist, we've got to decide what we're talking about: Are we talking about his art form, or are we talking about the publication that will carry his work? Cartoonists have always worked for publication, as opposed to painters, who work for galleries. It's the final vehicle that often determines "the challenge," as you put it. A painter's vehicle is the gallery. The painting he makes is "the product." The cartoonist, however, is creating something for reproduction. This has an effect on the challenge.

Let me step back here and answer the question in two parts. The cartoon art form—the art of treating an image impressionistically—will not fade. It will keep growing in popularity, because a cartoon is able to convey an idea as an image, and images are the means of communication that are proliferating. Communication in the future will be based on imagery, the transmission of ideas by images. The vehicle of transmission is changing under our noses and will influence how the artist deals with the medium. He'll configure his work to suit the method of transmission. Historically, print has been the major vehicle. The arrival of the Internet has provided the cartoonist with another vehicle of transmission, which has a different set of requirements. The relationship with the reader, which is primary to the entire business of communication, has to be accommodated. In print, you can count on the fact that the reader will either glance at your work or dwell on it for a great length of time. You therefore can develop what I call a "contract with the reader" during the time he or she has it in their hands. In electronic transmission, we have no way of knowing how long a reader stays with you or what their retention time is. We're dealing with a totally different relationship.

Having said all of that, I suspect that the Internet cartoons will increasingly begin to resemble animation. In the end, we may wind up with animated cartoons, because the rhythm of reading on the Internet is not like that of a hand-held page. It requires a dimension of realism to abet a continuation of the action suggested by the image.

Heintjes: One of the pleasures I get from enjoying cartooning is a tactile one, and I miss that on the computer screen.

Eisner: I have the same reaction. I enjoy the brush work, and I enjoy inspecting the pen-and-ink techniques. But I've been in debates with some younger cartoonists who argue that the day of the paper cartoon is coming to an end. They believe there will come a time when readers will have lost the experience of looking at things on paper, so they won't have the same frame of reference that we do today. They'll only have looked at things on a screen. I argue that the tactile experience of holding a book will be very hard to diminish, but it is an argument that a lot of Internet-oriented cartoonists do not easily accept. I was having this very same sort of discussion last year at a panel at the San Diego comics convention, and one of the cartoonists told me I sounded like a medieval monk who sneers at the future of this guy Gutenberg with his movable type.

The bottom line is, technology is doing something to the comic-book business. Comic books as we knew them in the 1940s, 1950s, and 1960s are experiencing a continuing drop in sales.

Heintjes: Do you think that the difficult economics of publishing traditional comics is hastening cartooning's retreat to the Internet? People can publish their work online for very little cost.

Eisner: Well, there's no viable economic model for publishing comics online. Obviously, cartoonists are always looking for a new reader, a larger audience. They know now that a website can secure 100,000 hits overnight, but no one has figured out how the creator can make money off of that. This is not encouraging cartoonists to leave print. In fact, there are more cartoonists looking for print work than there ever have been. Perhaps the marketplace for cartoons is shifting. I'm not wringing my hands, because it's simply a new phenomenon that we have to deal with. I've probably been looking at this as a cartoonist and find it very hard to abandon print, so the more I look at it, the more it looks like animated cartoons to me. Now, the computer is a tool that can provide a tremendous amount of technical support—you can get all these colors, you can morph and combine images.

A young cartoonist I know showed me how he works on a computer. He was doing a magazine cover, and he was shifting all the elements around on his screen until he got the composition he wanted.

Heintjes: Isn't that like doing roughs?

Eisner: That's what I said. I told him, "I don't need to do that because I do a few quick pencil roughs to get to what I want to do." My biggest problem is how to execute the idea I have in my head. In comics, very little happens accidentally. It's not like Jackson Pollock dripping paint on a canvas—"voilà, this looks good, I think I'll save it."

A lot of students confuse the technology with the art itself. There's a separation that must be understood between the execution of the art and the business of executing that art for a specific medium.

Heintjes: But to clarify my question: Is cartoonists' retreat from traditional print publication hastening the demise of the printed comic?

Eisner: It isn't the cartoonists who are hastening the demise of printed comics. It's the competition from the new technology. The audience is moving toward electronic media. The best evidence I can give you is the absence of "kiddie" comics, the Mickey Mouse type of comic books. They're no longer around. The retailers I talk to tell me that they don't get young kids coming into the store anymore. They're home playing with the computer games, or they have Nintendo or whatever.

Heintjes: Nor can kids go to the corner drugstore to get their comics, and that used to be the point of entry for kids' interest in comics.

Eisner: That's also another thing. It's the same problem that newspapers are struggling with. Newspapers used to be sold in kiosks on street corners. My father used to stop off on the way home from work and pick up a newspaper in the subway. That no longer happens. It's delivered to your door, so it's a totally different kind of distribution that has evolved. It affects the reader relationship.

These are the forces that are altering what the creators are doing. Remember, the creator's primary function is to provide the material for "the vehicle," and I consider the Internet to be a vehicle. When I was doing comics for the newspaper in 1940, the paper that we were printed on was so rough and porous that the artistic style everybody used was rigid. There were no vignettes, so the flat benday coloring could be contained. Reproduction today permits oil painting or air brushing. Cartoonists have always learned to accommodate the technology as it changes. The reader also has different demands. Today's reader has been exposed to MTV and has grown up on a fusillade of images. Their life experience is different. The books I write are for people with some life experience. Not artificial or virtual experience, but real life experience. A large part of the young audience today is getting life experience artificially through the television or through the computer. These are experiences that are contrived.

Heintjes: What effect do you think today's media have had on the way people perceive stories?

Eisner: The media have had a tremendous effect on storytelling. A young reader's sense of wonder is very quickly satisfied by electronic media. It will generate things that a more limited medium like comics can only allude to. For example, a comic strip about space travel cannot compete with the experience delivered by the film *Star Wars*. So you have to deal with this generation in terms of its own experience, and part of that experience is MTV. I've been trying to watch MTV to figure it out, but I can't watch too much of it or my eyes bump into each other. What they're doing is using visual clichés over and over. You can connect into their message by using the experiences you've had watching other films or videos. The message doesn't come from your own real-life experience. It comes from artificial experience. But those of us who are trying to tell a story must pay attention to that.

Heintjes: Historically, when comic books entered periods of slumping sales, one survival technique was to have a broad appeal, so you had material geared toward a variety of demographics: funny animals for children, romance comics for girls, teenage comics for young teens, as well as the usual superheroes, monster, western, war, and science fiction material. Now, with a few exceptions, mainstream comics have given themselves over almost entirely to superheroes.

Eisner: Perhaps that may explain the malaise. It's interesting to look at Japan. Some of their comic books sell at the rate of 8 million copies a week, and the subject matter is enormously diversified. They have comics for expectant mothers, comics for adults, boys and girls, all different ages. It's a huge industry, but their culture has grown up with a language that is basically pictorial.

Heintjes: Japanese comics don't struggle with the social stigma that ours do.

Eisner: That's a big problem. I'm involved in that struggle. Rumor has it that I write comics for people who don't read comics. My readers don't come into comic-book stores. Here in the United States, comics is a despised art form, way down at the bottom of the artistic hierarchy. In Europe, a cartoon is regarded as a higher form of art, because it occupies a greater historical role. You had cartoonists like Daumier taking up arms against political oppression, so they're regarded as important creators. I remember talking about it to Harvey Kurtzman in the '60s after we had come back from Europe. He said, "Wasn't that wonderful? They treated us like real artists!"

Heintjes: How different are your experiences as a creator in the United States compared to those in Europe?

Eisner: I seem to get a warmer response to my work in Europe and in Latin America. I think the difference comes down to content. Superheroes are not as popular in Europe as they are here. My stories deal with the human struggle for survival, and that seems to be a subject closer to the European world view than it is here, largely because most European countries have a history of being under the unremovable thumb of an aristocracy or dictatorship. In this country, politically, we can change the rulers we don't like. We have this freedom so we can alter this condition.

Heintjes: You're doing some work for European markets that is also being subsequently published here.

Eisner: One of the books that was just published in Europe and in Brazil—*Don Quixote*—is being published here by NBM. Usually, after I finish a heavy book like *Family Matter*, I find that doing something very light is a great antidote. For a long time I've wanted to adapt classics to comics form. My Danish publisher, who is also my agent over there, has tried for a long time to get me to do this series, because I had these stories in dummy form. And his market had changed dramatically. The bulk of the sales was in libraries, and they were looking for classics.

Heintjes: I understand the European comics market is also slumping.

Eisner: Yes, it is. If someone stopped me on the street, grabbed me by the lapel and asked me, "What's causing all this?" my quick response would be "content." The content of comics is not keeping up with the demands of the readers. In Europe, as in the United States, the novelty of comics has worn off. It's no longer a novelty. When my former company in the '60s, American Visuals Corp., was selling comics for industrial and educational purposes, one of my salesmen called up American Motors and said, "We'd like to do a booklet for you on the new Social Security laws," the man at American Motors replied, "We already have a booklet." My salesman said, "No, we're going to do it comics form." The guy at American Motors said, "Oh, great! We'll be glad to talk to you about that." To them, comics was a novel vehicle and a novel medium. The idea of a comic book is no longer new. You can't sell it just because of what it is.

You sell it because of what it contains.

There was a time when movies were novel simply because they were moving pictures. Now, you take the medium for granted. You don't go to a movie because it's a movie. You go because of the content. That's the one thing I always tell students and other young cartoonists: It's content. If you have nothing to say, then you're just selling wallpaper. It's almost like pornography. They're not selling a story; they're just selling images.

Heintjes: Why do you think Europeans, with their own rich artistic history, have such a special appreciation for the work of certain American creators such as Carl Barks, Steve Ditko, Jack Kirby, and yourself?
Eisner: As for myself, I can tell you that the reception I get is based on my stories, not so much on the artistic technique. The other creators you mention are all important representatives of major genres that are big over there. Jack Kirby represents America—the thrust and the drive and the excitement. Crumb is highly esteemed in Europe. He's only the second American to win the annual prize at the Angoulême festival.

Heintjes: Who was the first American to win it?
Eisner: Will Eisner. [laughter]

Heintjes: Oh, him.
Eisner: When I first saw Crumb's stuff, he was still doing undergrounds, and I didn't quite get it. I thought it was just bigfoot stuff, very crude illustration. Then I read one of his stories, "Yeti," and it blew me away. I began to pay attention. He's done some very sensitive stuff, like the poster he did, "A Short History of America."

Heintjes: You've produced most of your recent work through Kitchen Sink Press, a company that gave you creative carte blanche. Now that Kitchen Sink is no longer publishing, do you see getting that same degree of creative autonomy in today's turbulent marketplace?

Eisner: I will have absolutely no trouble retaining creative autonomy. I've signed a contract with DC Comics to reprint *The Spirit*, and they're keeping my graphic novels, collectively called "The Will Eisner Library," in print. We also have a handshake deal in which I give DC first look at any new books I do. Of course, I'm still an independent. For example, the children's line I'm working on is with Terry Nantier at NBM.

One of the reasons I'm giving DC the first look is because they have the best chance of getting my work into bookstores. Of all the publishers today, they have the most muscle, and they've done very well with the Vertigo line.

Heintjes: You like the Vertigo line?

Eisner: I like the editorial thrust of the Vertigo books. The fact that Vertigo is producing the kind of stuff they are is a plus. It's helping the industry by publishing material that would not be generated by the old DC or the old Marvel or any other major publisher. As they said in *Death of a Salesman*, "Attention must be paid."

Heintjes: You had always been reluctant to allow *The Spirit* to be reprinted in a deluxe format. Why now?

Eisner: The reason I finally agreed is that, with the death of Kitchen Sink, the possibility of *The Spirit* being reprinted is almost out of the question. I originally objected to it with Denis [Kitchen, Kitchen Sink's publisher] because I felt that a big *Spirit* book would be like a mausoleum. Then I finally agreed to allow him to do a series of new *Spirit* stories in *The Spirit: The New Adventures*.

Heintjes: How did you feel about that series?

Eisner: It was a little like putting your child up for adoption. I was astounded at what some of them were doing with him. Clearly, I would never have done stories the way these guys did. Guys like Alan Moore and Neil Gaiman are very much in touch with today's reader, and they were talking to them in that vein. I had no sense of violation or concern; they just saw The Spirit from their perspectives. When I created The Spirit, I never had any intention of creating a superhero. I never felt The Spirit would dominate the feature. He served as a sort of an identity for the strip. The stories were what I was interested in. The Spirit was just a walk-on in a lot of the stories. Sherlock Holmes is an example of what I mean. You read Sherlock Holmes stories for the stories. The stories endure, not the idea of a super-detective. The Spirit stories are very much like the Sherlock Holmes stories: The stories endure despite their setting in a world long ago and far away. At least, that's what I hope.

Heintjes: DC Comics is owned by Time Warner, and big media companies are interested in synergy between properties. Has there been any discussion of doing anything else with The Spirit? Will we be seeing The Spirit join the Justice League of America?

Eisner: There's been no discussion about that. The preservation of The Spirit as a character really means very little. What's important to me is the 300-and-some-odd stories that I wrote myself. Nothing will change those. They'll still be around. If DC came to me and said, "How about a crossover between The Spirit and Batman?" it would depend on how they intended to handle it and who would do it. If I were doing it, The Spirit might make a fool out of Batman [laughter].

Heintjes: After all you've accomplished in your career, what continues to drive you?

Eisner: Oh, there's so much that is undone in this medium. I want to do it. I've got a book coming out called *Last Day in Vietnam* in which I eschew the use of balloons altogether. It's a collection of true incidents that happened to me in my visits to Vietnam and when I was in Korea. But it's done with a totally different approach. I only used this once in *The Spirit*, where the reader is a participant, and the characters are talking to the reader. At the time, I felt it was successful, but I never followed it up. I'm constantly experimenting. As we're talking, I'm dummying up another book that has to do with folk tales back in Dropsie Avenue.

Glenn Miller used to say he was still looking for "the sound." That's how I feel. Actually, I'm still looking to achieve what I set out to do fifty years ago: to achieve a literary level in this medium. One of the problems is in marketing. Maybe one of the problems is that the adult reader is turned off by the form. He sees a lot of pictures, and he sees balloons, and he sees a book that he pays fourteen dollars for, which gives him maybe a half-hour's worth of reading time. For that same money, he can get a book by Stephen King or John Updike that would give him hours and hours of reading time. Perhaps the solution is not in form but in content. This is something I'm struggling with, trying to seize the adult reader.

Heintjes: What trends do you see in the work of today's aspiring cartoonists?

Eisner: A preoccupation with special effects. A lot of them are preoccupied with creating new superheroes. Recently some young black creators showed me a new ethnic superhero. What a waste of creativity! We don't need another ethnic superhero—we've got plenty of them. Show me something about ethnic life in America today. That's what we don't have enough of. But they're thinking of where the money is at, and they know they're not going to get anywhere fast by doing my kind of stuff. They're going to get instant money by doing superheroes of some kind.

Heintjes: Looking back at your body of work, which are you proudest of? By the way, you're not allowed to say, "My next one."

Eisner: You intercepted me [laughter]. It's hard to say, but . . . I guess *A Contract with God* is like my first child. "Gerhard Shnobble" in *The Spirit* is a favorite story, because it was the first time I attempted a philosophical point. From a technical point of view, I think *A Life Force* was well structured. *Dropsie Avenue* was, for me, a technical tour de force because I attempted something I didn't think was possible in this medium, and that is to do a proper history of a neighborhood. In each case, I've always attempted to climb a hill, and sometimes I succeed and sometimes I don't.

Heintjes: Of course, we all want you to climb many more hills, but when the time comes for Will Eisner to live with The Spirit in Wildwood Cemetery, what provisions have you made for your literary estate?

Eisner: I've made provisions in a will to leave my work to certain places and to certain charities. I have a son, and he'll oversee my estate. And my wife will oversee it as well. In the case of my graphic novels, DC is committed to keeping them in print, so they'll be around. That's important to me, which is one reason I went with them. Oh, Tom—the whole subject is premature.

Heintjes: Well, I hope those mortal considerations are a long way off. You realize that you're eventually going to be the one who writes the history books—no one's going to be around to contradict anything you say. It'll just be you and Al Hirschfeld.

Eisner: Someone was pointing that out to me the other day [laughter]. It's not a bad position to be in.

The Spirit of Comics: The Will Eisner Interview

DANNY FINGEROTH / 2003

From *Write Now!* No. 5 (August 2002), 3–10. Reprinted by permission of Danny Fingeroth. Copyright © Danny Fingeroth. All rights reserved. www.twomorrows.com.

Danny Fingeroth: I want to thank you for taking the time to do this interview, Will. What are you working on right now? I know you're in the middle of a project.

Will Eisner: I just completed a book that Doubleday is publishing called *Fagin the Jew*. It will be published in September, I believe. I just sent off the final art the day before yesterday.

Fingeroth: That's not part of the DC Library?

Eisner: DC lost the bid on it. They wanted it, but Doubleday made me an offer I couldn't refuse. DC always gets "first look" at any graphic novel I do.

Fingeroth: And are you starting something new now?

Eisner: Well, I always have . . . I have a file here that says "do me now." [*laughter*] I'm just starting another book now.

Fingeroth: My understanding is that you don't like to talk about projects you're working on.

Eisner: I generally don't, and the reason for it is it dilutes itself if I talk about it, because while I'm working on it, I'm developing ideas and so forth. It just dilutes itself in my mind.

Fingeroth: At this point, how many hours a week do you devote to work?

Eisner: I work pretty steadily. When I'm not traveling, I work from nine to five.

Fingeroth: Wow.
Eisner: Every day, five days a week.

Fingeroth: What, you take the weekends off? How dare you? [*laughs*]
Eisner: My wife says Saturday and Sunday are her days.

Fingeroth: Well, that seems to work for you. I'm going to ask you a bunch of questions that range from the pretentious to the picayune. So if there's anything that you think is too stupid to answer—
Eisner: I'll give you stupid answers.

Fingeroth: Thank you. [*laughs*] Well, okay. You've been doing comics and graphic storytelling for an amazingly long time and your stuff is still wonderfully fresh, innovative, and exciting. Would you say there is an overall theme or purpose or direction in your work, from the beginning to now? Or has it changed over the years?
Eisner: Well, the direction has always been to explore areas that haven't been explored before. I guess that's the way to put it. I believe that this medium is a literary form and that it has not been used as fully as it could. So all of my experience, all the things I've been involved in since 1950, certainly, have been an effort to employ this medium whose language is sequential art—that's the medium that we're talking about—in areas that it had not tried before. For example, when I was in the military between 1942 and 1946, I realized that the medium is usable as a teaching tool, very effective as a tool. So I sold the military on the use of that. It was very successful. I went back to doing *The Spirit*, by 1950 I realized I had done all I wanted to do on *The Spirit*, and the opportunity to expand into teaching material with sequential art presented itself. So I started a company producing instructional material in sequential art, or comics, as you might call it. It lasted for about twenty-five years, and then in 1972, '73, I stumbled into Phil Seuling's conventions and discovered that the underground artists—I'm talking about Robert Crumb and Art Spiegelman and Spain Rodriguez and Denis Kitchen and a couple of others— were really using comics as a pure, literary form, in that they were addressing the establishment mores and morals of the time, and that encouraged me to go back to the area where I wanted to spend my life, which was producing comics or sequential art for adult readers, with grown-up subject matter.

Fingeroth: Now, the stuff you'd been doing in the interim twenty years was in comics format but in an educational milieu?

Eisner: Yes, what you might call the comics format. Actually, it was the sequential art format. It is the arrangement of images in a sequence to tell a story, and whether you do them on three tiers or two tiers, with nine or six panels to a page, is irrelevant. It's how you arrange the images in an intelligent and readable sequence to convey an idea or tell a story that is really the heart of the definition, if you will, of what I want to do. And in 1975—or '76, I guess, somewhere in there—I began doing what I believed was a novel form addressed to adult readers. And out of that came *A Contract with God*.

Fingeroth: You'd always aimed at adult readers, even with *The Spirit*.
Eisner: Yes. Writing for young readers was one of the problems that I had during the Eisner and Iger Studio years, and one of the reasons I went in for *The Spirit*—which was quite a gamble at the time, for various reasons. I wanted to talk to an adult audience. A newspaper readership would give me that. I was always very impatient talking to the very young readers. I didn't really know what to say to them. [*laughs*]

Fingeroth: You mean talk to them beyond just the basics of superhero action/adventure?
Eisner: Well, candidly, superheroes are one-dimensional characters. You can't do very much with them. And life experiences are filled with story material. Everybody's concerned with survival and the life experience is concerned with that and how to deal with it. So it's a wide-open area, there.

Fingeroth: Now, in different hands, these can be very bleak subjects, but you certainly seem to do them joyously.
Eisner: Well . . . that's an interesting point you just made, calling them "bleak." Every once in a while people do say to me, "Your stories are bleak," or "there's a *noir* quality to them." That's French, you know. [*laughter*] I don't see it that way. First of all, I'm not a moralist. I'm not really writing books to define human morals. I consider myself doing reportage, reporting to my fellow man the things I see. I see a man lying in the street, nobody paying attention to him is something I want to turn to my fellow man and say, "Hey, look at that, look at that. He's lying there, nobody's paying attention." The other thing is, I think it's necessary to explore the purpose of life. That's what drives us in living. In one of the books I did, there's a story called "The Big Hit." At the end of the story, I have this one guy saying to the other fellow, "Living is a risky business." Really, the whole business of living and survival is very much a part of how we think as human beings, so if you can talk about

that, it has resonance, it means something. It's useful. What I want to be is useful, obviously.

Fingeroth: Do you think that focus, that direction, comes from the Depression era and World War II era experiences?

Eisner: Living through the Depression has made me sensitive—as it did with all the people who also lived through the Great Depression—sensitive to the human struggle for survival. This is really the heart of all living. Everybody's concerned with survival. Anytime you discuss it, it is of importance to an adult reader. Now, one of the problems with writing to young readers is that I cannot discuss heartbreak with a fourteen- or fifteen-year-old kid, because to him, heartbreak is if his father didn't give him the keys to the car or something like that. Or maybe his girlfriend decided he was a nerd.

Fingeroth: That's heartbreak for that kid.

Eisner: That's heartbreak, true. Youngsters are not concerned with survival.

Fingeroth: But it's different.

Eisner: It's a different kind of heartbreak. But in one of my books—I think it was *A Life Force*, where this man is trying to decide what life is all about—I discuss the meaning of living, what is it, what it's all about. He compares himself to a cockroach. It gave me a chance, again, to expand the capacity of the medium.

Fingeroth: It seems that certain subject matter that, say, in *The Spirit*, you may have been addressing in a more metaphorical way, you've been getting with more directly, or at least with a different sort of metaphor system, since *A Contract with God*. In other words, it seems that you did have some of those same concerns when you were doing the *Spirit*, but your way of dealing with them changed when you "came back"—what it seemed to the public was coming back—with *A Contract with God* and so on.

Eisner: Well, one thing we don't realize is that the artists and writers, like everybody else, grow. They grow up. [*laughter*]

That's a very interesting point, however, because one of the reasons I never really wanted to do a daily strip was, I discovered that daily strips would not allow the artist to experiment and grow, necessarily. He remained pretty much the way he was when he first started. If you look at the daily strips over the years, the ones that have survived for fifty years, they're pretty much the same as they were when they started, and there's no room for experimentation. The joy, for me . . . the truth of the matter is, you've got to love what you're doing, you've got to enjoy what you're doing in order to do it well. If you don't like what you're doing, you don't do it well. Nothing good is ever done without enthusiasm, really. And for me, the opportunity to cut new paths is to try new things. The real excitement for me is to do something that nobody has ever done before, if I can do it. Unfortunately, it's very hard to invent the wheel, because somebody has already done that, but . . . [*laughs*]

Fingeroth: There's steel-belted radials, though.
Eisner: [*laughs*] Okay. But the point I'm trying to make is that the excitement in any medium is to explore new territory, with all the risk that's involved. And it's a great risk, because you could spend a whole year working on something only to discover that it's a bomb. [*laughter*]

Fingeroth: To me, looking at your work over the years, one significant change is that you yourself describe as going from a cinematic style to almost more of a theatrical awareness, where people are more "on stage."
Eisner: That's an interesting point, very perceptive of you, because I have always been influenced largely by live theater. And the reason for that is that live theater is closest to reality, and all the work I do is pressing for reality. All my work starts out by saying, "Now , believe me . . . " Even *The Spirit* was an attempt to create a believable hero, even though he wore a mask, which was kind of an idiot thing. [*Danny laughs*] I tried to make him believable. Now, the cinematic stuff I did early on was really a practical approach, because while you're writing, in this medium, anyway, you've got to be aware of the fact that reading patterns are influenced by other media, and in the '30s, movies came along and began to influence reading patterns. They added to the reader's understanding a whole new visual language, influenced graphic literacy, if you will. Movies began using the camera as the reader, so to speak. Or the audience became the camera, and the camera would look through somebody's armpit, or look down from the ceiling. You had bird's-eye-views, you had worm's-eye-views, and so forth. Those are part of the language they were introducing. So I employed them, because I'm always eager to reach my reader, and this was a new visual language.

Now, when I started back into the graphic novel, I moved back into the live theater/real stage format, which I've always found to be the most sure way of communicating with my audience. One other thing I should say is that live theater has a sense of reality that movies do not have. You sit in the theater and people are doing something on the stage, they're real people, they're *real*.

You are looking in on a real incident. In movies, you are looking at something that only *seems* to be real. It's an artificial reality.

Fingeroth: Comics can mimic film or they can mimic theater. You've taken those elements and, in at least two eras, created a whole new vocabulary for people. What's the appeal of the visual in presenting your message? You have things you want to say and messages you want to get out. Why not straight prose? What's the appeal of the picture in there?

Eisner: That's an interesting point. Prose is a different medium. I write with pictures. Now, when people ask me what I do, to answer it as quickly as I can, I say, "I'm a writer. I write with pictures." This is my medium, and I think there is an advantage to sequential art, because, first of all, it communicates more rapidly than text alone. Text cannot be dismissed, because text is capable of revealing the great depth that single images or static images cannot do. And that's one of the challenges of this medium. This is something that's challenging me all the time, how to better transmit internalization—which text can do. For example, someone writing with prose or text alone can say, "Sam Brown entered the room. His whole life experience taught him that there was danger here, and he sensed it" and so forth, and it goes on and on. Well, doing that visually, you are unable to step aside and tell all about Sam Brown's long life experience and the dangers he's been through. So these are the challenges that text deals with. But, nonetheless, we're living in a time, what I call a "visual era," in which text alone is under siege.

Fingeroth: That's a polite way of putting it.

Eisner: Well, I think it's about as accurate as you can be. Whenever you try to describe something, you have a tough time trying to get an accurate word. [*laughs*] The era we're living in now is characterized by the fact that a huge amount of information is being poured out on us at this geometric rate of growth, and we don't have time to read. I remember when I was teaching at the School of Visual Arts, I was trying to get my students to read, and I discovered that most of them had not read the novels that I was forced to read as a kid. They weren't even reading short stories, which sort of went out of fashion. Used to be very fashionable in the thirties, which really taught me how to write this kind of stuff, because I was a great reader of short stories. But the times we're living in, communication is largely done by imagery. And I've got to be conscious of that and aware of it. I believe that is what I feel I'm providing in working in this medium, what everybody working in what you call "comics" is providing. I hate the word "comics," it's a misnomer. But it's like "Kleenex," you know? You don't say facial tissue . . . so it has stuck.

Fingeroth: I guess the other shift I noticed in your work over time—and again, I'm sure I'm not the only one nor the first one, but I thought I'd mention it—is that in *The Spirit*, you had to get your personal statements in as metaphor through the characters, through clever storytelling devices. Now you go directly to the personal and to the memoir. But, in other interviews— and I'm sorry to throw quotes at you, but I've been reading nothing but interviews with you for three days [*laughs*]—you've talked about how painful it is to delve into these memories and put them on paper . . .
Eisner: Oh, it is.

Fingeroth: But there must be some appeal to it for you to keep doing it. What's exciting about that process for you?
Eisner: I don't know how other writers work, but I can only write about things that I know. Either things I've seen firsthand, experienced personally, or received maybe through a third party. As a matter of fact, one of the reasons I've been unable to write science fiction stories is because I've never met any aliens from another planet. I don't know any androids.

Fingeroth: [*laughs*] As far as you know.
Eisner: [*laughs*] I don't know, maybe I have. Some of the publishers I ran into very early on were probably from another planet. So I prefer to write from what I know. And it allows me to do some things which are very realistic and very understandable by my readers. For example, I've always used climate or rain—which, by the way, Harvey Kurtzman used to tease me about and call it "Eisenshpritz."

Fingeroth: [*laughs*] There should be a TM after that.
Eisner: I should copyright that, I guess! People understand climate, they understand weather, they understand rain. Everybody has felt rain, so if I can employ that in the process of conveying an idea or telling a story, I do that. So as far as philosophy is concerned, the first time I became aware that I could possibly, in this medium, deal with a philosophical idea or a morality concept was in *The Spirit*, with the story of Gerhard Schnobble, a little guy who could fly. I did that and to my surprise it worked out well, it came across well, and it got a good response. And I was pleased. And it survives. As a matter of

fact, the story has remained memorable among the *Spirit* stories. People keep constantly talking to me about it. In Denmark, there's a building wall with a painting of Gerhard Schnobble on it. A city-financed mural.

Fingeroth: And yet, I don't think today you would do a story about a guy who thought he could fly who gets caught in a shootout. Today you seem much more involved in recounting—
Eisner: Real stories, yes. The Schnobble story was really a philosophical statement, if you will. But now I prefer to deal with reality.

Fingeroth: But reality often from say, the '30s, '40s. '50s.
Eisner: Well, those are the years that I know. But apparently it doesn't really matter, because the principles of the thing stay the same. The last book I did, the one that came out last year, *The Name of the Game*, which is a discussion on the whole idea of marriage and so forth, spanned two generations. *Dropsie Avenue* was an attempt to do a history of a neighborhood, that dealt with generations. But as a matter of fact, I prefer to do things set in the past because that will not change, where today is liable to change on me. [*laughs*]

Fingeroth: Is there some inner drive you feel to get this down on paper, to record a certain time and place in history?
Eisner: No, no, it's just an environment that's very comfortable for me to write in.

Fingeroth: Because my parents are from the Bronx of those years, where many of your stories are set, it's fascinating for me to see what in your work intersects with stories I've heard from them and from my other relatives.
Eisner: We all want to know how it was. In fact, in doing the autobiography *Heart of the Storm*, I remember my father telling me about his life in Vienna. He was a young painter in Vienna, an artist. And I was so eager to find out how it was then. As a matter of fact, many years ago I stopped off in Vienna when I was traveling around Europe on a business trip just to walk the street, the Prada, that he walked on. Just to get the feel of it. It's a thing to do. I know other people do the same thing. I know Art Spiegelman went to Europe and I think he visited one of the concentration camps just to get a feel of what it felt like, what it looked like. I think one has to do that to convey a sense of honesty in your work.

Fingeroth: This is just a pick note, so feel free to ignore this question. I can understand changing the names of real-life based people in your stories, but why do you change the names of streets and neighborhoods that exist or existed? Just so nobody will give you a hard time about not getting an exact likeness?

Eisner: No, no. Because . . . It's the way Faulkner created his own county . . . it's almost a metaphor. It's "an example of." And again, it enables me to connect with the reader. If I use an actual street, with a name that truly existed, I'd lose some of the intimacy I would expect from the reader. So if it's a street that's got a *fictitious* name, it could be a street that he remembers or she remembers. As you can see, my entire preoccupation is to connect with the reader. That's one of the reasons why I don't like to work in color. I prefer to work in a single line in black and white. I'll sometimes print my books in brown because I think it's a way of making it softer and easier to read, but I prefer not to work in color.

Fingeroth: But the *Spirit* was published in color.
Eisner: Well, that was necessary in those days. My attitude with *The Spirit* was totally different than my attitude today.

Fingeroth: Are there authors who influenced you years ago and today? Anybody you can cite as a particular influence?
Eisner: As far as cartoonists are concerned, Milton Caniff was a very strong influence on me. Segar's *Popeye* taught me a lot. Usually, the guys who influence me are people that I try to learn from. For example, *Krazy Kat* by George Herriman I discovered very early. As a matter of fact, I came upon him while I was selling newspapers in the street during the Depression, and the stuff was being published by King Features in the Hearst papers. And I was blown away by that. I thought, "Wow, this is great!" And I've always remembered that he had the capacity of engaging the reader in a way that enabled him to avoid or eliminate panels. As a matter of fact, he was rarely consistent in his backgrounds. One scene had a moon and a tower, and the next scene, they were still talking in the same dialogue, but it was a rock of some kind. If you've seen it, you know what I'm talking about.

So those three authors really taught me an awful lot. I learned an awful lot about storytelling from Caniff. And of course I had many years of reading short stories. O. Henry was a tremendous influence on me. So was Saki, the French author . . .

Fingeroth: Guy DeMaupassant?
Eisner: DeMaupassant. And I read a lot of Russian short stories. The short

stories of the '30s were really tremendously influential, and really, literally, taught me how to write *The Spirit*. Remember, doing a seven-page complete story every week was a lot more difficult than I thought it would be. [*laughter*] I discovered something early on. I started off with an eight-pager and then I discovered I was working at a rate of a page a day. [*laughter*] But I discovered there were only seven days in the week. And I had to cut back to seven-page stories.

Fingeroth: And you filled out the other nine pages with other people's stuff?
Eisner: Yeah.

Fingeroth: Can you talk a little bit about how you create a story? From what I've read, you don't use a typewriter or a computer.
Eisner: I don't use a typewriter. I do the text and pictures at the same time.

Fingeroth: Do you do an outline in longhand first?
Eisner: Sometimes I will. I'll do like a laundry list of—I'll start off with the ending. Before I begin, I know what the ending will be. I work my way up to the ending, which is my way of doing the story.

Fingeroth: Does the ending ever change as you're working your way toward it?
Eisner: The ending doesn't change, but I will alter the path with which I get to the ending, because as things happen, they suggest another happening which works into it. I usually prepare a pencil rough first, a readable dummy, from which I sell the book, actually. For example, at one time I had about four or five publishers in Europe and a couple publishers in this country and I would send out a dummy to them. Nobody really knows which you read first in a sequence, whether you see the pictures first or read the text first.

Fingeroth: I can't believe nobody's done a study on that.
Eisner: I believe you see the images first and then go to the text, because I think this is how it works in real life. For example, just visualize a man lying on the street and a fellow comes over to him and says, "Charlie, are you all right?" It comes afterward. For that reason, for example, I don't like what I call "umbilical balloons." Harvey Kurtzman and I used to argue about that all the time because he liked to do balloons and text and have two or three

balloons coming out of the same person. And I believe that's all wrong. I don't think it works. So each of us has own style and technique and preference. A lot of people are using umbilical balloons, but I don't use them.

Fingeroth: Have you ever drawn from anybody else's script?
Eisner: I have difficult writing from a script that belongs to somebody else. The problem is, I would probably change it. [*laughs*] No, the way I work is I have a kind of a roadmap that I've set up in my mind, or I have a list. To give you an example of how it might work, say, would be the case of the *Spirit* story where this man comes from another planet, finds it difficult to live here, and then returns to the other planet. This was the basis of the story, and I wrote down a whole list of steps. How he arrives, he gets a job in the weather bureau, and my next and my next step, he meets this lady, and so forth. And at the end of the book, he goes off to another planet. All that's listed down. Then I start writing my stories. Now, each page for me is a *megapanel*. I try to contain a number of cohesive incidents on a single page so the page has a containment in itself. But that's also because I'm very conscious of the technology of the reading of this medium, so, for example, I believe that when you turn a page, you lose the reader for a millisecond. Unless you recognize that, you're going to lose the thread of the story for them. I used to warn my students about the business of having someone on the last panel of page one, let's say, start saying, "I am going to . . . " And on the next page he says, "Chicago." You lose the reader that millisecond, as they're turning the page. That has to do with the technology of the medium. Now, that may change when we arrive at the point where all comics will be displayed electronically, over the Internet, so you'll have a totally different kind of thing.

Fingeroth: Do you think that's going to happen?
Eisner: Well . . . that's been a long-running debate between me and Scott McCloud over this subject. A friendly debate, but an enthusiastic one, anyway. And I believe that what's going to happen is that comics—or cartoons as still images, which print lives on—will become animated. So what you're going to wind up with is animated cartoons.

Fingeroth: Something like the "webtoons" that were popular, or were trying to be popular, a few years ago?
Eisner: I don't know what they were, what are webtoons?

Fingeroth: You know, like the stuff that Stan Lee was doing with Stan Lee Media.
Eisner: Oh, yeah, when he got into flash-animation?

Fingeroth: Right, the flash-animation stuff.
Eisner: They'll progress into pure animation, which is being produced in Hollywood today. So I think still images, which is what comics in print deals with all the time, loses something when it's projected over an image through the Internet. They've been trying to do that, a lot of guys have done that, and it doesn't work as far as I'm concerned.

Fingeroth: Well, it's a different medium.
Eisner: So that's where it's going. I'm not very interested in movies. I've never really been interested in getting involved in the production of a movie. In fact, I've never really been eager to have any of my work made into a movie. I'm satisfied with the way it's been done with print. I love print, and as far as I'm concerned, as long as I am able to work I will continue to work in print. I've had offers, as you can imagine, from time to time, to do a movie, to get involved in making a movie, and was really not interested at that time. Of course, one should never say never . . . eh?

Fingeroth: Because of positive things about print, or negative things about Hollywood . . . ?
Eisner: No, no. Well, Hollywood's a story all in itself. It's because I have really not licked print altogether. There's a lot yet to conquer.

Fingeroth: Well, if you haven't, nobody has. Take my word for it. [laughs] You have had, certainly, a long and remarkable career. I imagine there have been setbacks along the way. Any advice for people about how to deal with career setbacks that would feel like impossible obstacles?
Eisner: Stay with it. Don't quit. Have faith in yourself. Believe in what you're doing. Failures are a way of learning things. As a matter of fact, I was telling a story, last week I was speaking to a group of librarians and someone asked me the same question. One of the difficulties of this business is that you have to learn to deal with rejection. Every kid coming out of school, sooner or later, will walk into an art director's office or a publisher's office and the editor will look at his work and say, "now, don't take this personally . . . but this is the stupidest, crappiest work I've ever seen."

Fingeroth: "But don't take it personally." [*laughs*]

Eisner: "Don't take it personally." Well, it happened to me, I remember, as a young kid. I showed my work to a magazine and the editor looked at this work and laughed and said, "These are the stupidest faces I have ever seen." And I walked out of there very dejected. And sitting out in the waiting room, waiting to see this editor next after me, was Ludwig Bemelmans the famous illustrator. A foreigner. And he said to me in broken English, "Don't vorry, boy, somebody vill like your vork."

Fingeroth: [*laughs*] Did he look at your work?

Eisner: No. I was carrying my big black portfolio, looking like the world had fallen in on me.

Fingeroth: Now who was this guy?

Eisner: Ludgwig Bemelmans. He was a very famous book illustrator and painter.

Fingeroth: It was wonderful that he said that to you.

Eisner: Yeah, it was very encouraging. I walked out feeling a little better.

Fingeroth: Any books or courses that you recommend to aspiring comics writers and artists? I imagine *Comics & Sequential Art*. [*laughs*]

Eisner: Well, I would recommend that. I think that's a very good book. [*laughs*] And *Graphic Storytelling and Visual Narrative*, too. Those books, by the way, are different from Scott McCloud's book, *Understanding Comics*, which is very important, in my opinion. Scott's book is addressed to the broad public, and explains the phenomenon of comics, the technology and the structure of it and so forth. What I tried to do with *Comics & Sequential Art* and *Graphic Storytelling* is provide something for someone who is working in the medium or teaching it. So I suggest those. But there are lots of good books . . .

For those who want to learn anatomy—because it's very important to be able to manipulate the human figure if you're going to talk about it and write about it—I think the anatomy books by George Bridgman are very, very valuable. And they're cheap and easy for you to get. Everything I know about anatomy I learned from him. I took a course with him back at the Art Students League in the '30s.

And writing, I think everybody who wants to write should read short stories. Go back to the old short stories of the thirties, wonderful things. I've always believed that the best comic book, graphic novel, or sequential art, whatever you want to call it, is done by the same man who writes and draws it. And barring that, I think that someone who writes should be able to think graphically when he writes a book, in order to deal with the artist. As a matter of fact, I was talking about this with Neil Gaiman once, and he told me that he writes with the skills and the style and the talents of a specific artist in mind. So before he starts writing, he wants to know who the artist will be. So that's a good tip.

Fingeroth: Of course, if you're Neil Gaiman, you can have some say in that. A lot of people just get whoever they're assigned by the editor.
Eisner: Well, no, I think even for a young writer who's just starting to work at one of the major houses certainly, it would be in order to say, "Who is going to illustrate this, so I can write it better for this person." There's some guys who can't draw horses. So why do a story that involves a lot of horses? [*laughter*]

Fingeroth: This is true, this is true. Anything you've never been asked? Anything you've always wanted to say for publication that you've never been asked about? [*laughs*]
Eisner: Gee, no. I've been talking about this medium so long that I think I've gotten out everything I've had to say. Listen, your questions are good, very provocative.

Fingeroth: Thank you. That means a lot. Your answers have been incredible and inspired many of the questions. Before we wrap this up, is there anything you want to plug? I know you're going to be speaking at the Library of Congress soon.
Eisner: I'll be going there next week.

Fingeroth: That's very exciting.
Eisner: Your article will come out long after that. The only thing I want to plug, I think, is *Fagin the Jew*, which is being published by Doubleday this fall.

Fingeroth: Okay. And maybe when I send you the transcript, after you've done the Library, maybe we can do one or two follow-ups by e-mail or something just so you can tell me about that, if you have the time, because that's a very exciting thing.
Eisner: Well, I'll be talking about graphic novels.

Fingeroth: Are you excited about speaking there?

Eisner: What I'm doing now is accepting invitations to talk about the graphic novel. At long last the graphic novel has arrived. It's being discovered by libraries around the world, all over the country. And I'm very eager to talk about that. I want to correct something. A lot of the people, librarians, and other publishers, people who publish or buy graphic novels—I'm not talking about the readers—regard a graphic novel as nothing more than a collection of comics with a flat back. If it's thick, if it's got more than a hundred pages, it's a graphic novel. So I've been running around trying to correct that and point out that the graphic novel is a literary form. It is written with a structure very similar to the classic novel. As a matter of fact, *Signal from Space*, a book I wrote . . . I wrote that book not because I wanted to write about science fiction, but wanted to prove or show or demonstrate that a graphic novel could be written following the disciplines of a standard text novel, prose novel.

Fingeroth: The structural disciplines, you mean?

Eisner: Yeah, the same structural disciplines. It really worked. Anyway, that's my conclusion.

Fingeroth: Thanks for your time, Will, and for sharing your knowledge. And for all the great work.

Eisner: Thank you, Danny.

Auteur Theory

MICHAEL KRONENBERG / 2004

From *Comic Book Marketplace* No. 115 (September 2004), 36–47. Reprinted by permission of Gemstone Publishing, Inc. All rights reserved.

Comic Book Marketplace: For many years you've had complete autonomy over your projects—how does it feel to have carte blanche to explore and push the limits of the medium?

Will Eisner: Great!! It feels good, I'm enjoying it. The reason I struggled to retain my property in the first place way back was I felt it was the only way to maintain control of the content, the intellectual control. That was the reason I did that in the first place. I was really more interested in that than the potential of money because in those days comics didn't have as great a future as they have today.

CBM: Do you miss the collaborative effort of comic books?

Eisner: Well, there was a collaborative effort when I was doing *Spirit*, but it was less collaborative than it was supportive. I had a staff of people who were intellectually competent and I was able to produce the material with their support. I don't miss what you call the collaborative effort because I'm working alone today very deliberately. I feel I have total control over what I am doing.

CBM: When you had your studios early in the '40s, were you also in control of the projects that you were doing?

Eisner: Oh, yeah. In the Eisner and Iger Studio what I did was design the individual characters at the beginning and then turn them over to people on the staff who would continue them. You know the function of these things is really production support. What I do today has no need for a timed production. It takes me about a year, year and a half, to do a graphic novel and I work at my own pace, create my own deadlines. I'm not servicing a publisher. I guess that's the best way to put it.

CBM: You do have an agreement with DC, right?

Eisner: The only agreement I have with DC is that I've licensed them to continue producing archival editions of *The Spirit*. And with the Vertigo division I show them my new novels and give them the opportunity to bid on it. They have first look, actually.

CBM: I noticed on the DC website that they are selling some of your back graphic novels.

Eisner: That is called the Will Eisner Library.

CBM: In this vein, do you have any desire to work with any of today's writers or artists?

Eisner: No, not really. I think there are a lot of good ones around, but they are independent, working on their own. I don't have any desire to work on a story with any of them. I'll work together on something like a discussion on comics. I just did a book with Frank Miller. A one-on-one book where we sat and talked for three days, and someone recorded what we talked about, and they are putting it into a book. Dark Horse is publishing it.

CBM: As many of your contemporaries struggled to hold onto their properties, much less stay employed in the industry, how did you survive and prosper?

Eisner: Why, hard work, and luck.

CBM: You know, you read about how Siegel and Shuster sold their rights to Superman; I guess maybe Bob Kane would be one of the exceptions, but even Carmine Infantino right now is suing over his property.

Eisner: Actually Bob didn't get equity back into it until much later. Before he first sold his property, they owned it. It was a trade practice in those days. Nobody really questioned it. When you say they fought or struggled to get their properties or to hold onto their properties, that's not true. Nobody really made even an attempt. I'm the only one that even made an attempt. And I just gave you the reason for that—I wanted control over the editorial contents. Besides *The Spirit* was designed for newspapers, not a comic *book*. The standard trade practice in the comic book industry was that you sold an idea, like Bob brought Batman to DC, they owned it. Siegel and Shuster brought

Superman to DC—they owned it. And there was no question about it. Like Siegel and Shuster signed the check that they got and on the back of the check was stamped the words "For all rights and title." When Bob Kane signed his contract, I was at his house (we were high school buddies), and it very clearly said that they, DC, owned Batman. It wasn't until years later that he was able to get them to agree to put his name on the property. They give him a royalty, but they own the property. They never gave the property back to him. Bob never really struggled to get the rights.

CBM: I find it amazing that you really were the only person who seemed to think about this at the infancy of the industry. Did you see the potential for the medium back then? Look what it's become with the graphic novels, the ability for self expression, there's movies and television shows—did you see this?

Eisner: Yes, I always saw it. As a matter of fact as early as 1940 I had an interview with the newspaper *The Baltimore Sun*, and I said that this was an art form that was a really valid art form. I always believed that this medium had literary potential or was a literary form. I believed it from the very beginning. One of the reasons I went into *The Spirit* was because I wanted to get out of what I felt was the "comics ghetto" and the newspaper syndication gave me the opportunity to write to adults. It was always what I really wanted to do. But I always believed this medium had a tremendous cultural future.

But that is not the reason why I struggled in that negotiation to retain ownership. The reason at the time I wanted to retain the ownership is that I wanted to maintain the integrity of the content. The only way to do that is to own the copyright. The business of copyright ownership is questionable. To simply own a copyright doesn't mean you're going to make a lot of money. It depends on how much exploitation you're able to do with it. So it's a totally different kind of thinking.

CBM: Have you been influenced by movies, and was *Citizen Kane*'s release in 1941 an important influence?

Eisner: Wow! I was always influenced by the literature around me. I was influenced by classic literature; I was very influenced by the short stories of the '30s. The '30s were the big short story era. I was tremendously influenced by early pulps—they taught me how to write short stories. Everything around me has always influenced me. I think that's true of every writer, every artist, everybody that works in the field. But I never sat down and copied, if you will, or imitated, or emulated any of those things. I simply drew from everything

I saw around me those things that were necessary for what I was doing. For example, *The Spirit* had a cinematic quality, largely because I reasoned at the time that during the early '40s the readership was all influenced by the movies. Consequently I had to write in a "moving" language. I see pictures, sequential art as I call it, as a language.

CBM: Looking over *The Spirit Archives* and going back to when I first encountered your art when I was thirteen years old and picked up the Warren magazines of *The Spirit*—it's always had that feel of film.

Eisner: I was intrigued by graphic language. But, actually, my interest is live theater. As a matter of fact, all my graphic novels are influenced by live theater. But there's a big difference between theater and film. In film you're simply part of the mechanics—they tell you how to look at things; in live theater you are there and you see real people. You're a witness to a real event.

CBM: Were you in New York when there was the explosion in the theater, and Arthur Miller was writing, and Tennessee Williams? Were you able to see those?

Eisner: Sure. A big influence on me was the WPA theaters during the Depression. They taught me an awful lot about stagecraft. In those days, the WPA theaters . . . you know what I'm talking about? The Works Progress Administration? I learned a lot about stagecraft from them because they were very poor. They did not have enough money for fancy stage scenery so what they would use was a very minimal stage scenery which involved audience participation and made the audience use their own imagination. For example, in one of the plays, I think it was an O'Neill play, they had a single streetlight in the center of the stage and the actors would move inside or outside of the streetlight to indicate being inside of the house or being outside of the house. It was very, very fascinating. I learned a lot about that. I learned how to employ the kinds of backgrounds that would involve my readers.

   Another influence on me in that whole area was the work of George Herriman and his *Krazy Kat*. You examine the work he did and you'll find that he had an incredible ability to engage the reader from scene to scene. These are the things that I learned from. I really don't call that influence, I learned from them.

CBM: There were great artists in the WPA also—Thomas Hart Benton and Grant Wood. It was kind of a renaissance of American art as well.

Eisner: Leyendecker was a strong influence on me. The crosshatching in my shadows I learned from him. He designed and developed what he called transparent shadows. I used that a lot in my line of work.

CBM: At what point in your career did you feel that you had gained creative control to tell the stories you wanted? Was it when you secured the rights for *The Spirit*?

Eisner: I've always had creative control in all my work all my life, in everything I've done, except where I've done comics that were used for instructional material. There I had a certain amount of creative control, but the medium was being used to teach. For example, the work I did during the '50s and '60s with the military—when I produced training material.

CBM: Who do you look on in the time that you've been in the industry as people who have been writers and artists, people who have had the control that you enjoy?

Eisner: Well, it's hard to do because there are so many of them. Today there are a tremendous amount of people who are producing their own work. Many of the artists who began self-publishing are an example; if you list all the guys who are self-published, they have total editorial control. It doesn't come cheaply, it's at a price. Self-publishing fellows work very hard at marketing their own books, taking the gamble of producing a book and hoping they may sell enough copies to pay the printer and survive. Editorial control comes at a great price. But when you're working for a publisher, when you're doing *Superman* for example, you have to give up a certain amount of control because it is somebody else's property. You can do innovative things, like Miller did with Batman. But nonetheless the property is not his.

CBM: But you also have to get to a certain point, you have to have a name as you do, or Frank Miller does, to even be able to do what he did. Which is not easy to do as it is.

Eisner: Well, I don't think "name" has anything to do with it. I think what you do has to do with an innate desire to do it.

CBM: I guess what I mean is that a big company that has a property would even let you bring about a change or something a little more unusual to their property—they're so protective of their property.

Eisner: Obviously, and they should be. They entrusted the property to Miller because he had been working with them. He had demonstrated a great deal of ability and had probably convinced them that he could do something with it. I don't know what the conditions were, what was in the mind of DC when they entrusted the property to him. But whatever it was, they made a good choice because what he did with Batman was very unusual.

CBM: So what do you see in comics today that you like?

Eisner: Oh, I like the new stuff that is coming along—the very young people who are developing new, experimental work. I think they are the future of the business. And I'm very happy to see the young graphic novelists producing very serious material. So I am very optimistic about the future of the medium. I think we are in a wonderful time. Plus the fact that in the last two years the public libraries and the schools have recognized and accepted the graphic novel, which is really the thing I've been waiting for for thirty years.

CBM: What do you see that you dislike?

Eisner: What I dislike, that I used to caution my students against, is the slavish imitations. A lot of artists go into the field thinking, "Well, this is a quick way to make money so I'll do a superhero." We have plenty of superheroes. I dislike it when artists and writers that come into the field are not producing material that comes from their own experience. A lot of the fellows have nothing to say, or at least don't attempt to say anything. That is the only thing I regard as wasteful, really. But the rest of the field is booming and it's alive and it's very productive. New people, young artists are coming in. I think it is a wonderful time for the comics.

CBM: I think creatively in the industry it's a great time. There are people crossing over from other mediums—whether it's film or novels. And they're coming in and either writing or doing art. I think that the crossovers are pretty amazing. I don't think I've ever seen anything quite like it.

Eisner: I agree with you. It's tremendous, very exciting. I'm very enthusiastic about it. And the only thing that makes me sad is I wish I was twenty-five years younger.

CBM: (Laugh) You *act* like you're twenty-five years younger.

Eisner: Well, I feel twenty-five years younger. It is a wonderful time.

CBM: I guess what I want to ask you also is that readership is not what it was—say, I know it is hard to compare to the '40s when *Superman* or *Detective Comics* would sell nearly a million copies a month—but readership is down and comic book shops have been closing although things are getting better lately. Is there anything that you see that could bring readership back up or anything that the medium could do or change in their direction?

Eisner: Well, let me tell you how I see the field now. I think what has happened to the readership is that it has been fractioned. What you have now is what they call "niche publishing." There are segments so that you have superhero comics, you have story comics, like *Bone*, you have satirical work like the stuff done by Batton Lash, his super-creature lawyers, and the younger fellows like Thompson who did the coming-of-age *Blankets*. Each one has a market of its own, so what you have is total readership that is a lot greater but it is segmented into what I call special interest. The same thing is happening in literature, where you have people who like science-fiction stories, you have people who like romance novels. Each of the fields have a segment of their own. That's what is happening in this field today. There is something else that is happening, of course, is the sudden discovery by the moving picture people—discovering comics as a source of material, source of ideas and story material.

CBM: Hopefully they will stay loyal to what has been done. I read recently that *The Spirit* was picked up. Can you talk anything about that?

Eisner: Well, the contract that I have is that they must adhere to the configuration of the characters. So the business of *The Spirit* flying around between buildings is not likely to happen. That's all I know about it.

CBM: At one time the newspapers were flooded with creative comic strips like *The Spirit*, when Alex Raymond was doing *Flash Gordon* and Foster was doing *Tarzan* and *Prince Valiant*, Caniff was doing *Steve Canyon* and *Terry and the Pirates*—what do you think has happened to them?

Eisner: Well I'll tell you, for a short while I was president of a newspaper syndicate so I have some experience. What happens is the comic strips are no longer the major source of circulation. Way, way back in the early part of the century comic strips were the producer of a great amount of circulation. That was because there was a lot of competition, there were many competitors in New York City. When I was selling newspapers, I had seven different newspapers on my little table. What has happened in the last thirty or forty years is that there is usually just a single newspaper in town, generally owned by a large conglomerate, so they no longer have newspaper competition for this kind of circulation. Their competition is TV and the Internet. As a matter of fact, recently one of the major newspaper chains demanded that the newspaper syndicate lower their prices by a tremendous amount. Obviously they don't really care if the newspapers pull the comic strips out. So that's what has happened—comic strips generally now are in newspapers at the pleasure of the editor, and they reduce the size of them continuously. You have a whole page of comics squeezed together getting smaller and smaller.

CBM: It is still ironic that the '40s, '50s, maybe even the early '60s, there was a time where it was looked down upon to do comic books and doing a newspaper syndicated comic strip was a thing of pride. From what I've read there was almost a hierarchy where the newspaper strip artist kind of looked down on comic book artists.

Eisner: That is quite true. As a matter of fact, some of it still remains. Newspaper comic strip creators are regarded as having the larger circulation of people, more sophisticated and closer to mainstream. Remember, the role of comic strips over the years has been a very strong cultural role. The early comic strips provided a way for immigrants to be able to read and identify with humor, society, and our culture. The role of the comic strip has diminished into a form of pure entertainment now—much of it satire. But there is still a sense of hierarchy that lingers. It is slowly being eaten away; the National Cartoonists Society is now including comic book artists which they didn't do at the beginning. As comic books get a little bit more sophisticated and begin to become more influential, the artists and writers who are working on them become more influential themselves.

CBM: Can you take us through the creative process of working on one of your graphic novels? Do you write a full script before you start?

Eisner: No, the way I work is I start with the ending; I know what the ending is going to be. Then normally what I do is I write and draw the whole thing out in pencil roughs on a sheet of typewriter paper. I don't use the typewriter to write. I write with a sequence of pictures including balloons for dialogue. I compose scenes with balloons in place first. I know exactly where the story is going because I know what the ending is. So I'm constantly working my way up through a maze of events into the ending. Any innovation I do along the way is a way to bring me to the next level. Sometimes I will plan the whole thing like a laundry list—I'll just list events that I want to go into. I write and draw at the same time—the dialogue and the pictures at the same time. When you compare that with a book of text, the pictures or the images are metaphors and the dialogue is a conversation between the people in the thing. I rarely overuse narrative unless it's a special kind of book like *Fagin the Jew* in which I used a lot of connective narrative. I'm using a lot of that now, more than ever. In *The Name of the Game* I also used a connective narrative where I was discussing connective history because this native is incapable actually of dealing with time. The word "meanwhile," which we used for years, is no longer enough.

CBM: I know you were drafted. Did you see combat in World War II?

Eisner: No. I was at the Pentagon during World War II producing training material. I did see a lot of military action after the War. At the start of the Korean War the Amy asked me if I would contract to do a continuation of the magazine (*Army Motors*) that I did during World War II called *P.S. Magazine*, and I agreed to do it. I would travel to the combat area in Korea and Vietnam during those wars. I was in Germany and several other places.

CBM: How did your time in the service affect you, and how did it affect your work?

Eisner: It matured me. The early *Spirits* were done by a young cartoonist like me who had had no real life experience. I was just out of high school and I was drawing and drawing. I spent my days and nights drawing. During the War and my experience in the military taught me a lot about life, so when I got out in 1945 the stories I began to write were really stories based on life experience.

The thing that people don't really factor in their thinking about comics is that the artists grow up like you do. One of the reasons why I never really wanted to do a daily strip is because in a daily strip you have to be the same all the time.

CBM: During World War II, what did the realization of the Holocaust do to you and how does that affect your work?

Eisner: Like all Jews I was terrified by the Holocaust. As a matter of fact, when I was drafted I tried to get into combat because I wanted to do something. The natural reaction is that you want to do something active against this terrible thing. The military wouldn't let me because apparently what I was doing was something they felt was more useful to them.

It did affect me. We had relatives who disappeared in Europe, but my parents had immigrated to this country long before. My father came to this country about 1914, and my mother was born on the boat coming over about the same time. I had no immediate relatives in Europe, but nonetheless I was horrified, shocked, enraged, and somewhat terrified because if Hitler had won I might not be here today.

There are some of us who have very close connections like Spiegelman whose parents were actually in the concentration camp. A lot of Jews in this country had very close connections. My wife is a fourth-generation Jew; her grandparents came over during the Civil War. So she only knew about what was going on in Europe by reading about it. Those who had direct connections felt it much more deeply, of course, but all Jews were terrified. It was a frightening time.

CBM: During the Golden Age of comics when you had your studio, and people like Bob Kane, Simon and Kirby, and Siegel and Shuster were working, did you encounter any anti-Semitism from either publishers or other writers or artists?

Eisner: No, there was none of that, I never encountered it. The reason you remember a lot of Jewish artists was only largely because when comic magazines (in those days they weren't called comic books) started there was new territory. It was easy to get into it, so a lot of the Jewish cartoonists who were on the periphery moved into it. Also, Jews have a long history of storytelling; very much like the Irish, only more Biblical. So this is a natural and very attractive medium for them. We never encountered any anti-Semitism at all. As a matter of fact, none of the Jews I know, including myself, even attempted to introduce Jewish culture, which is something that a lot of people involved in the Jewish community think we did, but it's not true. Mostly the characters we made were Gentile; the Spirit was Gentile. Oh, Jules Feiffer said that everybody knew he was Jewish even though he had a turned-up nose and an Irish name, but that was a joke. All the characters that were created by Jewish cartoonists were WASPs.

CBM: In many ways the same thing occurred in film where a lot of the screenwriters were Jewish and when they were writing about these private detectives or heroes they were all Gentiles.

Eisner: It's only in the last number of years when you've got a Spielberg and people like that who are doing things from the Jewish cultural background.

CBM: And yourself and your graphic novels.

Eisner: What I'm doing now are interesting stories. Actually the last two books I've been doing, *Fagin the Jew* and the one that's going to come out next spring, *The Plot*, are departures for me. They're polemics; they're really not designed as fictional or entertaining storytelling. In *The Name of the Game* I did the history of a wealthy Jewish family just to show the transition and growth—I'm always interested in historic growth as I did in *Dropsie Avenue* when I took on the history of the street in the Bronx. So I'm constantly experimenting, or pushing the envelope if you will. That, for me, is the excitement and adventure of what I'm doing.

CBM: You're also keeping that spirit of New York and that experience of New York and that life at that time alive, which I think was really an important cultural time.

Eisner: You've got to understand that I write only about the things that I know about. The reason I don't do science fiction or space stories is because I don't know anything about aliens from another planet. I write about the things I know. New York City is a marvelous place. It's real theater. It's the center of the Earth. Things are happening here all the time. It's just bubbling with story material so you just really have to dip in there and pull out stories. You can walk down 42nd Street and by the end of the street you can have fifteen or twenty stories. I know big cities, I know New York.

CBM: Are you able to get back to the City?

Eisner: Yes, I get back to the City twice a year at least. For about eight years I was commuting there from Florida when I was teaching at the School of Visual Arts, so I stayed in New York almost every week.

CBM: Mr. Eisner, I thank you.

Eisner: You're welcome.

INDEX

CANISIUS COLLEGE LIBRARY

3 5084 00533 1171

Book Shelves
PN6727.E4 Z92 2011
Will Eisner : conversations